AMERICAN CATHOLIC RELIGIOUS THOUGHT

edited by
Patrick Carey

PAULIST PRESS
New York/Mahwah

The Publisher gratefully acknowledges use of the following materials: "To Our Readers," May 1933, p. 4; "CW Stand on the Use of Force," *Catholic Worker,* September, 1938, p. 4. Permission to use these materials has been granted by Mrs. Tamar Hennessy. J.C. Murray, S.J., "Civil Unity and Religious Integrity." *We Hold These Truths.* Permission to use this material has been granted by Sheed & Ward, 115 E. Armour Blvd., Kansas City, MO 64141. John A. Ryan, "The Church and the Workingman," *Catholic World* 89 (April/September, 1909), pp. 776-82. Permission to use this material has been granted by Sister Mary John Ryan, CSJ. Virgil Michel, OSB, "The Liturgy the Basis of Social Regeneration," *Orate Fratres* 9 (1934/35), 536-545. Permission to use this material has been granted by *Worship* and The Liturgical Press.

Library of Congress Cataloging-in-Publication Data

American Catholic religious thought.

    Includes bibliographies.
     1. Catholic Church—United States—Doctrines.
2. Catholic Church—United States—Doctrines—
History. 3. United States—Church history.
I. Carey, Patrick, 1940-
BX1751.2.A796 1987   230′.273   87-2546
ISBN 0-8091-2884-5 (pbk.)

Published by Paulist Press
997 Macarthur Boulevard
Mahwah, N.J. 07430

Printed and bound in the United States of America

Contents

Part IV: Americanism and Modernism, 1880-1910

Part V: Social Justice, 1840-1940

Part VI: Neo-Thomism and Catholic Culture, 1920-1960

Preface

This text developed as a resource for a course I have been teaching on American Catholic life and thought. I prepared it to meet a need that no other book met. American Catholic life has been adequately presented in a number of histories of American Catholicism, but American Catholic religious thought has received very little attention. This text introduces students to the intellectual tradition that unfolded within American Catholic history.

The book is divided into two major sections for easy use in a class. The first section contains a brief introduction that outlines the historical context for the selected documents that follow. The selected documents, representative of American Catholic thought at particular periods in its history, are preceded by a brief introduction to the author and text and are followed by a selected bibliography for further reading and research.

I dedicate this text to the numerous graduate and undergraduate students who have taken my courses on the American Catholicism and who have contributed much to the creation of the work by their helpful evaluations and criticisms.

Introduction

The charge has been made repeatedly that American Catholics, with a few rare exceptions, have failed to produce any creative and systematic theological response to their American environment.[1] This generally accepted accusation no doubt has a good deal of truth. Such indictments, however, tend to overlook those few American Catholics who in fact responded to the wider currents of American thought, understood and explained their religious experiences in ways that reflected the general intellectual movements of their times, and creatively helped American Catholics identify themselves religiously in the world of American culture. One looks in vain in the major histories of American Catholicism, however, to discover what thought American Catholics did develop—whether creative or not. What is currently needed, therefore, is a study of the kind of religious thought that did evolve. Drawing attention to these patterns of thought will encourage, I hope, more analysis of this development.

This introduction outlines developments in American Catholic thought from John Carroll's (1735-1815) 1784 apologetical work, the first major American Catholic writing in defense of Catholicism, to the publication of John Courtney Murray's *We Hold These Truths: Catholic Reflections on the American Proposition* (1960), the last major American Catholic apologetic prior to the Second Vatican Council. This text does not examine the American Catholic experiences at the Second Vatican Council (1962-1965) nor the post-conciliar developments in religious thought within American Catholicism because an examination of them demands another volume.

American Catholic thought, like other Christian thought in this country, has its deepest roots in the Christian experience of the incarnation, life, death and resurrection of Jesus Christ. For almost twenty centuries, Christians have reflected upon the meaning of that experience and have tried to relate it to their lives in the worlds in which they lived.

3

American Catholics from the eighteenth to the middle of the twentieth century have lived in both the world of post-Tridentine European Catholicism and in the world of American culture. American Catholic thought, therefore, has generally been a reflection upon the meaning of the Christ event within the context of European and American cultural and intellectual settings. Much American Catholic thought, it is true, was in continuity with European Catholic thought, but it was not a simple repetition of that thought. The American environment had its effect. In 1855, a German priest in Wisconsin noted: "All the resolutions made in Europe dissolve as soon as one feels the breezes of the American coastline; every tie, including the one with God, must be retied here and must undergo the American 'probatum est' [i.e., testing] before it can be said that it is secure."[2] American Puritanism and republicanism created an environment for Catholics that demanded, in terms of style and content, a religious response that had no effective European model.

American Catholic problems were indeed different from those of European Catholicism, and American responses to those problems were not simply borrowed from European Catholicism. American Catholics were most certainly involved in the Protestant-Catholic polemics of the period after the Council of Trent (1545-1563), but even in these controversies the situation in the United States made the rational defense of Catholicism specifically American. Their theological concerns, moreover, were not limited exclusively to internal Christian debates, but extended to the theological significance of peculiarly American issues: the compatibility of republicanism and Catholicism, religious liberty, separation of church and state, the nature of Christianity and the church in a pluralistic society, and the public responsibility of the church for issues of peace and justice in a capitalistic society. The Catholic experience of Christianity and the American experience mutually conditioned theological reflection upon these and related issues. The Catholic responses to these questions were to some extent attempts both to understand the ultimate significance of the American experience from the Catholic perspective and to interpret the meaning of Catholicism from the American perspective.

As members of a minority religion, American Catholics were forced to reinterpret their understanding of Catholicism to meet the inherent challenges of a republican mentality and the overt charges of nativist and Protestant polemics. As a result of this situation, American Catholic religious thought became primarily pastoral and apologetic (sometimes irenic and sometimes polemical). It was pastoral in the sense that it was chiefly concerned with identifying, defining and preserving for Catholics their religious identity in the midst of a voluntary and pluralistic religious country. It was apologetic in the sense that it tried to vindicate Catholicism in relation to the republican and Protestant tradition.

This introduction argues that an American Catholic intellectual tradition did exist and that it was related to the intellectual currents of this country and to the larger historical tradition of Christianity. The purpose of this text, therefore, is to locate significant Catholic responses to American problems and to examine the American Catholic theological tradition in its historical setting. This text shows how Catholic writers have used the dominant climate of thought in the United States to further their own apologetical cause and to give Catholics a sense of their American as well as their Catholic identity. From 1784 until the Second Vatican Council Catholics have in turns appropriated elements of the Enlightenment, Romanticism, Liberalism, Social Christianity, Neo-Thomism and other currents in American and European thought in their attempts to relate their understanding of Christianity to the society in which they lived.

The persons whose writings were selected for this anthology do not exactly reflect the dominant religious thought in the Catholic community (theologians and opinion makers rarely do), but they do mirror some of the key religious, intellectual and social concerns of their age, and they do give a Catholic response to those concerns. I have chosen eleven American Catholic writings on the grounds of the above criteria, but I am well aware that a number of others could have been selected as well.[3] The principle of selection here is admittedly broad, but it is applied to single out some of the acknowledged leaders of American Catholic thought. Such a text could not have excluded, I believe, writings from John England, Orestes Brownson, Isaac Hecker, Martin John Spalding, John Ireland, John Hughes, Edward McGlynn, John Ryan, Dorothy Day, Virgil Michel and John Courtney Murray—i.e., the major articulators of Catholic concerns in the United States.

ENLIGHTENMENT CATHOLICISM, 1784-1842

It is a truism to say, as Walter Ong, S.J., has noted, that "the United States was conceived and cradled in the age of Reason as no European country had ever been."[4] American Catholicism, one might with equal truth claim, was formed and developed within this same context. Although Catholics had a long history in America before the ratification of the United States Constitution, still they were not formed into an episcopally-organized church until 1789. During the pre-Civil War period, Catholics were a tiny minority of the population. Embattled from within over ethnic and ideological issues and attacked from without by the "Protestant Crusade," they struggled to develop a form of Catholicism that would preserve ties with the European Catholic tradition and at the same time adapt Catholicism to American ways and patterns of thought that were significantly influenced by the Enlightenment. Thus, the initial formation of American Catholicism took place within the environment of the Enlightenment. Catholic relations to this American mentality were firmly rooted and developed from the time of John Carroll's first major apologetical writing in 1784 until the death of John England (1842), the Bishop of Charleston, South Carolina (1820-1842) and the last great American Catholic representative of the Enlightenment mentality.

Although American Catholic apologists, like many of their American Protestant neighbors, were not totally identified with the Enlightenment mentality, they did appropriate Enlightenment values to present their understanding of the Christian tradition to the American people. In other words, I am arguing here that there was an American Catholic way of appropriating the Enlightenment. "The Enlightenment," of course, is not easily defined and indeed had a variety of very different forms in Europe and in the United States. For purposes of this brief introduction, however, I am using the term Enlightenment and Enlightenment mentality to refer to that sweeping movement in European and American thought, particularly during the eighteenth and early nineteenth centuries, that emphasized the following: the autonomy or semi-autonomy of the individual; a Newtonian conception of a harmonious, law-governed universe; the use of the empirical, experimental and inductive reason of Francis Bacon and John Locke in understanding that universe; the idea of historical progress; and the perfectibility of human persons. The American values of republicanism, religious liberty, separation of church and state, voluntaryism and denominationalism were products to a great extent of this mentality.

During the antebellum years, a number of American Protestants and nativists charged that Catholicism was irreconcilable in practice and principle with these enlightened values of the day. Among other things, they maintained that Catholicism and American republicanism were historically, practically and theoretically incompatible. Catholics, they complained, were basically monarchists in their political theory as well as in their ecclesiology, opposed to religious liberty and separation of church and state. These opponents also asserted that Catholicism had no place for the individual, being an irrational religion based upon blind submission to an arbitrary teaching authority. American Catholics responded to these indictments by demonstrating through their apologetical writings and through the creation of some republican-like ecclesiastical institutions that Catholicism was indeed compatible with Enlightenment values.

Like their European co-religionists who were educated in post-Tridentine scholasticism, like their American neighbors who had institutionalized the age of reason in their political constitutions, and like their American Protestant adversaries who were nurtured in Scottish Common Sense Philosophy,[5] Carroll and England, the chief American Catholic apologists during the early national period, fit into the broad spectrum of the Enlightenment. They not only accepted much of the Enlightenment's anthropology and political philosophy but also appealed to empirical reason and employed the inductive method to defend Catholic claims. They revealed their Enlightenment perspectives most clearly in their responses to nativist and Protestant charges against the Catholic understanding of: (1) the state and society, (2) ecclesiastical government, and (3) the individual's role within Catholicism.

The Enlightenment understanding of the autonomous individual as one who possesses natural rights and a free conscience provided a foundation for an American Catholic understanding of the state and society. On the basis of this Enlightenment anthropology, Catholic apologists accepted a contractual or compact view of the state, and by articulating this perspective in their writings, they hoped to convince their opponents of their political republicanism and Americanism. Throughout the nineteenth century Catholics maintained that Catholicism and republicanism were compatible both in theory and in practice. Catholics were not, for example, theoretically opposed to a republican theory of the state, as some of their opponents maintained. According to Bishop England, one's political theory was not a matter of revelation; Catholics, like other Christians, therefore, were free to accept any idea of government which the autonomous mind could devise. The Catholic Church itself had no teaching on the true nature of political government. Catholics, and Catholic theologians in particular, however, had constructed a variety of theories of the state—but they did so on the basis of natural reason, not on the basis of faith.

Not only were Catholics free to develop political theory in accordance with perceived truth, but historically and practically they were at liberty to live in a variety of forms of government. In fact, the historian could easily discover that Catholics had initiated, lived under and supported numerous forms of government, among which were republican states.

Although apologists made it clear that Catholics were free to accept any theory of government they found most reasonable, they were also careful to indicate that the theory American Catholics preferred was republican. John England, for example, tried to show that Thomas Aquinas (1225-1274), Robert Bellarmine (1542-1621), and Francisco Suarez (1548-1617) believed in some type of republican theory of government. At least, they all held that the people were the only legitimate source of all civil authority and government. England himself, like John Carroll before him, maintained a "social compact" theory of government.[6] Popular sovereignty was the basis of England's understanding of republicanism and he asserted that "no doctrine of CATHOLICISM" was opposed to this.[7]

Carroll's and England's understanding of popular sovereignty and their consciousness of the individual's rights and freedom within society produced a constitutional view of the state. For them the powers of government were limited. The state had powers only to regulate public policy; it had no power, for example, to interfere in a person's religious relations. The powers of the state, therefore, were not coterminous with the powers of society. Religious liberty was, thus, an individual's and a community's right, granted by nature, and not merely a governmental concession or grant. Since religious liberty was based on nature, it was universal in application.[8]

Such a theory also implied an acceptance of the fact of religious pluralism in America. All individuals and all religions had the right to their own religious opinions, beliefs, communal structures and forms of worship. Such a state of religious pluralism could be recognized without destroying the social fabric and without admitting that all religions are theologically equal (i.e., religious indifferentism). Social or political unity did not depend, as some European Catholics believed, upon the acceptance of one religion in the state. Social and political unity depended rather upon the republican virtue of the people, i.e., according to John England, upon the people's zeal for the common good.[9] Religion, of course, was an essential component of society, in that it was one of the primary teachers and advocates of republican virtue.

This did not imply, however, that all religions were theologically equal. John Carroll made a distinction between what he called "*theological* or religious intolerance, which is essential to true religion, and *civil* intolerance."[10] Civil intolerance, i.e., civil legislation against certain peoples because of their religious beliefs, was illegitimate because the state was incompetent in religious matters and could not impose any civil disabilities because of a person's religious convictions. Theological intolerance was another matter. It did not affect one's ability to live in political and civil harmony. To be theologically intolerant simply meant that every person had a perfect right to accept only those religious beliefs and institutions one considered most in conformity with the truth. Theological intolerance meant, for example, that Catholics could legitimately assert and believe that the Catholic Church was the only true church without ever imposing this belief upon others through political or civil measures. Theological intolerance also meant that one did not have to accept one's neighbor's religious truth claims and beliefs; one could, in fact, deny the grounds of those convictions without violating a neighbor's political or civil rights to hold them.

For Carroll and England, universal tolerance was the only effective way of achieving Christian unity. In fact, John Carroll argued that if universal tolerance could be preserved "America may come to exhibit a proof to the world, that general and equal toleration, by giving a free circulation to fair argument, is the most effectual method to bring all denominations of Christians to a unity of faith."[11] Religious beliefs, too, since they were voluntary, could be propagated solely by rational inquiry, free discussion, and religious persuasion. Religious beliefs could not be justly forced upon anyone. Here again, confidence in rational persuasion and voluntaryism reflected the faith of the Enlightenment.

Religious liberty did not necessarily imply separation of church and state. Separation, however, was a cherished idea among a number of American Catholics. For Irish-American and Anglo-American Catholics who had, as John Carroll indicated, "smarted heretofore under the lash of an established church," separation was the only just way to preserve religious liberties; Catholics, Carroll told one correspondent, should be "on our guard against every approach towards establishment [of religion in the United States]."[12] Separation implied not only that the state had limited powers, but also that the church was limited in the political arena. The church's powers were purely spiritual. John England, the primary Catholic apologist for separation in the early nineteenth century, wrote: "It is heresy in religion; it is an absurdity in politics to assert, that because a man possesses political power, therefore he possesses ecclesiastical jurisdiction: or that because he has spiritual power, he therefore has magisterial rights in the state. The doctrine of the Roman Catholic Church and the principles of the American Constitution are in unison upon this subject."[13] In another place England asserted that he was "convinced that a total separation from the temporal government is the most natural and safest state for the church in any place where it is not, as in the papal territory, a complete government of churchmen."[14] In the "papal territory" popular sovereignty had accepted the rule of churchmen and therefore that exception to the principle of separation was itself based upon a republican notion of government.

The contractual view of a limited civil government had implications for an understanding of ecclesiastical polity. Ecclesiastical as well as civil government was limited and, in the view of some American Catholic apologists, ecclesiastical government should reflect the broadest possible participation of church members in areas that concerned them most directly. Throughout much of the nineteenth century some apologists attempted to show their Protestant and nativist neighbors not only that American political republicanism and Catholicism were compatible, but also that Catholic ecclesiology possessed republican elements. This apologetic was carried out in two ways: first, by apologetical writings; second, by the organization of some republican-like ecclesiastical structures.

Apologetical literature throughout the nineteenth century reveals a preoccupation with republicanism as a theological problem. Even within a defensive posture American Catholic apologists were acknowledging that the new historical and democratic consciousness of American culture presented a valid problem to Catholics. Catholics, they were implicitly acknowledging in their defenses, must come to theological terms with the experience of republicanism within the church. The Enlightenment anthropology and the social contract view of the state held by Catholic spokesmen like John Carroll and John England, when filtered through a Gallican ecclesiology and the Anglo-American constitutional experience of government, created a specifically American approach to ecclesiology. Within this political, philosophical, and theological framework these Catholics tried to create a new understanding of the individual's relationship to the church (especially making more room for participation in the church's life), to reconcile in a new way the local to the universal church, and to provide an apologetic that emphasized the republican aspects of the church's history and structures.

John Carroll, like John England after him, believed that in the United States the church should function in a way that was suitable to republican forms of government. On the local parish level this meant that members of a congregation had certain rights to control and manage ecclesiastical temporalities. In fact, when Carroll was superior of the American missions he told the lay trustees of St. Peter's congregation in New York City that "Whenever [canonical] parishes are established no doubt, a proper regard, and such as is suitable to our government, will be had to the rights of the congregation in the mode of election and presentation of pastors: and even now I shall ever pay to their wishes every deference consistent with the general welfare of Religion."[15] Although Carroll acknowledged the right of the congregation to nominate a pastor, he became skeptical about the practical possibility of such a practice in the United States after he experienced a number of hostilities in parishes that demanded the right. Later in his career, he opposed a type of lay participation which he called "ecclesiastical democracy," i.e., "an overbearing interference of the people, in the appointment of pastors."[16] Such a practice he repeatedly identified with "Presbyterianism," or "Congregational Presbyterianism." He did, however, accept lay participation in the local congregations as long as the involvement did not make the pastor a "victim of the most capricious despotism."[17] Thus, allowing lay participation, he also tried to protect the rights and freedoms of the clergy, as well as the prerogatives of the episcopacy in the exercise of ecclesiastical government. His attempts to balance the rights and duties of all members in the administration of the Catholic Church in the United States reflected, of course, the influence of republicanism upon his ecclesiology. John England made similar, but more explicit, attempts by establishing a constitutional form of ecclesiastical government for his diocese.[18]

Carroll perceived that republican government in the United States would have "necessary effects"[19] upon ecclesiastical structures and therefore sought the appointment of a bishop to restrain the inevitable desires for lay and clerical independence and participation in the church. But, because of the republican atmosphere and the fear of foreign intervention in American affairs, he and other clerics wanted the bishop to be elected by the members of the American clergy. After Rome approved his election to the episcopacy he tried to keep from the public the fact that the Bull erecting Baltimore as a diocese stipulated that the clerical right to elect an American bishop was restricted to the first election; other bishops were not to be elected by the American clergy.[20] Thereafter, Carroll protested against the restriction to his friends and asserted that even though he opposed Ecclesiastical democracy (of the kind condemned by John Milner[21]), "yet I wish sincerely, that Bishops may be elected, at this distance from Rome, by a select body of clergy, constituting, as it were, a Cathedral chapter. Otherwise, we never shall be viewed kindly by our government here, and discontents, even amongst our own clergy, will break out."[22]

In 1783, even before Carroll had become superior of the American missions, he created a "Constitution of the Clergy" for the explicit purpose of protecting ex-Jesuits' property rights, i.e., to protect their lands from being expropriated by the government or confiscated by the Roman Congregation Propaganda Fide. The proposal for the corporation[23] reveals a number of American republican preoccupations: it provides for structure and accountability regarding property rights; it authorizes a system of checks and balances of powers among the clergy over use of property; it makes a clear distinction between the temporal and spiritual powers within the clerical community, explicitly denying that a bishop or pope have a just claim to the ex-Jesuits' "temporal possessions"; nor did they have any powers to "invest any persons with the administration of them"; it stipulated that the temporal administration of ex-Jesuit properties was to be conducted by the common consent of the clergy; it explicitly acknowledged that the body of clergy was to be governed by the rule of law and not by individual whim. Even in the area of ecclesiastical, as opposed to purely temporal, administration, Carroll believed that the ex-Jesuits needed a new form of government that would restrain the powers of the religious superior, as the former Jesuit constitution had done.[24] The "Constitution of the Clergy," formed between June 27, 1783 and October 11, 1784, reflected many of these republican ideals for the administration of the church.[25]

The concern for a constitutional balance of powers within the church and for wider participation in the actual government of ecclesiastical temporalities was manifested in a variety of other ways during the national period. Lay and clerical trustees of various congregations articulated this republican mentality during the troubles of trusteeism (1785-1860).[26] Although the lay trustees failed to create any permanent structures of lay and clerical participation in the American church, they did reflect the influence of the Enlightenment upon the American Catholic population. Not until after the Second Vatican Council (1965) would American Catholics again try to structure parishes and dioceses on a participatory basis.

Another manifestation of the influence of the Enlightenment upon ecclesiology is evident in the conciliar form of government that was established in the United States as a direct response to the tensions of trusteeism, to the need for order and structure, and to the American political and ecclesiastical forms of government. Undoubtedly the use of episcopal councils to govern the church was an ancient Christian practice, but it can be and has been appropriated to affirm a variety of different approaches to the exercise of authority in the course of Christian history. It can be and has been used, for example, both to restrict and to reinforce or enlarge ecclesiastical authority. During the period of the American Catholic Enlightenment, Carroll and England perceived the conciliar exercise of government, among other things, as an attempt to define and limit ecclesiastical authority. Although the episcopal conciliarism that did emerge after 1829 excluded the participation of the laity and the clergy in ecclesiastical decision making, it did reflect an accommodation to the American republican experience.[27]

During the nineteenth century, this conciliar form of government also tried to balance the roles of the episcopacy and the papacy in the church. It did not separate the roles as sharply as did Gallicanism (i.e., the movement in France that supported national ecclesiastical freedoms, emphasized episcopal rights, and maintained considerable independence from Roman and Papal legislation and jurisdiction), nor did it collapse the roles as did Ultramontanism (i.e., the European Catholic movement that stressed the rights and juridical powers of the pope over those of the local or national bishops). The constitutionalism that was part of the American way of life influenced the bishops in their attempts to preserve a sense of local identity and autonomy without denying or confusing the connection between local and universal jurisdiction in the church. The conciliar form of government revealed a conciliar theology of the church that was modified and conditioned by the experience of American republican values. In fact, in the early nineteenth century in particular, the conciliar understanding of the church, filtered through the British and American constitutional experience of government, gave many Catholic apologists a theological basis for their claims that republicanism and Catholicism were theoretically as well as practically compatible in the United States. Thus the American Catholic approach to ecclesiology in practice as well as in theory differed greatly from either the purely Gallican or Ultramontane practices in Europe. The constitutionalism inherent in conciliar understandings of the church and the American theory of government combined to create a particular American Catholic ecclesiology. The episcopal councils in the early nineteenth century, their successors in the three plenary Councils of Baltimore, the organization of the National Catholic Welfare Council (later referred to as "Conference") during the First World War and its twentieth-century successors, are the more permanent manifestations of American Catholic ecclesiological structures that have accommodated themselves somewhat to American republican ideals of government.

The Enlightenment anthropology that underlay Carroll's and England's understandings of the state and the church was also responsible for their respect for the individual's conscience in matters of belief within Catholicism. A good Catholic was a reasonable Catholic and one who was Catholic by rational conviction, not merely cultural association. Such an emphasis upon the individual and reason also grounded their attempts to demonstrate the reasonableness of Catholicism and its claims to be the true Christian Church.

Both apologists emphasized the role and capacity of the individual's reason in religion as well as in politics. An individual was obliged through rational inquiry and critical examination, not merely through education, "to exert himself for the discovery of truth" and to submit only to truthful and reasonable authority. Even in the realm of revealed religion, reason was capable of uncovering the "fact" of supernatural revelation and the factual existence, structure and authority of the Catholic Church. By using the general laws of historical evidence (i.e., by examining the various witnesses, documents, monuments, artifacts, miracles and prophecies of history) reason could adequately demonstrate the fact of revelation and the Catholic Church's authoritative magisterium. This theological or apologetical method, John England repeatedly said, was not metaphysical speculation; it was inductive, reasonable and scientific. Although revealed religion disclosed a knowledge of God that reason alone could not discern, nonetheless revelation itself was not contrary to reason. No one, therefore, was bound to accept revelation "without such evidence as will be sufficient to satisfy the mind."[28] Miracles and prophecies, in particular, were sufficient evidence that God had revealed himself, thus establishing the authenticity of the scriptures and of Jesus' mission to establish his church. Since rational investigation of the historical record demonstrated adequately that God had established the Catholic Church as the authentic interpreter of his word, submission to Catholic teachings was not an irrational act. Thus, Catholicism could be considered a reasonable religion since it demanded reasons for the very acceptance of the possibility of belief and historical proofs for the authority of the Catholic Church.

Although reason provided grounds for belief, it was not itself the basis of faith. According to John England, "Faith is, then, the belief upon the authority of God, of what reason cannot by its own force discover." Reason, thus, was not superior to faith, nor was it the ultimate judge of what should be believed within Christianity. Once a person had discovered the Catholic Church as the only true infallible guide to revealed religion, reason ceased to be the primary agency of understanding. Faith, or belief upon the testimony of God, took over where reason left off. Reason could indeed establish grounds for credibility but it could not itself produce faith. Faith was still a gift of God; but it was not an abject slavery of the mind nor an irrational assent to unintelligible propositions; it was an acceptance of truths based upon God's testimony which human reason could not itself discover. Reason and faith, therefore, were not two opposing avenues to truth. Upon "patient inquiry," reason and faith "will always be found mutually to aid each other."[29]

This rationalistic, individualistic, objective and extrinsic view of revelation as intellectual propositions led to an almost exclusive emphasis upon faith as an intellectual assent to the doctrinal propositions derived from revelation but defined and articulated by the ecclesiastical magisterium. This Catholic apologetical stress upon the question of the church (corresponding to the equally extrinsic and rationalistic Protestant emphasis upon the question of the Bible) as the infallible guide made Carroll's and England's apologetics what Orestes A. Brownson would call a "method of authority."[30] That is, apologetics became a means of ascertaining through the inductive method the facticity of God's revelation and thereby the supernatural character of ecclesiastical authority. All other theological questions, therefore, depended upon the correct understanding of this "rule of faith." This emphasis upon the reasonableness of faith (which, in fact, many times made reason the bar for revelation) not only reflected a theological continuity with European Catholic responses to deism but also appealed to the basic Enlightenment values in American society and established a common ground of discussion with those Protestants who had taken up the Scottish Common Sense Philosophy. The entire purpose of this approach, of course, was to reveal Catholicism as *the* reasonable form of Christianity. Submission to the church's teachings, therefore, was perceived as a rational and not a blind obedience.

ROMANTIC CATHOLICISM, 1830-1888

The early national period's emphasis on reason endured throughout much of nineteenth- and twentieth-century Catholicism. This fact alone led Walter Ong, S.J. to note that "the American Catholic has been exceedingly slow to register the romantic emphasis. He has in many ways reacted more slowly than the European Catholic because of his American rationalism and more slowly than other Americans because of his Catholic rationalism."[31] This judgment needs to be modified by what I argue took place in American Catholicism in the middle of the nineteenth century, from the establishment of the Provincial Councils of Baltimore in 1829 to the death of Isaac Thomas Hecker in 1888. During this period, changes in institutional structures and shifts in patterns of thought occurred that reflected what could be called the romantic impulse.

Romanticism is most certainly difficult to define with any precision because the movement poured itself into a variety of different political, intellectual and religious orientations, liberal as well as conservative, Protestant as well as Catholic, American as well as European. In fact, the argument over whether or not there is anything that can be designated

romanticism and precisely what might constitute the romantic tempera-
ment has been going on for years. Nonetheless, like a number of historians, I find the term useful, even though not always very precise, for
describing some of the shifts in consciousness that were taking place in
American Catholic apologetics and theology during the middle of the
nineteenth century. I am using the term here to characterize that movement in thought and culture that viewed the universe as a comprehensive
harmonious synthesis of the infinite and the finite. The divine is at the core
of all reality and manifested itself in and through all created existences. For
Catholic romantic theologians and apologists, this view of the universe
revealed a more harmonious relationship between grace and nature than
had been realized in the previous age's excessively rationalistic separation
of the two.

The romantic theologians reemphasized the doctrine of the incarnation and placed it at the center of their understanding of nature, history,
the church and society. For the romantic, the infinite was present in every
period of history as well as in nature. Thus, history was conceived in terms
of its organic continuity and development. Every age had its own uniqueness, intrinsic significance, characteristic excellence, and its own contribution to make to the richness and progress of humanity.

The infinite manifested itself in particular communities as well as in
historical epochs. Such an emphasis gave rise to an appreciation of the
spirit of different nationalities and to an organic view of the church.
Within Catholicism this stress upon the organic unity of the church led to a
reassertion of authoritative ecclesiastical structures as primary means and
symbolic representations of that unity. The rise of neo-ultramontanism
was a significant part of the romantic movement. Among other things, it
was a reaction to Gallicanism, Josephism and other forms of ecclesiastical
individualism and localism which had failed to preserve a sense of the
church's organic and universal unity.

This organic totality of infinite life with which the romantics felt
themselves to be one was apprehended, in this post-Kantian age, by intuition and feeling rather than analytic reason. Thus, romanticism, especially within European Catholicism, was a movement that emphasized the
doctrine of the incarnation, reasserted an organic understanding of nature, history, tradition and authority, restored intuition and feeling to theology and piety, and reacted to the excesses of the rationalism, moralism,
individualism and ecclesiastical nationalism of the previous age.[32]

What was happening in European Catholic romanticism was likewise
occurring here and there in American Catholicism. For the most part,
American Catholics did not develop any systematic romantic theology, but
they did selectively appropriate some romantic impulses in three areas of

ecclesiastical life during the middle of the nineteenth century: ecclesiastical polity, piety and apologetics.

The gradual change from Enlightenment to Romantic emphases is evident first of all in the changing practices and perceptions of ecclesiastical polity and in a new stress placed upon the papal role in the church. In the section on Vatican I, I discuss the American Catholic understandings of the role of the papacy in the church. Here I outline briefly the shifts in the understanding of ecclesiastical polity. Increasingly after the First Council of Baltimore in 1829, the American bishops effectively reasserted the episcopal structure of the American church at the national level in reaction to the congregationalism of trusteeism and in opposition to prior American Catholic apologetical attempts to explain Catholicism as a quasi-republican system of government. In fact, episcopal conciliarism represented in the United States what neo-ultramonantism represented in Europe—i.e., a centralization of authority in the church. In Europe, neo-ultramontanism was, among other things, a reaction to ecclesiastical nationalism and Catholic pluralism; in the United States, episcopal conciliarism was, among other things, a reaction to the congregationalism and divisiveness of trusteeism.

Some American bishops also tried to strengthen the episcopal structure of the local diocesan church after the First Provincial Council of Baltimore. Bishop John Hughes (1797-1864), for example, represented a Catholic romantic reaction to what he perceived to be excessive individualism within American Catholicism. When Hughes assumed the episcopal reigns of the Diocese of New York in 1840, he believed that the time had come for the American Catholic Church "to return to the ordinary and regular discipline of the Church."[33] For too long, he asserted, American Catholicism had appropriated elements of republicanism and individualism that were inconsistent with universal Catholic discipline and church order. The trustee form of local church government, in particular, was nothing but a capitulation to Protestant ideals. If the Catholic Church was to be in continuity with its true past, it had to reassert the episcopal monarchy of the Roman Church.

In the realm of piety, the "Catholic Revival" of the middle of the nineteenth century also reveals the romantic impulse. That revival was an attempt to overthrow the cold rationalism of Enlightenment piety, or, as some would have it, to make American Catholics active participants in the total sacramental life of the church, i.e., a practice that many American Catholics prior to the 1830s had not experienced regularly. The renewal of what Jay P. Dolan has called "sacramental evangelicalism"[34] was an attempt to balance or synthesize the personal and individualistic experience of conversion with the communal and sacramental identification, thereby strengthening the converts' ties with the institutional church. Ann Taves, too, has argued that the popular devotional life of the American Catholic, as that is revealed in the various prayer books published during the period, emphasized the miraculous and promoted an emotional awareness of the life of Christianity in its various forms. This romantic piety resurrected a variety of personal devotions, including those to the Eucharist, Mary and the saints. Eventually Rome standardized these religious devotions, thereby enhancing uniformity of those religious practices which emphasized what was uniquely Catholic and reinforced ties to the church.[35]

The romantic emphases, evident in American Catholic polity and piety, are most clearly reflected in the area of apologetics. Although American Catholic apologists throughout the nineteenth century continued to use the historical and rationalistic apologetics of the Enlightenment era, they also increasingly appropriated elements of romantic thought in their attempts to vindicate Catholicism in American culture.

John Hughes, Martin John Spalding, Orestes A. Brownson and Isaac Hecker in a variety of ways and with different degrees of sophistication represented the romantic strain in Catholic apologetics and helped to transform American Catholic consciousness. Some of the leading American Catholic romantics, particularly Brownson and Hecker, read Vicomte Francois René Chateaubriand (1768-1848), Joseph-Marie Comte de Maistre (1753-1821), Friedrich von Schlegel (1772-1829), Johann Adam Möhler (1796-1838) and other European Catholic romanticists as well as the American Transcendentalists. Such reading and the American experience combined to produce new ways of perceiving and defending Catholicism within American culture. With the exception of Brownson, Catholic apologists in the United States reflected neither the learning nor the depth of the Europeans or the American Transcendentalists, but their apologetics did reveal a shift from the rational, objective and individualistic concerns of the Enlightenment to the intuitive, subjective and organic concerns of romanticism.

The romantic apologetic had two major emphases. First, the romantic rehabilitated the organic value of tradition and history, emphasizing the internal and corresponding external continuity of Catholicism. These apologists presented Catholicism, therefore, as the guarantor of high culture and the primary agent for the development of Western civilization. A theology of the incarnation was at the heart of this apologetic. Second, some of the more philosophically oriented romantic apologists emphasized the fact of consciousness as the starting point for doing theology and apologetics. These tried to restore intuition and religious subjectivity to theology and apologetics while simultaneously preserving the objective grounds for the subjective religious experience. In other words, these romantics sought to synthesize, balance and correlate the subjective individual religious experiences and the objective communal religious experiences.

Bishops John Hughes and Martin John Spalding represent transition figures in the American Catholic movement toward a new apologetic. Although these bishops, like other American Catholic apologists during the period, still tried to demonstrate the Catholic Church's apostolicity by logic and objective historical sources, nevertheless they increasingly accentuated the historical and cultural effects of Catholicism upon the development of Western civilization. This shift from a static preoccupation with the church's nature and structure to a dynamic concern with its mission in society reveals an affiliation with the romantic concerns of the age.

A number of John Hughes' attempts to vindicate Catholicism reflect a romantic interpretation of history and a romantic return to the past, particularly to an idealized pre-Reformation Christendom.[36] A doctrine of the incarnation informs Hughes' understanding of history.

> And the great idea of the great lever which Christianity presented for the elevation of the human race, was the doctrine that the Divine Son became man, and in becoming man elevated human nature by its union with the divine nature in the same person! This is the origin; and if you start from the fountain and behold these waters of regeneration bursting forth from their primitive source, and watch them as they meandered and divided, now into one stream of benevolence, now into another, now into the improvement of legislation, now into the mitigation of the civil condition of the slave, and as they passed from nation to nation, and age to age, you will see in all their branches this power and efficacy, because God had ennobled humanity by the "Word" being "made Flesh and dwelling amongst men."[37]

Through the incarnation, a new force, impulse, or principle had been released in history and had in a variety of ways transformed human culture. The gradual development of Western civilization, of course, was an indirect and secondary, not a direct and primary result of the incarnation. The regeneration of the human heart was primary. Through this renewal, however, "a principle was planted in the heart—it is a conviction—a religious conviction—it is a sentiment" that gradually leavened the whole mass.[38] This would eventually create social regeneration. According to Hughes, all cultural and moral progress "is the result of some *latent* principle, deeply, though perhaps silently working in the mass of the people, which *thus* finds a vent and a medium of expression."[39] The improvement of industry, the amelioration of the social conditions of humankind, the evolution of human rights, the development of representative and deliberative political assemblies, the institution of the common law, and the elevation of women, for example, were all signs of the impact of the Christian spirit upon Western civilization.[40]

Martin Spalding was also interested in the historical influence of Catholicism upon the development of Western culture. Using the philosophy of Friedrich von Schlegel, "that master spirit of the present age," Spalding argued that Catholic Christianity, under Divine Providence, provided the regenerative impulse and ultimate meaning for the advancement of humanity in universal history. Divine Providence, made manifest in Catholicism, was continually directing the course of history to enable free men to realize most fully the aspiration of a human nature "stamped originally with the image of God."[41] The Catholic spirit brought art, literature, and education to Western civilization and, therefore, the Catholic Church was indeed the mother of true progress and liberty.

For Hughes and Spalding, the gradual unfolding of Western culture took place through the offices of the pre-Reformation church which had gradually integrated the Christian spirit into all areas of life. Increasingly, Hughes and other mid-nineteenth-century Catholic apologists presented the medieval church, and the papacy in particular, as the friend of the poor and the oppressed, and the institutional barrier against political and economic tyranny. God had a predilection for the weak and the outcasts of society and the institutional church put that preference into practice. Such an idealized view of the pre-Reformation church provided Hughes with a model for criticizing the defects of the modern world and for blaming the evils of contemporary society upon the effects of the Protestant Reformation. The Protestant principle of justification by faith alone, in Hughes' judgment, was responsible for divisiveness in Christianity and for selfish capitalistic theories and practices. When the unity of the medieval church was broken, these twin evils of the modern world were inevitable.[42]

Although Hughes' use of the idealized past provided grounds for criticizing contemporary values, it offered no realistic solutions to contemporary religious and economic problems. But to criticize these romantics and their interpretations of history as idealized and unrealistic (which they were) would miss the point they were trying to make in their apologetics. Their semi-apocalyptic interpretation of history which made Protestantism ultimately responsible for the evils in society and church and Catholicism the ultimate and continuous source of divine good held out hope to a poor, oppressed and persecuted people and gave them a sense of history that would ultimately work out in their favor. This romantic and apocalyptic view of the past was really a hopeful view of the future for those who were suffering in the present. We do not understand the apologetic if we interpret it only as idealized and unrealistic, just as we might miss the point of St. John's Apocalypse if we interpreted it without considering the persecuted community it was intended to encourage.

Even though Hughes and Spalding had appropriated a romantic and apocalyptic approach to history in their apologetics, neither was self-consciously romantic and neither had explicitly criticized the weaknesses of the older rationalistic apologetic. This was not the case with the converts Orestes Brownson and Isaac Hecker. They self-consciously dialogued with the romantic movement and tried to transform the older apologetical method. Brownson in particular integrated the impulses of Romanticism into his theological thought patterns more systematically and more consistently than any other American Catholic thinker of the period. Throughout his Universalist-Unitarian period (1826-1844) he was influenced at first by the rationalism of the Scottish Common Sense school of thought and then by the romanticism and transcendentalism of the French romantics and eclectics. During his Catholic period (1844-1876), although he continued to accept the insights of romanticism, he tried to steer his theological train between the excesses of Romanticism and Enlightenment Scottish Realism. Like the romantics, he emphasized the unity but not identity of grace and nature, the organic nature of history and the church, and intuition in the human knowledge of God. Unlike some romantics, he rejected both the superficial attempts of some of his fellow Catholics to restore medieval Christendom and the "excessive" subjectivism of the Transcendentalists and their "pantheistic" synthesis of the finite and the infinite. Like the Scottish Realists, he upheld reason's capacity to reach the truth and to discover an objective order. He criticized, however, their overly objective, external, historical and rationalistic apologetics.

Throughout his Universalist-Unitarian period, Brownson had searched for a philosophical and theological concept that could resolve the intellectual problems he gradually uncovered in the thought of some contemporary American and European philosophies and theologies. At one time, like some others, he had believed that every human person had an inherent religious sentiment and therefore religious experience was universally possible as long as individuals discovered within themselves the grounds of their religious experience. He very quickly began to question this position, however. He asked himself: Does what I experience really correspond to anything real outside of myself? The problem of reconciling the relationship between subjective experience and objective reality (on the levels of epistemology, ontology and theology), i.e., the problem of the post-Kantian world, would be a primary intellectual concern for him for much of his life. The problem, of course, appeared in a variety of forms. How does one preserve the distinction and simultaneously save the union that exist between apparent contradictions in human life: i.e., between the infinite and the finite, grace and nature, object and subject, revelation and reason, liberty and authority, progress and stability, church and state?

During his Unitarian days, after reading Victor Cousin, Benjamin Constant and the French Saint-Simonian, Pierre Leroux, Brownson uncovered a fundamental theological concept that could synthesize as well as distinguish the above polarities—i.e., his doctrine of life by communion which he appropriated from the thought of Pierre Leroux. This doctrine not only synthesized the objectivist concerns of the Enlightenment with the immanent and subjective concerns of romanticism, but it also removed many of his intellectual difficulties with Catholicism, eventually enabling him to become a Catholic. Although he did not consistently articulate this doctrine after his conversion, he did hold onto it "with variations, either consciously or unconsciously for the remainder of his life."[43]

The point of departure for Brownson's doctrine of life by communion was in human consciousness where the self's recognition of itself and the non-self existed in indissoluble unity. In fact, for Brownson, one starts the quest for understanding from a unity that already exists and discovers both subject and object in the unity of thought and life. Just as no thought is possible without the prior synthetic presence of subject and object, so also no act of life is possible without that indissoluble unity.

For Brownson, to live is to manifest. This means that life itself is defined as the interaction or intershock of the me with the not me. "Man lives and can only live by communion with what is not himself."[44] That which provides for the unity of as well as the distinction between subject and object in thought and life is, Brownson eventually discovered, the divine creative act. Thus, for Brownson the doctrine of life by communion was ultimately grounded in the divine creative act whereby God is "immanent as first cause in all creatures and in every act of every creature."[45] This act is the "great dialectical principle," the medium of the dialectical harmony of God and man, grace and nature, revelation and reason, the spiritual and the material.[46] Through the medium of God's creative act, man lives by communion with God himself, other men and nature, giving rise to three institutions: religion or the church, society or the state, and property.[47]

Although Brownson's doctrine of life by communion, grounded as it was in the divine creative act, provided some objective grounds for knowledge of God as cause, and explained how sin could be transmitted from one generation to another and how human persons could influence one another, it could not explain how God could intervene in the historical process. To explain God's historical interventions Brownson had recourse to the doctrine of providence. His doctrine of providence complimented his doctrine of the divine creative act and gave him an intelligible explanation for the possibility of the incarnation, tradition and the Catholic Church.

When God created Adam, Brownson held, he created him to live under a supernatural providence. God revealed to Adam from the beginning that there was an order of life above our natural human life and this primitive revelation was communicated to the entire human community through tradition. This primitive revelation contained intimations of a God-man as a fact that was to take place or that has already taken place. This primitive revelation, though at times obscured and latent, has reached all the sons and daughters of Adam.[48]

This primitive revelation is awakened and kept alive from time to time by God's special free interventions into human history. The actual incarnation, then, was the fullest manifestation of God's providential care for his people and the primary means through which he establishes a union between the human and the divine, thus raising and elevating humankind to a new level of divine life. Christ communicated his life immediately and directly to his apostles and disciples and through communion with them this life is transmitted to others in the church. The church becomes then the visible manifestation of this divine life, and thus the divine life in the church is authenticated not by some arbitrary and extrinsic act of authority or history, but by an internal principle of tradition which is itself the Incarnate Word. Union with this divine internal tradition in the church is not automatic, however, but is realized through a subjective conversion. Still, it is the action of the object, i.e., the divine presence of Christ in the communion of the Church, that makes possible the subject's act of conversion.

This doctrine of communion eventually made it possible for Brownson to see the Catholic Church as the visible continuation of the incarnation. Ten years after his conversion to Catholicism, he began to argue that this doctrine of life by communion could provide Catholics with a new apologetic because it represented the generative principle of Catholicism and was able to embrace all truth in its unity and universality. The older method was unconvincing because it relied almost exclusively upon authority, logic and motives of credibility which were drawn from the external facts of history. The doctrine of life by communion offered Protestants an explanation of the internal principle that holds together the various expressions of Catholicism.[49] This new apologetic puts Brownson in the romantic camp.

Isaac Hecker, Brownson's disciple, also reflected the romantic influence in his apologetical emphases.[50] Hecker's apologetical method was an attempt to synthesize or harmonize the inner, subjective religious yearnings and aspirations of the individual and the human community with their outward and objective revelations and realizations. The theological *point de départ* for Hecker was no longer reason, authority, or history, as it was for scholastic apologetics, but the religious wants, needs, and experiences of the individual. Hecker was primarily concerned with the "instincts" and "aspirations" of human nature.

The subjective "Questions of the Soul," according to Hecker, found their response in objective revelation located in the sacramental experiences of Catholicism. Thus, Hecker tried to correlate the subjective quest for meaning with the objective revelation in the church. In fact, the quest, implanted by God, was itself a revelation of the nature and destiny of man. For Hecker, as for Brownson, no dichotomy existed between subject and object. One could not, however, collapse the two and destroy the distinction, as some Transcendentalists were wont to do. "In the production of life, subject necessarily connotes object and is correlative with it. Oneness is barrenness."[51]

The age as well as the individual was yearning for some kind of fulfillment. The instincts and aspirations of the age revealed for Hecker a cultural movement toward Catholicism. Transcendentalism, the Brook Farm experience, Fruitlands, Valle Crucis, and other American religious and social quests proved to Hecker that leading Americans, those on the cutting edge of the future, were articulating the inadequacies of Protestantism and reflecting the needs of modern man for more spiritually satisfying experiences and answers to the basic problems of humankind.

To Hecker the Holy Spirit was working within individual persons and within American culture leading them and it toward the revelations of the Holy Spirit within the Catholic Church. Thus, Hecker correlated the subjective inclinations with their objectives and sacramental realizations. The Holy Spirit speaking within corresponded to the Holy Spirit coming from without. The subjective and incarnational élan of romanticism was thereby combined with the objective preoccupations of the Enlightenment. His apologetical emphasis, however, was placed upon the subject rather than the object, as the starting point for any analysis of the religious dimension of life.

VATICAN I AND PAPAL AUTHORITY, 1869-70

American Catholics, whether influenced more by the Enlightenment or by Romanticism, repeatedly had to answer American nativist and Protestant charges against the papacy. Popes were indicted for immorality, papal interference in purely political affairs and religious despotism in their claims to primacy of honor and jurisdiction. The papal office was monarchical, the nativists also charged, and therefore contrary to republicanism. American Catholics, therefore, could not logically nor consistently maintain a double allegiance—one to a foreign papal monarch and another to the American republican government.

While responding to these and other charges, American Catholic apologists developed two schools of thought on the nature of the papacy and the extent of papal power and authority. The two schools of thought resemble, although they are not to be equated with, the Gallican and ultramontane positions on the papacy that were current in European Catholicism prior to Vatican I. In Europe, Catholics had for centuries debated the problem of the precise locus of ultimate teaching authority in the church. During the fourteenth and fifteenth centuries, some (the conciliarists) argued that ultimate ecclesiastical authority resided in the universal council; others (the ultramontanists) held that the pope possessed such authority. The seventeenth-century Gallicans and their subsequent followers, successors to the conciliarists, upheld the authority of the national church and the national episcopacy; the ultramontanes and neo-ultramontanes of the nineteenth century favored the centralization of ecclesiastical authority in the papacy and fought vigorously against the conciliarist and Gallican views throughout the post-Tridentine period. The Gallicans seemed to have had momentum on their side until the French Revolution. After the Revolution, because of the devastation of the Gallican Church, the impetus shifted to the ultramontanes, culminating in the definition of papal infallibility at Vatican I (1869-1870).

Prior to Vatican I, American Catholic positions on the locus of ecclesiastical authority were neither as sharply debated nor as much a reaction to the French Revolution as were those in Europe. The two major European positions certainly influenced the formulation of American perspectives on the papacy, but the American experiences of nativism, republicanism, separation of church and state, and the episcopal conciliar form of American ecclesiastical government after 1829 significantly altered those two traditional approaches to the papacy. The two major pre-Vatican I American perspectives on the papacy, therefore, reflect much more the American than the European circumstances.

The American constitutional view of the state and the experience of the separation of Church and State clearly separated the American from the European perception of the papacy. Although the American Catholics were divided in their assessment of papal powers, they were united in their acceptance of the papacy as the purely spiritual center and symbol of Catholic unity. They agreed among themselves upon papal primacy of honor and jurisdiction within the universal church and asserted that the popes had no divinely-instituted temporal authority or mission. They were also united in their strongly expressed affections of loyalty to the persons of the oppressed pontiffs during the nineteenth century. The permanence, constancy and spiritual independence of the papacy in opposition to oppression from the French Directory and Napoleon became a rallying cause for many American Catholics who felt similarly oppressed.[52] Under the unanimous expressions of affection for and loyalty to the papacy, however, lay two divided positions on papal authority.

The first school of thought, the Enlightenment or episcopal school, represented by Bishops John Carroll, John England, Peter Richard Kenrick (1806-1896) and others, balanced the primacy of the papacy with the rights, prerogatives and powers of the national episcopacy. Influenced by the Enlightenment, constitutionalism, conciliarism and a form of Gallicanism that was filtered through the British and American constitutional experience, they emphasized the constitutional limits of papal prerogatives in matters of jurisdiction and teaching. This school also denied that papal infallibility was Catholic teaching; it was a theological opinion, but one, they believed, not well grounded in scripture or tradition. The church was indeed infallible, but that infallibility was located in the college of bishops united with the pope. England expressed this collegial perception of the episcopacy in his Diocesan Constitution: "We [i.e., Catholics] believe and acknowledge the majority of the bishops of the church, who are successors of the apostles, in union with their head aforesaid [the pope], to be an ecclesiastical tribunal appointed by our Lord Jesus Christ to decide by his authority, with infallible certainty of truth, in all controversies of doctrine, and to testify truly to us those things which have been revealed by God and man. We also recognize and acknowledge in that same tribunal full power and authority, by the same divine institution, to regulate and to ordain the general ecclesiastical discipline of the whole Church of Christ."[53] The Second Plenary Council of Baltimore in 1866 agreed with this general description of the locus of full authority in the Catholic Church, although the council preferred to use the term "inerrancy" rather than infallibility to describe the nature of that authority.[54]

Many in the conciliar school were ardent Americanists and republicans in politics. They repeatedly asserted, against the nativists, therefore, that every well-ordered republican society demanded a central authority. The papacy represented in the spiritual order what the American presidency represented in the political order—i.e., an office unifying the community, and directing the decision-making powers of the community. As the president was the head of the federation of states, so the pope was the head of the federation of dioceses.[55] Thus, the pope's position as the symbol of unity, and his office as president of the episcopacy made him more a constitutionally-restrained governor than an absolute monarch. His powers were purely spiritual; he had no temporal authority granted to him by revelation. Thus, American Catholic allegiance to the papacy was no threat to Americanism. Catholics could be as American in their political allegiance as any other religious persons. The conciliar school's approach to the papacy was more than simply a theological defense of the nature and function of the papal office in the church. It was also, maybe even primarily, an apologetic for Catholic Americanism and Catholic republicanism.

During the First Vatican Council, Peter Richard Kenrick, the Archbishop of St. Louis, expressed the conciliar position in opposition to the infallibilist forces. Prior to the council he neither felt the need nor had the opportunity to discuss the issue of papal infallibility, but during the council he asserted that the doctrine was not definable because the evidence of scripture and tradition was either silent on or opposed to the doctrine. He argued against a definition of the doctrine, furthermore, because of his understanding of a council's role in the church. A council's task was to witness to the faith of the church and not to debate theological opinions. Papal infallibility was a legitimate theological opinion, but, in Kenrick's view, it was not a part of the church's faith communicated from the beginning. He was against the definition, moreover, because he saw such a definition as a fundamental threat to the divine right of the episcopacy and the episcopal order in the church. Such a definition, he feared, would reduce the bishops to being simply vicars of the pope, making them dependent upon the pope rather than the Holy Spirit for their offices. Kenrick also feared that if the doctrine were defined there would be no way of setting limits to papal authority nor of establishing conditions for the exercise of this infallibility. The potential evil consequences of such an absolutism argued against the definition. He also opposed the definition for practical reasons. Such a definition would frighten Protestants and confirm their gravest fears about Catholicism. It would make liars, too, of those English and Irish Catholics who for centuries swore on oath that the doctrine of papal infallibility was not a part of Catholic faith or tradition.[56]

Kenrick left Rome before the First Vatican Council voted in favor of the definition of papal infallibility. Although he eventually accepted the Vatican Council's teaching on papal infallibility, he never formally rejected his original objections to the definition. He submitted to the definition on the grounds that the church's collective wisdom is superior to that of the individual and on the grounds that Christian doctrine can and does develop within the Christian tradition.

Kenrick was in the minority in the 1870s. The wave of the future was not with the former conciliarist positions. Vatican I represented the victory of the neo-ultramontane school which had been developing since the French Revolution. In the United States, this second school of thought, the Romantic or neo-ultramontane school, was represented by Bishops Francis Patrick Kenrick and Martin John Spalding, F. X. Weninger, S.J., and Orestes A. Brownson. These shared many of the views of the Enlightenment school, but emphasized the extension, rather than the limits, of papal prerogatives in matters of jurisdiction and teaching. These apologists believed that papal infallibility, in particular, was a legitimate Catholic theological opinion and advocated it as an authentic Catholic position grounded in scripture and tradition. They were also careful to point out the interdependence of spiritual and temporal affairs, rather than stressing their separation.

In the midst of the Oxford movement in England and the United States, Francis Patrick Kenrick, Bishop of Philadelphia, wrote the first American treatise on the papacy, *The Primacy of the Apostolic See Vindicated* (1845). Although this work was intended as an historical justification of the primacy and not a detailed nor precise canonical or scholastic explanation of papal powers, nonetheless it did acknowledge that papal infallibility was in accord "with ancient tradition."[57] Martin John Spalding, educated like Kenrick in Rome, also believed that "Though not an article of faith, it [papal infallibility] is, however, the general belief among Catholics: and I myself am inclined strongly to advocate its soundness, chiefly on account of the intimate connection between the Pontiff and the Church."[58] Brownson, too, was a strong advocate of papal infallibility. He saw the doctrine as a clear manifestation of the superiority of the spiritual to the temporal. Catholics were not obliged to believe it as a doctrine of faith, although he himself believed the doctrine to be "the sounder theological opinion."[59] In 1862, he asserted that "the pope is infallible *ex cathedra*, that is, with the church, and the church is infallible with the pope, though neither is infallible without the other." As an individual, however, the pope does not in his private capacity possess the prerogative.[60]

The neo-ultramontane school believed, in the words of Orestes Brownson, that the American conciliarists (Gallicans, in his view) had attempted to "restrict the Papal power as much as possible" and that in doing so they had conceded "far more to Protestant prejudice and cant than is necessary."[61] In a republican country, Francis Patrick Kenrick noted, people are "naturally prejudiced against an authority which resembles a monarchy."[62] The theologians of this school, therefore, sought to reassert against the stream of American "prejudices" the authority of the church and the fullness of papal powers. The true question for this school was not "whether the Papacy be or be not compatible with republican government, but, whether it be or be not founded in divine right."[63] Once it was clearly established by scripture and tradition that the papacy was founded in divine right then it could logically be maintained that the papacy "is supreme over whatever is founded only in human right."[64]

For Kenrick, who was not particularly concerned with outlining the precise prerogatives of papal authority, it was "difficult to assign precise limits to a power which must be adapted to the exigencies of the church in an endless variety of circumstances."[65] Thus, this school repeatedly asserted the superiority of the spiritual over the temporal, without maintaining that the church could interfere directly in political affairs. The church's non-interference in political affairs, however, was conditional. The church teaches obedience to all lawfully constituted political authority, but if a government would issue "laws contrary to the principles of eternal justice," it would negate the limits of its power and could not receive obedience from religious persons. The church, in such a case, would not contravene its powers by releasing its subjects from obedience to such laws.[66] Temporal and spiritual matters are so often "mixed up in this life, and all here is so subordinated to the great ends of our existence hereafter, that it is not in all cases easy to draw the line, nor prudent to be over-particular in saying where the spiritual authority begins or ends."[67] This school was careful to assert the independence of the church from political authority, while at the same time reaffirming the superiority of spiritual over temporal authority. Such a position did not, these apologists pointed out, violate the American separation of church and state. American Catholics, for example, could believe in papal supremacy and papal infallibility without denying the separation of church and state, because that supremacy and authority governed ecclesiastical affairs and the ultimate religious ends of humanity, not political policies unrelated to those ends.

Bishops from the United States brought their divided opinions to Rome in 1869 and 1870 in response to Pope Pius IX's convocation of the First Vatican Council. Of the forty-eight American bishops and one abbot who participated in the council, about seven consistently either spoke out, signed petitions, or wrote against the proposed dogma of papal infallibility; about four were vocally and articulately in favor of it. At the end of the discussion, twenty-four American bishops and the one abbot voted in favor of the definition, one, Edward Fitzgerald, Bishop of Little Rock, Arkansas, voted against it, and twenty-two had left Rome before the vote, either because they could not for personal reasons remain in Rome any longer or because they did not wish to vote against a position that was obviously favored by the majority of bishops.[68] The final vote on July 18, 1870 was five hundred and thirty-three for papal infallibility and two against it. Thus, the pope, as head of the church, was declared to possess the charismatic gift of infallibility when he explicitly defined matters of faith and morals for the entire church to believe.

After the definition was promulgated, all the American bishops, even those formerly opposed to the definition, formally accepted it. The submissions, however, were not the same.[69] The American infallibilists as well as the former anti-infallibilists, once they returned to the United States, interpreted the dogma of papal infallibility in a moderate way, indicating the limits as well as the extent of the papal powers.[70]

Apologists like Brownson and even Hecker saw the definition as a victory for the supremacy of the spiritual over the temporal in a world that was increasingly denying religious authorities. Hecker also saw the definition as the culmination of the church's efforts since the Protestant Reformation and especially since the French Revolution to reassert the authoritative powers of the church. Now that such a definition was accomplished, the Catholic Church, which had been excessively preoccupied with issues of authority for three centuries, could begin to reassert the importance of the Holy Spirit in the interior life of the individual. In fact, the definition of Vatican I had "prepared the way for the faithful to follow, with greater safety and liberty, the inspirations of the Holy Spirit."[71] The coming centuries, in Hecker's opinion, would pay increasing attention to the internal dimensions of the Christian life, as the former centuries had paid considerable attention to external authority within the Christian community. Hecker's interpretation of Vatican I indicated how some Catholics could enter into the optimism of the late nineteenth century without denying the teachings of Vatican I. In fact, some, like Hecker, would see Vatican I as a turning point in the history of Catholicism. The Holy Spirit was preparing the church for new options in the future.

AMERICANISM AND MODERNISM, 1880-1910

By the late nineteenth century the Catholic community was by far the largest single denomination in the United States and well institutionalized from coast to coast. From 1880 until the 1920s, the community experienced wave after wave of new immigrants, reinforcing the image of the church's foreignness. The new immigration, moreover, increased the internal ethnic dissensions and intensified the external nativist attacks. The Catholic community not only experienced its own tensions but also lived in the midst of a Protestant community that was encountering a series of its own conflicts. The challenge of evolutionary theories and the new sciences to traditional religious perspectives, the battles between the liberal theologians and their conservative or fundamentalist opponents, the awareness of social and economic inequalities—such difficulties within the Protestant community also affected the American Catholic community. The general cultural optimism and the developing awareness of America's destiny in world affairs, moreover, influenced those Catholics who identified themselves with American ideals.

According to Walter Ong, S.J., "there was a time at the turn of the century when Catholic consciousness in America seemed on the point of taking explicit intellectual cognizance of the forward-looking habits endemic in the American state of mind."[72] American Catholics, of course, had previously in the nineteenth century taken "explicit intellectual cognizance" of the American mentality. In fact, the previous romantic consciousness—which had reasserted and reformulated the doctrine of the incarnation and providence, renewed the organic and providential view of history, the church, and society, and stressed the role of the Holy Spirit in individual religious experiences—laid a foundation for later American Catholic religious developments. At the end of the century, this consciousness produced two related but distinct movements: Americanism and modernism.

The Americanists (e.g., Archbishop John Ireland of St. Paul, James Cardinal Gibbons of Baltimore, Archbishop John Keane of Dubuque, Bishop Dennis O'Connell of Richmond, and a few Suplician clerics) tried to create a rapproachement between Catholicism and contemporary American life. These liberal Catholics accommodated themselves, in particular, to the American zeitgeist. In a practical-pastoral and non-systematic way, the Americanists accepted an optimistic and evolutionary world view, a cultural and religious immanentism, an ecumenical spirit, and a religious concern for the economic problems created by industrial expansion. The Americanist Catholic responses to the spirit of the times developed not only within the context of the Leonine papacy (1878-1903), which many Catholic liberals at first interpreted as a papacy in support of modern movements, but also within the context of the perennial nativist attacks upon Catholicism as foreign to intellectual freedoms and the American way of life.

The Americanists created a climate of opinion in American Catholicism that encouraged some scholars to examine theoretically and systematically the problems created by the scientific method, evolutionary theories, and historical and biblical criticism. From about 1890 to 1907, these quasi-modernist American Catholic scholars called for a greater use of the scientific method and the social sciences and advocated a more systematic appropriation of historical and biblical criticism in theology. These modernist tendencies in American Catholicism were limited to a small group of American Catholics and, therefore, did not significantly influence the direction of American Catholic thought. When these tendencies came under suspicion in the papal encyclical *Pascendi* (1907), the American modernists quietly quit their endeavors to create a dialogue between theology and modern thought patterns and either pursued careers that were no threat to orthodoxy or, as in the case of two or three, left the Catholic Church.

This Americanist and modernist enthusiasm for the age was certainly not shared by all American Catholics. Those who generally opposed the Americanist programs (e.g., Archbishop Michael Corrigan of New York, Bishop Bernard McQuaid of Rochester, Bishop Frederick Katzer of Milwaukee, and many Jesuit and German clergy) were much more critical than the Americanists of American values and had a more conservative approach to accommodation. Most of these conservative Catholics saw the liberal mentality and programs as threats to the integrity of Catholic authority, the certainty of Catholic doctrine, and the unity of the American Catholic Church, and as capitulations to the secularism and naturalism of the times. They frequently quoted Pope Pius IX's and the First Vatican Council's declarations against liberalism in their criticisms of liberal Catholic attempts to reconcile the church and the age.

They criticized in particular the liberals' one-dimensional view of Americanism, their excessive nationalism, cultural chauvinism, and their tendencies toward rationalism, egalitarianism, progressivism, ecumenism and socialism. In cultural matters, they charged, the Americanists were chauvinists and in theology the modernists were minimizers. Because the conservatives valued diversity within American Catholic unity and because they wanted to protect the value of the particular in culture (against what they considered the leveling and universalizing tendencies of the Americanists), they advocated an ecclesiastical program of gradual assimilation for the new immigrants. The conservatives, moreover, criticized liberalism in theology, because the liberals, using the scientific methods, social sciences and biblical criticism, tended "to limit and reduce the authority of the magisterium of the Church as far as possible."[73] The liberals in the United States, by capitulating to the spirit of the times, had sacrificed Catholic truth, "usually under the mask of an exaggerated patriotism."[74] The authority and doctrine of the Catholic Church had to be repeatedly reasserted, especially in times when such authority was rejected outside the Church and attenuated within.

The liberals, in the midst of their conflict with the conservatives, led a movement to reconcile Catholicism and American ideals. These men wanted Catholicism to shed its foreign cultural identifications, to enter into the spirit of American institutions, to be a leader in the advancement of research and modern scientific learning, to become the visible foundation of American democracy, to further America's role in leading the world toward greater liberty and justice, and to cooperate with other religious bodies in solving the contemporary social and economic problems. The Americanists' vision of American Catholicism and their practical programs for relating Catholicism to American ideals were not established upon any systematic theological foundations. Their periodic speeches and addresses, however, reveal their acceptance of five themes that dominated the liberal spirit of the age: (1) a quasi-immanentist or incarnational view of the natural order; (2) a corresponding perception of the Christian's inherent responsibilities for that order; (3) an equally corresponding willingness to accommodate to the spirit of the times; (4) a providential, but also evolutionary or developmental understanding of human history; (5) an openness to the use of the new sciences within religion and theology. Their enthusiasm and optimism for the age prepared the ground for more systematic modernist attempts to use the new sciences in theology.

A quasi-immanentist understanding of the relationship of the sacred to the secular lay behind the Americanist call for Catholics to identify themselves with American ideals and institutions. Although the Americanists emphasized repeatedly the interdependence of the natural and the supernatural, they never collapsed the distinction between the two. Nature and grace could not be separated. The age and the church alike pulsated with God's presence. The God of nature worked in the one and the God of supernatural revelation worked in the other. In its depths, the age was instinct with Christian emotions and it only waited for contact with Christ's Church to acknowledge itself Christian. Grace built upon nature, they would say, and therefore the Catholic Church must be concerned with the natural as the womb of the supernatural. This meant that Catholicism could not be a solely sanctuary religion—a religion exclusively concerned with the future world beyond death, a world divorced from temporal concerns. The Church, and therefore the Catholic, could not be only concerned with salvation in the future because the Church was "the source of salvation to men in their present as well as in their future life." The Catholic Church could not separate or distinguish too radically "the interests and the work of the Church from those of society." Jesus himself went about preaching the Kingdom of God, and for him that meant that "Nothing that was of the welfare of man in this present life was alien to His love and power." The church's primary work, like that of Christ, was "to bring souls to God," "but simultaneously with this there went always the work of stripping, as far as it was possible, of ignorance and pain, the natural life of humanity, and promoting it by most efficient aid to ascents toward higher planes of intellectual light and material well-being."[75]

The Americanist believed that Christians had an inherent responsibility for the natural order because that order was not removed from the order of grace. For Archbishop John Ireland, as for other Americanists, salvation was a present as well as a future work. This meant that the church should first humanize and civilize before it could effectively and efficiently Christianize. Thus, the liberals called for the church to become well acquainted with the modern spirit, with its research, knowledge, and science. If the Church were responsible for the betterment of human society, it would have to acquire the secular tools that would enable it to contribute to the liberation of modern man from poverty, ignorance and injustice. Catholics were called to enter the contemporary world in order to preserve what was good in it (e.g., American democratic traditions in social and economic as well as in political life) and to remove the obstacles (i.e., ignorance and poverty) to the fullest realization of these American values.

Although this twofold mission belonged primarily to the Catholic Church because its spiritual and infallible authority provided certain moral guidance to its people, nonetheless it should also share this mission with other American Christians. Ecumenical cooperation in social betterment could certainly be achieved "without the smallest peril to one's particular religious faith." If religion was to be in the forefront of human progress, then, according to John Ireland, American Catholics should also encourage a fair exchange of religious ideas. Catholics, for example, need not fear such an exchange at the World's Parliament of Religion in Chicago in 1893 because "Truth is not timid, and upon an occasion so great and important should not truth court publicity, in order to be better known and better loved?"[76] Bishop John Keane agreed with Ireland's estimate of the Parliament, maintaining that "it is only by a friendly and brotherly comparison of convictions that reasonable men can ever come to an agreement about the all-important truths which are the foundation of religion."[77] Ecumenical dialogue and cooperation, thus, was another aspect of the Americanist program.

The Americanist willingness to accommodate Catholicism to the spirit of the modern world was itself based upon an understanding of the world as the arena of God's saving activity. This did not mean that the church must conform to the age, but it did mean that God was present in the world and therefore the church had something to learn from the world. The church needed to learn the wants of the modern world and needed to adapt the church's mission to meet those aspirations. The church was, after all, a mixture of the temporal and the eternal, the changeable and the permanent. Some accidentals in the church's structure and mission could easily be modified and changed to meet modern needs.

Like many of the romantics, the Americanists had a providential and organic view of history, but one that was significantly conditioned by the evolutionary mentality of the day. The impact of the evolutionary impulse is especially evident in the addresses and speeches of Archbishop John Ireland. The code words "progress," "development," "change," "newness," the "future," "destiny," and "mission" are frequently found in his attempts to reveal the Catholic Church as the agent of Western civilization and American Catholicism as the harbinger of modern developments. For him, as for a number of liberal Catholics, the United States and American Catholicism stood on the cutting edge of the future. Both had a God-given destiny to lead the modern world into a future of freedom and justice for all. He looked to the future rather than the past as the arena for the concentration of Catholic intellectual and social endeavors. His eager optimism, however, was at times an uncritical acceptance of the pulse of the times.

As the world changes so also the church's consciousness of itself and its teachings change. For Ireland, following perhaps John Henry Cardinal Newman's view of the development of doctrine, the church has always brought out new interpretations of its principles, but they are new "only because the emergencies calling for them had not before arisen."[78] Although these ideas lay undeveloped in Ireland's writings, they do reveal an openness in his thought to the theological implications of change and evolution. Some of these implications would be developed in a more systematic fashion by John Zahm.

The inevitable evolution of man and his "consciousness" of justice are hallmarks of Americanist optimism.

> Slowly . . . but ceaselessly, humanity was moving forward, gaining age by age in consciousness of rights; this consciousness being ever quickened by the influence of the Christian religion, and in particular by its teachings on the fatherhood of God and the brotherhood of man. Towards the close of the eighteenth century the spirit of democracy was hovering over the nations seeking to incarnate itself in a people. . . . At that time . . . the Republic of the United States of America rose into being and majesty.[79]

One element of the modern world that was clearly a manifestation of God's work in the world was the development of American democracy. It was itself the result of an evolutionary process that was in its origins ultimately Christian. America, too, was the "highest billow in humanity's evolution." The Catholic Church should be especially conscious of the progress that had taken place in the United States because "Progress is the law of God's creation."[80] The church, therefore, should be behind contemporary progressive democratic movements in economic as well as political life because those movements were basically Christian in their origins and ultimate destiny. The American Catholic Church, in particular, had also the special mission of carrying Catholic truth "on the wings of American influence" to the entire "universe."[81]

Because the Americanists had an immanentist view of the natural order and a providential-developmental view of history, they called upon Catholics to enter into the intellectual and scientific developments of the modern age. The church, they repeatedly asserted, must use the modern sciences to understand better humanity and the world. Although they were not themselves capable of using the new sciences, they were open to their use and that openness to modern patterns of thought prepared the way for modernist approaches within American Catholicism.

A few historians and theologians have denied any connection between Americanism and modernism "either by way of cause or practical preface." These would also maintain that Americanism was "largely devoid of theological content."[82] It is difficult to deny, however, that the Americanists were open to the theological implications of their programs. The very fact that they encouraged dialogue with modern research and science makes them at least unwitting forerunners of a modernist mentality.

American Catholicism did not produce anyone of the stature of the modernist Alfred Loisy, but at the end of the century it did produce a few scholars with modernist tendencies. These few could be called modernist or quasi-modernist if one accepts F. L. Cross' definition of modernism as "a movement within the Roman Catholic Church which aimed at bringing the tradition of Catholic belief into closer relation with the modern outlook in philosophy, the historical and other sciences and social ideas." Although the movement did not possess a shared vision, it was based upon at least three leading principles or ideas, according to Cross: (1) a critical approach to the Bible—i.e., the Bible was interpreted as the record of a real unfolding of divine truth in history; (2) an inclination to reject scholastic intellectualism in theology and to subordinate doctrine to practice; (3) a teleological attitude to history, finding the meaning of the historic process in its issue rather than in its origins.[83] Some of these tendencies are evident in a few American Catholic scholars.

From the 1890s to 1908, some Americans called upon their fellow Catholics to investigate more systematically the theories of evolution, to use more effectively history and the social sciences in theological education, and to take a more historical-critical attitude to biblical research than they had in the past. John Zahm, a professor and scientist at the University of Notre Dame, was one of the first American Catholics to analyze and criticize systematically the evolutionary mentality of his day. Like many of the Americanists, among whom he had close associations, he was an optimist, but he was more conscious than they of the need to examine the evolutionary theories critically from a distinctly Catholic perspective. For him the theory of evolution, at least in its theistic form, was clearly compatible with the Catholic intellectual tradition. Once properly understood from the theistic perspective, evolutionary theory could supply new insights for Catholic theology. It could, in fact, provide additional support to the religious perspectives that the world has an ultimate purpose and unity, that man has ultimate dignity and is the "highest term of a long and majestic development," and that God is immanent in the processes of history as well as transcendent to the entire development (in fact, the immanence of God in his works refuted the Deists of the Enlightenment who understood God to withdraw from his works once he had created them). Zahm also asserted that the "relations between the natural and the supernatural" are more harmonious than some perceive them to be. For Zahm, the world was "instinct with invitations to a higher life and a happier existence in the future."[84]

The modernists not only reflected the evolutionary and incarnational impulses of the progressive theologies of the day, they also demanded more critical historical methods and prudent uses of higher biblical criticism. John Hogan, S.S., a priest and teacher at New Brighton Seminary outside of Boston and later professor at the Catholic University of America in Washington, D.C., tried to lead American Catholic theology in the direction of historical theology. At least, he pointed to the inadequacy of basing all theological reflection upon "metaphysical principles." "The modern tendency, it is true," he wrote in 1898, "leads to the development of theology on the lines of history and philology, and its future as a living science is clearly in that direction."[85] Other professors, like William Kerby and John A. Ryan of the Catholic University, emphasized the necessity of using the social sciences, especially sociology and economics, in the seminaries and in theological discourse.

In 1900, for example, Kerby asserted that the scholar must take a "many-sided study" to the gospel in order to understand its meaning and scope. "The personality of our Savior, the conditions in which He worked and which He tolerated, attitudes which He took, the processes and limitations which He recognized in supernatural life, the laws of social growth, individual man and social nature, human limitations and the historical interpretation of the Gospel, all these elements must be taken into account before we can safely claim to have understood the role of the Gospel in life and its relation to the problems of society." For Kerby, "The theological sciences, as commonly taught in our seminaries, are not enough. The priest must know human society, its structures, laws, forces, and institutions; he must know also its history and its tendencies." The spirit and method of theology and philosophy, as presently taught, were not "entirely in sympathy with the actual situation." A more scientific method was necessary to give theology a fuller appreciation of the actual circumstances of modern life. "Moral, religious, economic, political and social forces combine in producing the social phenomena which we study—no one-sided view of them is ever safe." Thus, the social sciences must obtain "an integral position" within all theological education.[86]

Before the condemnation of modernism in 1907, a few American Catholic scholars were also engaged in the historical-critical study of the Bible. A few Catholic periodicals, e.g., the *New York Review* and the *Catholic University Bulletin*, raised the question of the Mosaic authorship of the Pentateuch. Some in fact asserted the "dominance of higher criticism over traditional views and opinions" regarding Mosaic authorship.[87] Others, like the St. Joseph's Seminary (Dunwoodie, New York) professor Francis E. Gigot, S.S. (1859-1920), who was perhaps the "most advanced Catholic scripture scholar in the American Church," called upon Catholics to use higher criticism: "The time is gone when the questions involved in the higher criticism might be simply identified with rationalistic attacks upon the revealed word. Again, one can no longer afford to be ignorant of topics which, perhaps more than any others at present, engross the attention of the intellectual and religious world."[88]

The budding interest in higher criticism came to a swift end with the encyclical *Pascendi* (1907), condemning modernism as the "synthesis of all errors." Even prior to this papal explosion, the dialogue between Catholics and America had been "abruptly killed off" by Pope Leo XIII's encyclical *Testem benevolentiae* (1899) condemning Americanism. Many Catholic scholars in the 1950s would have agreed with Walter Ong, S.J. that the letter "dealt a blow to American Catholic self-confidence from which the American Catholic mind has never effectively recovered."[89] The two encyclicals had at least the temporary effect of halting even the inchoate dialogue between Catholic theology and the new sciences.

The American responses to these condemnations depended, of course, upon one's prior disposition regarding the Americanist and modernist mentality. One American Catholic critic in 1908, for example, asserted that *Pascendi* indeed described the modernist mentality to which a few American Catholics were "well-disposed."[90] Charles A. Briggs, Protestant professor of scripture at Union Theological Seminary in New York, noted that after the encyclical "liberal Catholics" [i.e., Americanists] were being identified with modernists.[91] John Ireland, perhaps smarting from Briggs' comments, fired back that the encyclical condemned only those errors which the Catholic Church had always censured.[92] Such sensitivity revealed the threat the encyclical posed in liberal Catholic quarters.

For a number of years, the two encyclicals had a negative effect upon the development of historical-critical methods in theology and scripture studies. One historian has wryly observed, in fact, that with the condemnation of modernism, "original research became original sin."[93] Those critical methods, however, could not be repressed forever. In fact, in 1936, the American Catholic Biblical Association was founded, signaling a revival in American Catholic circles of a more critical approach to biblical studies. The new association was given positive reinforcement in 1943 with Pope Pius XII's encyclical *Divino afflante spiritu*. After that period, a new generation of critical scholars arose in the persons of Raymond Brown, Dominic Crosson, Bruce Vawter, Roland Murphy, Myles Bourke, John L. McKenzie and a host of others who have made historical criticism a significant part of American Catholic seminary and university education.

SOCIAL JUSTICE, 1840-1940

Although many Americanists were aware of the need for a social justice in the United States that would reflect, in Ireland's words, "the Fatherhood of God and the brotherhood of man," they did not develop any systematic analysis of justice in American society. Such an analysis, though, did arise during the late nineteenth century. Just as the so-called "Social Gospel" developed within the context of Protestant liberal theology, so also the Catholic "Search for Social Justice" originated within the context of Americanism and modernism and developed more fully during the early part of the twentieth century. The development of social Christianity was, of course, a response to industrialization, immigration and urbanization. In its Catholic form it also originated as a response to the evolution of European Catholic social thought (especially Pope Leo XIII's encyclical on the conditions of labor, *Rerum novarum*, 1891) and the rise of socialistic tendencies in American labor movements.

In the period before the Civil War, American Catholics—mostly poor, laboring class immigrants—were part of the "social problem" in American life. Catholic social thought during this period, therefore, concentrated upon their plight. They filled the cities with unemployment, crime, prostitution, orphans, disease and slum living. In the midst of these social disorders, American Catholic leaders, although primarily occupied with ecclesiastical expansion, helped to organize various Catholic charities, self-help programs, mutual aid societies and social institutions. Personal and communal charity, rather than social reform, was one adequate response to the social needs of the age. Moral suasion through Catholic evangelicalism, too, was seen as a means of rectifying the social problems Catholics experienced. For many, the social problems in American society were individual and attitudinal. Catholic leaders criticized, in particular, American acquisitiveness, materialism, and the identification of poverty as sin. To counter these values, which had affected the immigrants as well as the native Americans, they preached individual repentance and spiritual reform. Restoration of personal piety, therefore, could solve the difficulties of the incipient industrial age.

Although American Catholic leaders did not call for major social and economic reforms, a few did attack the laissez-faire economic theories and the excessive individualism of American society. According to Bishop John Hughes, for example, "the theoretical and practical, political economy of our age [1844] has encouraged and whetted the passion [of cupidity] instead of moderating and regulating its violence."[94] Hughes criticized the economic theory and practice that identified man with his material self-interests. The only proper way to understand human nature and destiny was through Christianity; such a perception would necessarily broaden the definition of human nature and thus subordinate material self-interests to the higher designs of human destiny. For Hughes, the ultimate source of the selfishness and individualism of incipient capitalism was Protestantism. Laissez-faire economic theories and practices that emphasized material self-interests exclusively had divorced revelation and ecclesiastical authority from economic life. Such theories were the inevitable result of the Protestant doctrine of justification by faith alone. This doctrine of justification removed the mediation of the church from the salvific process and freed political and economic works, in fact, all works, from their spiritual and ultimate relations. Thus, economic theory and practice became autonomous, thereby producing excessive individualism and consequent economic injustice. Justice and the communal sense could be restored, Hughes believed, by reintegrating a Christian anthropology into economic theory and by reviving the church's role in regulating acquisitiveness. Precisely how this was to be accomplished Hughes did not reveal.[95]

American Catholics were more concerned with the social and economic issues that faced the immigrants than they were with the issues of slavery and consequently they paid little attention to *the* moral problem of the age. When Catholics did speak out on slavery, they seemed to reflect the divided mind of the larger American society. Some argued that slavery was compatible with Christian values; others asserted that it was a moral evil contrary to the norms of justice and equity; still others maintained that it was primarily a political problem that should be resolved by state legislatures and not Christian leaders. The antebellum American Catholic record on this issue and the post-Civil War Catholic response to racism was anything but prophetic.[96]

Although many antebellum Catholic attitudes to social problems continued on in the post-war years, a new awareness of the social situation gradually arose among some leading Catholic spokesmen and a few prophetic figures proposed new measures for social reform. In the 1870s, T. Wharton Collens, a New Orleans jurist, proposed the establishment of lay religious communities voluntarily devoted to poverty and to a communistic sharing of property.[97] During these years, too, Catholics in large numbers were beginning to join trade unions and other labor unions. The cooperative principle was gradually accepted by laboring men, and Catholic leaders began to see the social problem in a new way. They began to interpret the social problems in terms of a faulty economic system rather than in the exclusive terms of individual moral corruption, and tried to shift Catholic energies away from the particular problems of the Catholic community toward the general welfare of American society.

From 1880 to 1920, Catholics began to develop what Aaron Abell has called "social liberalism."[98] Such a program combined a crusade for social justice, cooperation with non-Catholics in solving social problems, and rapid Americanization of the new immigrants. Social liberalism manifested itself in a number of ways and helped prepare the American soil for the reception of Pope Leo XIII's encyclical *Rerum novarum*.

James Cardinal Gibbons of Baltimore, along with Bishops John Ireland and John Keane, defended the right of Catholics to organize and join labor unions in order to obtain justice from the industrialists.

Father Edward McGlynn, a pastor in New York City, supported Henry George's single tax theory as a means of solving the unequal distribution of the goods of creation. Americanists like Ireland, as we have seen, were fully behind the crusade for social justice. In 1889, for example, he called "the amelioration of the masses" one of the major needs of the age. The church had the primary responsibility to engage itself in this task. Like Father Edward McGlynn and many of the Protestant social gospelers, Ireland appealed to the popular cry of Christian social reformers. Amelioration of the masses has been, he said, "the constant aim of Christian charity; it is the practical application of the Christian doctrine of the brotherhood of man and the fatherhood of God." Until the laborers' "material condition is improved, it is futile to speak to them of supermaterial life and duties." He called upon Catholics, therefore, to leave their sanctuaries and to become engaged in the struggle for economic justice because "Christ made the social question the basis of His ministry."[99]

Rerum novarum represented a turning point in American Catholic thinking on the problems of the industrial order. Before it was published, Catholic thinkers had no consistent or systematic framework within which to speak about the social order. The encyclical discussed the social problems of the day within a neo-Thomistic philosophical framework. Leo XIII's 1879 encyclical *Aeterni patris* had called for the revival of scholastic philosophy and the application of Thomistic philosophical principles to problems of modern science, culture and philosophy. *Rerum novarum* represented the attempt to apply Thomistic principles to the social problems and provided American Catholics with a philosophical framework within which to discuss American problems. Leo XIII's Catholic solution to the social problem tried to steer a path between the Scylla of excessive individualism (capitalism) and the Charybdis of excessive conformity (socialism).

Socialism, the most dangerous problem for Leo, magnified the role of the state in industrial life and provided no place for the rights of private property. Capitalism, or economic liberalism, on the other hand, rejected moral and political intervention in industry. It gave too much power to individuals and had no effective way of restraining greed. While it emphasized the rights of private property, it did not understand that property belongs first of all to God and is given for the benefit and use of all humankind.

Leo's solution to the economic problem was framed within the context of natural law and was based upon the nature and dignity of the individual person. He stressed two principles that came out of natural law: the inviolability of private property and the principle of subsidiarity. Every person has by nature the right to hold property as his/her own in "stable and permanent possession." In the economic situation of the modern world this meant a just wage for the employee. And the just wage was to be determined not simply or solely by the free bargaining of working persons and their employers, but by a "dictate of nature more imperious and more ancient than any bargain between man and man, that the remuneration must be enough to support the wage-earner in reasonable and frugal comfort."[100] In cases where employees and employers could not arrive at a just wage, recourse to the state was necessary. The state must step in to provide justice where classes of people might suffer injustice without such assistance. The church's responsibility in helping to adjust the differences in society between working men and their employers was primarily accomplished by reminding each of duties to the other, especially the duties of justice and charity.

A few American Catholics after 1891 responded to the pope's encyclical by continuing to call for social reforms and social legislation. The Americanists, the Catholic lay congresses, individuals like John Zahm of Notre Dame and Humphrey Joseph Desmond of Milwaukee, the American Federation of Catholic Charities and other groups took up the call of the encyclical. No Catholic, however, was as systematic nor as creative as John Ryan in attempting to construct what Richard Ely called a "Catholic system of political economy."[101]

From 1906, the date of his first major work on the topic, until his death in 1945, Ryan was the foremost Catholic systematic thinker on social problems. He used the papal encyclicals to develop his own theories of economic justice, but his emphases and methodology differed somewhat from the encyclical. He, like Leo XIII, emphasized the dignity of the individual, his natural rights to property, and his priority over the state; but Ryan stressed, more than Leo XIII, the limits of private property and used the positive science of economics to determine more precisely what a just wage might be in the actual circumstances of the American industrial society. For Ryan, the goods of creation exist for the use and benefit of all; this principle had a natural priority over the ownership and use of private property. Private property, moreover, was not in itself an inherent or intrinsic good, nor was it a metaphysical right (as the right to life and marriage). Under present economic conditions it was a social institution that provided for the public welfare and thus it was indirectly necessary for the individual's benefit but ultimately subordinate to human welfare itself. Private property was still a natural right, but, unlike the right to life and to marriage, it was historically and culturally conditioned by circumstances conducive to individual and social welfare. Human welfare was the primary criterion for establishing the right of private property and for determining the morality of any social or economic system.[102]

Human welfare for Ryan was not an abstract or metaphysical principle of social justice; it was concrete, historical and pragmatic, referring to the "well-being of all persons, considered individually and socially."[103] It was to be measured by Ryan's five canons for distributing the goods of the industrial order: i.e., equality, needs, efforts, productivity and scarcity. In the industrial system, furthermore, substantial human needs have a priority. One determined basic human needs inductively and empirically—primarily through the science of economics.

This did not mean, of course, that the right to a living wage was a positive right. It was not; it was "individual, natural and absolute" because it was derived from the individual's human dignity. The right was absolute in the sense that its validity was "not dependent on the will of anyone except the person" in whom it inheres. It was absolute, therefore, in existence, though not in extent. The right was certainly limited. The right "to liberty and property are not absolute in the sense that the individual may have as much of these goods as he pleases and do with them as he pleases, but inasmuch as within reasonable limits—which are always determined by the essential needs of personal development—these rights are sacred and inviolable."[104] The natural right to a living wage was always conditioned by history and the economic system. Thus, in order to determine the concrete nature of that right, one had to determine inductively the practical needs of individuals and families in their historical circumstances.

The science of industrial or economic justice, therefore, was tentative, and always open to further progress. Practical moral problems of the industrial society could not be solved solely by recourse to abstract principles of philosophy or to generalized appeals to scripture and theology. The ethicist had to know *what* public welfare meant in practice if he/she was going to solve existing social problems. Ryan used economics, therefore, to determine precisely what was possible and expedient in his moral theory of a just wage. This use of the inductive and empirical method made his natural law philosophy practical and useful in suggesting reforms for the industrial society. It also conditioned natural law theory historically and made it more open to the use of the inductive sciences than traditional applications of natural law, thereby creating what Leo XIII himself had called for in *Aeterni patris*, a dialogue between Thomistic or scholastic principles and the modern sciences.

Ryan's proposals for social reform, as articulated in *A Living Wage* (1906) and *Distributive Justice* (1916), found institutional expression in American Catholicism when the National Catholic Welfare Council, the national organization of the American Catholic hierarchy, published the "Bishops' Program of Social Reconstruction," written by Ryan, in 1919.[105] The "Bishops' Program" called for social legislation to secure a living wage, just working conditions and hours, social security programs, unemployment insurance, and other specific economic reforms.

Ryan was not the only significant American Catholic social thinker in the first half of the twentieth century, nor was his kind of mitigated capitalism (or democratic capitalism secured by state legislation) acceptable to every American Catholic social thinker. The German Central Verein, the Catholic Worker Movement, Father Charles Coughlin and numerous other Catholics also read *Rerum novarum* and *Quadragesimo anno* (1931), but they appropriated and emphasized sides of papal social thought that Ryan had not stressed.

After 1908, the German Central Verein, under the leadership of Frederick P. Kenkel, sought to establish social reforms on the basis of Catholic corporate structures. Using the principle of subsidiarity, the Verein emphasized the organic nature of the community, especially Catholic corporate communities, rather than the state, as the primary basis or agency of social reform. The church, rather than the state, could effectively teach social justice and organize, through its own divinely-established institutions, Christian agencies for social reform. Virgil Michel, O.S.B., the liturgical reformer, may also be classed with the Central Verein movement for social reform in that he saw the liturgy as the primary teacher and agency of Christian solidarity, and an efficient cause of social reconstruction. The liturgy was the celebration and realization of the organic structure of the church and society. It could make Christians socially conscious and activate them personally to respond to the economic and social needs of society. The Catholic Worker Movement, under the leadership of Peter Maurin and Dorothy Day, used the papal social encyclicals to buttress their philosophy of personalism and voluntary poverty as a means of social justice. Social reforms were of little value unless Christian individuals, obedient and committed to the transcendent demands of justice, personally touched the lives of individuals in real need. Charles E. Coughlin, the "radio priest" of the 1930s, asserted a different kind of social reform. For him, social injustices resulted primarily from financial and monetary disorders and not primarily from conflicts between employers and employees. Coughlin's solution to the problem was nationalization of banking, credit, currency, power, light, oil, natural gas, and of all God-given natural resources—"public necessities which by their very nature are too important to be held in the control of private individuals."[106]

In the period after World War II, as Catholics were gradually moving into the middle and upper middle classes, emphasis in social thought was likewise gradually shifting from exclusively economic and industrial problems to the broader concerns of community living: housing, health, cultural improvements, peace and discrimination. Social justice issues would also no longer be narrowly American, but would consider the international effects of American economic and cultural relations, with a special attention to the problems of social justice in the third world. The most recent pastoral letters of the American Catholic bishops on peace (1983) and economic justice (1986) reveal that the search for social justice has broadened considerably within the Catholic community in the last forty years and is much more clearly based upon biblical notions of peace and justice rather than exclusively upon natural law concepts.

NEO-THOMISM AND CATHOLIC CULTURE, 1920-1960

From the end of World War I to the presidential election of John F. Kennedy, a gradual shift was taking place in American Catholic life. Catholicism was transformed socially from an immigrant to an American Church. Catholics were gradually shedding some of their ethnic identity and becoming a part of the American mainstream. American legislation in the 1920s, of course, assisted this process by restricting the constant flow of immigrants. Throughout the period, therefore, Catholic ethnic consciousness was little by little decreasing as a means of defining one's place in American society and Catholicism was beginning to replace ethnicity as a means of social differentiation in the pluralistic society. In the American sea of diversity, Catholicism became the integrating ship of individual and collective identity.[107]

The restriction of immigration also helped to stabilize the development of Catholic institutions that continued to multiply. Now, however, that development was more and more controlled, especially in the large urban dioceses, by bureaucratic centralization, an imitation in part of American big business techniques.[108] In the post-World War II era, moreover, American Catholics moved to the surburbs in large numbers, deepening the Americanization process as they left behind the urban ethnic centers. Throughout these years Catholic anti-Communism and the popular "Life-Is-Worth-Living" spirituality of prominent preachers like Fulton J. Sheen demonstrated anew the Americanism of Catholicism. Thus, American Catholics were beginning to experience the United States as homeland. Their minority feelings were progressively replaced and they were beginning to identify more and more with the American ethos.

As American Catholics participated more fully in the economic, social and cultural mobility of the middle class and as they organized their multi-ethnic heritage into an American Catholic unity, Catholic philosophers and theologians began to articulate the ideological bases of that Catholic unity. The cultural and institutional movements toward religious solidarity were matched in philosophy and theology by an emphasis upon the integral nature of Catholicism. The Neo-Thomistic, liturgical and Catholic Worker movements of the 1920s and 1930s, for example, tried to create a Catholic culture in America. Although these three movements differed from each other in numerous ways, they all sought to redefine or restore the essential unity and integrity of the Catholic tradition. In one respect, these movements were implicitly, and many times explicitly, saying that American Catholics had lost or were losing a consciousness of their own uniqueness. Catholics, they pleaded, had to become more explicitly conscious of their own Catholic identity.

The Neo-Thomistic revival reasserted the capacity of reason to comprehend reality, the unity and harmony of the world, the unicity of truth, the transcendental moral order of the universe, the certitude of faith, and the authority of the hierarchy to bring about a uniformity of doctrine and discipline within the Church. It provided Catholic intellectuals with an ideology that expressed the intelligibility of the world and the Catholic community's optimism and Americanism at a time in American society when many prominent American intellectuals had denied that intelligibility and had become disillusioned with the optimism of the late nineteenth and early twentieth centuries.[109]

In some respects, the Neo-Thomistic revival was similar to Neo-Orthodoxy in American Protestantism. Both movements were a search for the fundamental roots of their religious perspectives. As Neo-Orthodoxy was a return to the principles of the sixteenth-century Protestant Reformation, so Neo-Thomism was a return to and reassertion of thirteenth-century Thomistic principles. Both movements, moreover, incorporated some of the liberalism of the late nineteenth- and early twentieth-century American intellectual and cultural developments. Neo-Orthodoxy accepted the historical consciousness of the age, biblical criticism, social consciousness and the use of science in the theological enterprise. Neo-Thomism continued the optimism and Americanism of the previous age. Both movements, furthermore, were critical of their own age. Neo-Orthodoxy criticized nineteenth-century liberal theology and the progressive era for a naive optimism, belief in inevitable progress, and a capitulation to the scientific method as the starting point for theological reflection. Neo-Thomism criticized the age for its skepticism, irrationalism, disillusionment, individualistic capitalism, and totalitarian socialism. Thus, both movements were, to a certain extent, counter-cultural in their criticisms of the liberal American intellectuals' assessments of the age.

Fundamental differences, of course, separated the two movements. Some of the differences corresponded to the traditional post-Tridentine religious perspectives. The Neo-Orthodox, for example, relied more upon scripture than natural law as a source of theological reflection. The Neo-Thomist had a more optimistic view of human nature and the capacities of human reason than did the Neo-Orthodox.

Although the Neo-Thomistic revival had its roots in middle-nineteenth-century European Catholicism and was officially sanctioned and promulgated in Pope Leo XIII's *Aeterni patris* (1879), nevertheless it did not reach the United States with any significant impact until the 1920s and 1930s. Before this period, it is true, a few Catholics were interested in at least a commentators' Thomism. As early as 1869, for example, Camillo Mazzella, S.J. (1833-1900), professor of dogmatic theology at Woodstock Theological College in Maryland, published a few neo-scholastic theological textbooks, but they had little impact upon the Thomistic revival in this country. Mazzella's form of scholasticism, in one recent authority's opinion, did not have "any real understanding of modern science and culture,"[110] and therefore could not show the relevance of Thomism for the modern world. In 1873, St. Louis University's Philosophy Department also began to exhibit another example of neo-scholasticism. These two early attempts to revive scholasticism, however, had little immediate effect upon American Catholic intellectual life.

Even after Leo XIII's encyclical *Aeterni patris*, American Catholics were still not moved in the direction of neo-scholasticism. Some philosophers, like Edward A. Pace of the Catholic University in Washington, D. C., founded a philosophy department in 1895 upon Thomistic principles, but his efforts did not begin to show results until the 1920s. From the 1890s until the condemnation of modernism in 1907, American Catholics were less than enthusiastic about the revival of scholastic theology. In fact, as already indicated, those like John Zahm who did speak up about a revival of American Catholic intellectual life were more interested in meeting the theological questions raised by history and science than they were in reconstructing a scholastic synthesis. John B. Hogan, S.S. and John Talbot Smith, too, were critical of the metaphysical speculations of scholastic thought. They wanted theology and philosophy to be presented historically.

After the condemnation of modernism, those American Catholics who had been open to a dialogue between Catholic theology and the modern intellectual movements of the day ceased publishing anything resembling a flirtation with modern thought. Increasingly after 1907, Roman declarations and canonical legislation almost institutionalized Thomism as "the only proper mode of Catholic thought." Pope Pius XII's *Humani Generis* (1950), like a number of pervious papal encyclicals, made Thomism the "most authoritative expression of Catholic thought and a safe intellectual route to orthodoxy."[111]

Early twentieth-century American Catholic receptivity to Neo-Thomistic patterns of thought was conditioned as much (if not more) by the changing social and cultural experiences within American Catholicism as by the papal declarations. After World War I, as they began to search for the intellectual unity of their Catholicism, American Catholics discovered that the Thomistic revival could provide them with an integral philosophy of life that could meet the demands of their social and cultural experiences. Gradually Neo-Thomism began to dominate Catholic seminaries, colleges and universities, so that by the late 1950s over fifty percent of the philosophers in Catholic colleges and universities would identify themselves as Neo-Thomists.

Although St. Thomas Aquinas was the unifying figure of the Neo-Thomistic movement, his thought flowered in a variety of ways in the United States as it had in Europe. The Neo-Thomistic movement was not monolithic. I believe that William Halsey's otherwise excellent study of Neo-Thomism in his *The Survival of Catholic Innocence* has not given adequate attention to the varieties of Thomisms, either in Europe or in the United States. He presents neo-scholastic thought as a monolithic form of "common sense" philosophy. That was certainly one of its manifestations, but there were other more sophisticated forms of the movement. In its earliest forms, Neo-Thomism was simply a continuation of what Gerald McCool, S.J. has called a commentators' Thomism, i.e., a continuation of the theologies of Cajetan or John of St. Thomas, the baroque commentators on St. Thomas' theology.[112] From the late 1930s through the 1950s, some American Catholics, following the lead of Jacques Maritain's "strict-observance Thomism," enriched and developed the commentators' traditional Thomism, and others, following Etienne Gilson, began to approach St. Thomas historically in order to recover Thomas' own philosophy and to discover the diversity of scholasticisms. Some American Catholics, too, sought not just a recovery of Thomistic principles but a creative application of those principles to modern problems. John Ryan, as we have already seen, and John Courtney Murray, S.J. applied Thomistic principles to the problems of social justice and political theory in ways that significantly transformed the Thomistic tradition. Not until the late 1950s and early 1960s did American Catholics begin to examine still another form of the Thomistic tradition: i.e., the transcendental Thomism of Joseph Maréchal, S.J., Karl Rahner, S.J., and Bernard Lonergan, S.J.[113]

The "common sense" form of Neo-Thomism that developed in the early 1920s and continued through the 1930s found in St. Thomas the symbol of Christian rationalism. The followers and advocates of this Christian rationalism saw in St. Thomas' theological and philosophical systems a uniquely Catholic contribution to the stability and rational development of American society. Post-World War I America had, many Catholic intellectuals believed, "lost faith not only in religious beliefs, social customs, and moral certainties, but even in reason itself." What the Thomistic tradition offered American Catholics was, in William Halsey's opinion, "an almost Enlightenment fascination with reason and its powers of construction."[114] The modern world entertained a fundamental uncertainty with regard to the capacity of reason, the nature of the universe, and the values and meaning of human association. Catholics, under the influence of Thomism, began asserting an "everyman's" confidence in reason. Some of these Catholic philosophers were not bothered by the perplexities of the modern world. They could say, with John O. Riedl of Marquette University: "Scholastic philosophers are somewhat unique among present-day philosophers. They still believe in Truth, in reality, in God, in the power of human reason to know real things, in an immortal soul, an after life, and the power of man to guide his own destiny. Oddly enough, they based their belief in these fundamental verities on the authority of reason alone. . . . Outside scholasticism there seems to be nothing but intellectual chaos and despair."[115]

For many of the "common sense" Thomists of the early 1920s and 1930s Thomism had demonstrated its "pliability" over the years by modifying and adjusting the accidents of the system to the "march of the physical sciences" and to the newer philosophies, but it had been "changed in no essential element from the splendid synthesis created by St. Thomas and his fellow-pioneers." Thus, the movement "back to St. Thomas" was "not such a far cry after all, since his genius has lived an unbroken life to this day, safe like so many other worth-while institutions in the Church's protecting arms."[116] The unchanging nature of the Thomistic synthesis meant for some that "wisdom has been achieved by man." Such attitudes had significant consequences for education whose primary purpose was to pass on this wisdom because the "humane use of the mind, the function proper to him as man, is contemplation and not research. . . . In sum, then, research cannot be the primary object of a Catholic graduate school, because it is at war with the whole Catholic life of the mind."[117]

The "common sense" philosophy followed by many American Catholic philosophers and theologians may have provided American Catholicism with the intellectual foundations for their sense of Catholic unity and identity in an age of "intellectual chaos and despair," but it did not creatively dialogue with the intellectual currents of the day (e.g., pragmatism, idealism, neo-orthodoxy) and thereby make their philosophy a partner in the intellectual discussions of the day. As early as 1921, Virgil Michel, O.S.B., like Orestes Brownson before him, had argued that the Neo-Thomistic revival would be ineffective if it disregarded contemporary patterns of thought. Neo-Thomism, he asserted, could not be developed in lonely isolation from modern philosophical movements. "If we refuse to see the standpoint of others, or ignore their sincerity, we are not only shutting off all possibility of assisting them, but we are actually building a wall around ourselves and closing to them all avenues of approach." Catholic philosophy, if it were to communicate to those outside of Catholicism, had to appear "in a garb that is intelligible and acceptable to the outsiders" and to show "so much appreciation of other viewpoints that it does not repel those of other belief at first sight."[118]

Michel's advice was not heeded by many Catholic philosophers and theologians. Although many American Catholics popularized Neo-Thomism by making it a philosophy of common sense for everyman, some Catholics begin to respond to the Thomistic revival in more sophisticated ways. Some followed Jacques Maritain and others Etienne Gilson in an attempt to articulate the values of Thomism for modern man and his problems. The founding of the *Modern Schoolman* (1925), *Thought* (1926), *The New Scholasticism* (1927) and the American Catholic Philosophical Association (1927) signaled a more rigorous historical and philosophical study of scholasticism and Thomism. The historical recovery of Thomism, in particular, was advanced in many universities and colleges. Such was the case, for example, at Marquette University from 1925 to 1965. Under the leadership of John F. McCormick, S.J. (1925-1933) and Gerard Smith, S.J. (1945-1965), who had been educated at Toronto under Maritain and Gilson, Marquette's Philosophy Department became a leader in the historical revival of Thomism.

Maritain, Gilson and their followers were not alone in their attempts to apply Thomism to modern problems. Some American Catholics were also creative in their applications of Thomism. As we have already seen, Neo-Thomism supplied the natural law tradition for

John Ryan's social ethics; it also provided the intellectual foundations for John Courtney Murray's understanding of church-state relations and for Gustave Weigel's, S.J. approach to Christian unity. Murray's position represents perhaps the most creative and explicit adaptation of the Thomistic tradition to American experiences. From the establishment of *Theological Studies* (1940), the first significant American Catholic theological journal since the *New York Review*, to his death in 1967, John C. Murray developed a modern Catholic understanding of religious liberty that had a significant impact upon the Second Vatican Council's Declaration on Religious Liberty. As European Catholic theologians during the 1940s and 1950s were developing a transcendental form of Thomism by a careful analysis of Thomistic principles in the light of modern philosophies, so Murray was developing an American Thomistic position on religious liberty by examining the Thomistic principles of natural law in the light of the American political experience and the political consciousness that had evolved during the previous two centuries in the Western world. He also showed through a critical and historical interpretation of official magisterial pronouncements that the Catholic Church could and should approve of the legitimate development of religious liberty in the modern world. As European Transcendental Thomism came to terms with the subjectivity of the individual as it had been developing in modern philosophy and theology, so Murray's Thomism came to terms with the evolving political consciousness of religious liberty and formulated a theory of church-state relations that met the practical and changing exigencies of modern society.

From the time of John Carroll, American Catholic leaders had repeatedly supported religious liberty and the American constitutional provisions for the separation of church and state. The Catholic understanding of these positions, however, had never been clearly or theoretically articulated. The problem, of course, arose because of the various unions of church and state in European Catholic countries, the nineteenth-century papal declarations against religious liberty and separation, and John A. Ryan's and Moorhouse Millar's publication of their understanding of the Catholic view of *The State and the Church* (1922). Ryan upheld in theory the obligation of the state to support the one, true Church, but pointed out that in practice this had application only in a completely Catholic state. Ryan, however, believed that such a circumstance did not exist in the contemporary world and it certainly did not or probably would not obtain in the United States. It could happen in the United States, though, that non-Catholic sects would dissolve to such an extent that a political proscription of religion would become possible.[119]

Such a position not only created problems for Alfred Smith's campaign for the presidency in 1928, but also contradicted the former American Catholic positions on the relationship of church and state and confirmed Protestant suspicions about Catholic designs upon America. Ryan's position was similar to the so-called "thesis-hypothesis" theory that had developed in nineteenth-century European Catholicism. The thesis-hypothesis position, simply stated, asserted that the ideal relationship between the church and state was one of union (thesis), but given the present historical situation of religious pluralism a constitutional separation could be allowed in order to secure public peace (hypothesis). Between 1940 and the 1960s the theory was warmly debated in American Catholic theological circles. Murray and Joseph C. Fenton, professor of theology at the Catholic University and editor of the *American Ecclesiastical Review*, became the primary theological opponents and proponents of the theory.

Murray presented the issue of religious liberty as a concrete and historical problem. For him, it was not first of all a metaphysical or abstract issue, as it was for advocates of the thesis-hypothesis position. His analysis of the problem began with a scrutiny of the historical situation, rather than with an examination of abstract principles. He noted first of all the historical growth of man's personal and political consciousness, and saw that "religious pluralism is theologically the human condition." In other words, the historical fact of pluralism was itself theologically significant. The historical demands of modern man for political and religious freedoms, moreover, were expressions of the demands of "natural law in the present moment of history."[120]

Religious liberty, for Murray, was primarily "a juridical or constitutional concept, which has foundations in theology, ethics, political philosophy, and jurisprudence." Constitutionally, religious liberty guarantees freedom of conscience and freedom of religion. From a juridical perspective, freedom of conscience "is the human and civil right of the human person to immunity from all external coercion in his search for God, in the investigation of religious truth, in the acceptance or rejection of religious faith, in the living of his interior religious or non religious life."[121] Freedom of religion is a corporate or ecclesial, as well as an individual, freedom, entailing the right of religious association and expression. The problem of understanding this religious liberty in the contemporary world revolved around a proper understanding of the nature of the state and political government.

Murray turned to natural law to uncover what he considered the truths of the political order—but natural law understood historically. Natural law advanced the "idea that government has a moral basis; that the universal moral law is the foundation of society; that the legal order of society—that is, the state—is subject to judgment by a law that is not statistical but inherent in the nature of man; that the eternal reason of God is the ultimate origin of all law." These absolutes of the natural law, however, are always experienced amidst historical contingencies. Although history does not alter the natural law, it does change "human reality." The "nature of man is an historical nature," and to fail to understand that "history continually changes the community of man-kind and alters the modes of communication between man and man" is to fail to understand the political order.[122]

The political consciousness of the civil and religious rights of human persons had been developing in the Western world for centuries. The American understanding of the constitutional state with its acknowledgement of religious liberty was one of the chief products of this development. The American political consensus which produced the understanding of the constitutional state was derived from "ethical and political principles drawn from the tradition of natural law," and this tradition had roots in the Catholic tradition.[123] The natural law tradition in regard to political principles is constantly open to human develop-ment because history changes the "human reality." Thus, one needs to pay close attention to the existing historical conditions to obtain a clear understanding of the state. Thus, too, the understanding of the state is relative to the evolving human consciousness and is absolute with regard to its ultimate foundation in the "eternal reason of God."

An historical understanding of natural law has consequences for the understanding of the state. Such an understanding begins not with an abstract notion of the state (as would be the case in some approaches to natural law) from which it deduces certain obligations, but with the existing concrete reality (i.e., the constitutional state). When one exam-ines the constitutional state, according to Murray, one discovers that the concept of the limited state is based upon three basic distinctions. It is important to understand these distinctions in order to understand reli-gious liberty as a constitutional provision. The first distinction is that between the sacred and the secular order of human life. Man has a tran-scendent as well as a terrestrial existence, and the government has no power to interfere in his transcendent end; government's powers are limited to man's earthly existence. The transtemporal principle of the primacy of the spiritual endows the church with its freedom in relation-ship with the temporal order. Since the temporal, historical order is ever changing, however, this particular historical manifestation of the church's freedom will necessarily change according to the times and cir-cumstances in which the church finds itself. The absolute principle of primacy, therefore, is always realized in limited historical situations. As long as the church's freedom is preserved, there can be no ideal relationship between church and state—no thesis, in other words. The state's only responsibility to the church in Murray's theory was to guarantee and to protect this liberty.

The second distinction behind the concept of the limited state was that between society and state, as that distinction was understood in the modern world. The concept of society was a much broader concept than that of state. The state, in contemporary consciousness, was a limited constitutional government; it was only one order within society, i.e., "the order of public law and political administration." The state, therefore, was not co-extensive with society. Society was the arena of personal and corporate freedom, the order of culture and the common good. In the arena of personal and corporate freedoms the state had no right to intervene, except to protect those freedoms.

A third distinction was that between the common good and public good. "The common good includes all the social goods, spiritual and moral as well as material." Society itself was responsible for defining and maintaining the common good. The public good, on the other hand, belonged to the order of jurisprudence and law; that is, it was the state's responsibility to provide for the public good: peace, morality, and justice. Thus, the state was subject to and servant of the common good; and it was not the sole judge of what was or was not the common good. That judgment belonged to society as a whole.

According to Murray, one understands the powers of the modern state to be limited when this threefold distinction, which belongs to the order of "political truth," is joined to the political principle of "freedom under law." The constitutional state has no authority, for example, over religion. The question of religious liberty, for Murray, arises in this context of the proper understanding of constitutional government. Thus, religious liberty is justified and not idealized "as a legal institution, a juridical notion, a civil and human right." It belongs to the primacy of the spiritual, the order of society, the common good, and to freedom under law.[124]

Once Murray established the idea that religious liberty was a constitutional provision that reflected the developing political consciousness of the contemporary Western world, he tried to show that the Catholic Church could and should endorse this development. Religious liberty could be confirmed, he argued, because it was recognized by natural reason, which had itself been developing on this issue over the centuries, and because it "represents a valid growth in the understanding of the [Catholic] tradition" itself.[125] The Catholic tradition's constant avowal of the distinction between the spiritual and temporal, of the superiority of the spiritual to the temporal, and its concern for the freedom of the church amid the vicissitudes of history provided the foundation for a Catholic ratification of religious liberty as a constitutional provision. When the Catholic Church creatively combined these elements in its own tradition with the church's recent developing consciousness of human dignity and individual rights, clearly manifested in papal encyclicals since Leo XIII, it could certainly approve the modern constitutional development of religious liberty. To demonstrate this point, Murray critically examined and interpreted the recent papal teachings, showing that they revealed an evolving awareness and deepening consciousness of human dignity and the necessity of peace and justice in the social order. These developments corresponded to those in Western constitutional states where religious liberty was acknowledged. The evolving Catholic consciousness of the needs of the social order and the application of Catholic principles to that order could legitimately be extended to the political order where religious liberty was accepted as a reflection of the awareness of human dignity and of the need for justice and peace in society.

Murray's Catholic solution to the problem of religious liberty provided grounds for public peace and opened up possibilities, so he thought, for intercredal discussions of and cooperation on issues relative to public welfare, but it did not in American practice or theory lead to religious indifferentism. It could not lead to indifferentism since religious liberty was a constitutional provision and therefore a political, not a theological, statement. Murray's distinction here, however, was not a solution to a specifically theological problem: i.e., the question of Christian unity in the midst of the most religiously pluralistic country in the world. In the United States, mutual religious hostilities and bigotries contradicted the ideals of Christian love, peace and unity. During the post-World War II era, Gustave Weigel, S.J., like Murray a professor of theology at Woodstock College in Maryland, became aware of the need for Catholics to address this problem of Christian unity.

Weigel, like Murray, had been educated in the Neo-Thomistic tradition. He brought that tradition to an understanding of Christian unity. In 1948, when he returned from teaching in Chile, Murray encouraged him to begin studying and writing on Protestant-Catholic relations in the United States. He began doing so in the 1950s, encouraging the American Catholic community to learn more about Protestants and Protestant America. Weigel's ecumenical goal was to move the churches closer to one another in preparation for some future day of convergence. Neither conversion nor compromise, however, was the means to the goal. The primary human means in the 1950s was mutual understanding. Thus, Weigel himself began to enter into theological dialogue with members of other Christian bodies as no other Catholic in the United States before him had done.

Although Weigel engaged in numerous ecumenical exchanges, he was skeptical about the immediate possibilities of church unity because of the tremendous religious diversity in the United States, the fundamental differences in theology, the divergent understandings of Christian unity, and an indifference to the role of doctrine in many of the American Christian Churches. He argued, nevertheless, that Catholics should be actively involved in the ecumenical movement, even though it was Christ's grace rather than human efforts that would eventually realize Christ's own will that all be one.

Weigel's own efforts in the ecumenical dialogue before Vatican II were significant in that they laid the groundwork for the tremendous flowering of ecumenical activity after the council. His own ecclesiology was still juridical, coming from his study of the scholastic theological manuals. Although his ecclesiology would be superseded by the council, his advanced ecumenical practices encouraged students who read his works in the 1950s to look more positively upon the religious traditions of their Protestant neighbors and to study them from their own sources.[126]

The Liturgical and Catholic Worker Movements

American Catholic religious thought from 1920 to 1960, although dominated by Neo-Thomism, developed other currents that were theologically significant for the Catholic community. The liturgical and Catholic Worker movements, although they too were influenced by Neo-Thomism, represented theological approaches to Christian life that were not evident in Neo-Thomism.

The liturgical movement had its origins in European Catholicism in the late nineteenth and early twentieth centuries. In the 1920s the movement was sparked in the United States by those like Father William Busch of St. Paul Seminary in Minnesota, Virgil Michel, O.S.B., of St. John's Abbey in Collegeville, Minnesota, Gerald Ellard, S.J., of St. Louis University, and a host of others who read the publications of the European liturgists, were educated under them, or were immigrants who had already experienced the movement in Europe before coming to the United States.

The American liturgical movement is important not only because it was eventually vindicated by the Second Vatican Council's Constitution on the Liturgy, but also because it, like Neo-Thomism, tried to create a Catholic culture in the United States. It reflected and incorporated, however, a number of theological emphases that quietly challenged the scholastic method of theology and the almost exclusive juridical ecclesiology within American Catholicism. The movement was not, as some had thought, a mere rearrangement of liturgical furniture, but a campaign to revive the liturgy as the indispensable source of the Christian life and the primary means for reviving the social consciousness of Catholics. Theologically, the movement focused upon the "Pauline doctrine of the mystical body of Christ," making all Christians, in the words of Gerald Ellard, "realize that they are not merely members of one another, but severally the members of Christ, the fullness of Him, who is wholly fulfilled in them all."[127] The emphasis upon the church as the mystical body of Christ, an emphasis shared by a few American Catholic thinkers during the 1920s, reasserted the ecclesiological concepts of interiority, organic communion and the priesthood of the faithful.

In 1930, Virgil Michel, the founding editor of *Orate Fratres* (1926), the organ of the movement, argued that "polemical needs and historical conditions have led us to a somewhat one-sided emphasis of the nature of the church—not a denial of, but a neglect of emphasis on, her essential nature." The liturgical movement was an attempt to restore a consciousness of the church's inner divine life and thereby to subordinate the juridical aspects of its fundamental nature. Michel believed that the lost consciousness of the church as the mystical body of Christ coincided historically with the loss of the "liturgical sense."[128]

Liturgical reformers in the United States, particularly Virgil Michel, also made a specifically American contribution to the movement. In the 1930s, after the promulgation of Pope Pius XI's encyclical *Quadragesimo anno* (1931) and in the midst of the Depression, Michel began to advocate the inherent relationship of the liturgy, as the practical and visible expression of the mystical body, to social justice. The liturgy, he argued, could renew the social consciousness of Christians and thus inspire them to work for social justice in the world.

As the movement developed from the 1930s to the 1960s, it also fostered and incorporated studies in positive theology, especially biblical research and historical theology. The renewal of biblical research, represented by the foundation of the *Catholic Biblical Quarterly* (1939), and the incipient interests in historical theology (especially in patristics and the study of the primitive church) enhanced the theological foundations of the movement and offered Catholics new ways of doing theology and religious education in the United States. To a certain extent, the liturgical movement resembled the so-called French "New Theology" with its campaign to "return to the sources."

The Catholic Worker movement, initiated by the lay Catholics Peter Maurin and Dorothy Day in the 1930s, reinforced many of the theological emphases of the liturgical movement, but is particularly important for drawing Catholic attention to Christian eschatological expectation and Christian personalism. The radical idea of the Worker movement, according to William Miller, the movement's principal historian, is opposed to that liberalism that equates time with progress and progress with the observable and useful things "that brought men ease and power." The movement was and is a return to the early Christian theme that Christ is at the center and core of all creation and history, and only in personally submitting to the Christ who is all in all will creation, history and humans find fulfillment. This Christian faith and hope is ultimately a rejection of that mentality which expects some kind of realization of human social fulfillment by technological and ideological change or manipulation.[129]

The true end and fulfillment of the Christian life is redeemed humanity. That end was of course realized in Christ and is now present in the mystical body of Christ, even though it is not completely realized in the present. The church's mission, thus, is to make the promise of a redeemed humanity as practically present as is possible, given the sinful condition of humanity. The Worker challenged the church, in particular, to realize this eschatological goal in the present by making Christians more practically conscious of the evangelical demands of universal peace, justice and brotherhood.

If Christian eschatological fulfillment was the vision behind the movement, Christian personalism was the means for realizing, if only partially, that vision in practical action. The movement is, thus, essentially an emphasis on a Christian practice that makes the mystical body a visible expression of the eschatological hope. Peter Maurin, the primary theorist of the movement, introduced Dorothy Day and others to the Christian Personalism of French philosophers like Emmanuel Mounier; the ideas of the Christian personalists became the fundamental ideological core of the movement.[130] Christian personalism stressed the necessity of each individual Christian's responsibility to live out the faith by assisting one's neighbor at a personal sacrifice. Personal holiness, grounded in the liturgy, expressed in practical action and dedicated to self-reform as a means of social regeneration was the hallmark of the Worker movement. Radical social change could never be accomplished without personal cooperation with supernatural grace and that always entailed moral regeneration manifested in voluntary poverty and the evangelical virtues of faith, love and hope. The reformed Christian individual, rather than social legislation, was the primary key to a Christian society of love, justice and peace.

Christian personalism stressed the active involvement of the laity in the Christian life. The demands of the evangelical virtues and the call of personal and social regeneration were universal; they belonged to the laity as well as to the clergy and religious. In the 1930s, the Worker, like the liturgical movement and *Commonweal* (1926) magazine, tried to raise the consciousness of the Catholic laity to their Christian responsibilities for a just society. At a time when many Catholics were calling for a more vigorous "lay apostolate" (i.e., lay participation in the mission of the hierarchy), these movements were asserting the personal and at times independent role of the laity in the regeneration of humanity and society. Lay participation in the Christian life, in the church and in society transcended the commonly-accepted definitions of the "lay apostolate."

The radical practice of Christian love was the core of Christian personalism. Transformed by divine grace, man was capable of carrying out the radicalism of Christian love and thereby sustaining the hope that Christ would be all in all. The experience and practice of love would itself be the assurance of the divine presence and promise. This kind of "love in action," in the words of Dostoevsky's Father Zossima in *The Brothers Karamazov*, frequently quoted by Dorothy Day, is

> a harsh and dreadful thing compared to love in dreams. Love in dreams is greedy for immediate action, rapidly performed and in the sight of all. Men will even give their lives if only the ordeal does not last long but is soon over, with all looking and applauding as though on the stage. But active love is labour and fortitude and for some people, too, perhaps a complete science. But I predict that just when you see with horror that in spite of all your efforts you are getting further from your goal instead of nearer to it—at that very moment you will reach and behold clearly that miraculous power of the Lord who has been all the time loving and mysteriously guiding you.[131]

This kind of love in action is not cost efficient; it does not seek any immediate gratitude, reward or even practical effects. This kind of love characterized the Worker's life style. The Worker's goal, in William

Miller's words, "is not success in the world, as the world accounts success, but to establish the reality of the spirit in the world."[132] It is no wonder that such an approach to an integral Catholicism did not gain many adherents and has remained from the beginning to the present a minority movement within American Catholicism. But, like many movements within the church, this movement did and does give practical witness to the eschatological dimension of Christian life.

Neo-Thomism, the liturgical and Catholic Worker movements, although different in a number of ways, fostered a vision of an integral Catholicism in the United States. All three movements were also extremely critical of what they saw as the intellectual chaos and despair of modern man, the individualism, materialism and secularism of American society, and the permeation of the church and its members with these values. As Catholics were moving into the mainstream of American life, therefore, these movements represented not only a criticism of American values but also a rejection of the direction many American Catholics were taking in their social and economic mobility. They were attempting to redefine the root and center of an integral Catholicism. The Christian rationalism of the thirteenth century, the liturgy, and Christian personalism were perceived as the vital sources of Catholic unity in the midst of tremendous American diversity. If ethnic Catholics were beginning to use Catholicism as a means of social identification, they needed to reflect more seriously on what it meant religiously.

American Culture and Catholic Anti-Intellectualism

In the 1950s, as these movements for a more integral Catholicism were criticizing America and American Catholic values, another series of criticisms erupted within American Catholicism. This time the target was American Catholic anti-intellectualism. While some Protestants from neo-orthodox perspectives were attacking the "piety on the Potomac" and the "peace of mind" religious movements, Catholics were beginning to point out the failures of their own religious tradition to develop a creative intellectual and cultural life—a criticism formerly made by nativists. The criticism broke out in John T. Ellis' "American Catholics and the Intellectual Life."[133] This was followed in rapid succession by Walter J. Ong's *Frontiers of American Catholicism* (1957), Gustave Weigel's "American Catholic Intellectualist—A Theologian's Reflection,"[134] and Thomas F. O'Dea's *American Catholic Dilemma* (1958). These writers castigated the Catholic schools and universities, among other institutions, for their sins against intellectualism. The criticisms themselves could be interpreted as signs of growing maturity, stability, and strength within the Catholic community.

Ellis opened his attack by quoting the observation of Denis W. Brogan, professor of political science at the University of Cambridge: "In no Western society is the intellectual prestige of Catholicism lower than in the country where, in such aspects as wealth, members, and strength of organization, it is so powerful."[135] Ellis went on to point out some of the historical factors that curtailed creative intellectual and cultural developments in American Catholicism. Nativism, immigrant status, general American egalitarianism, lack of serious reading habits in the young, emphasis on material success in church and society, rote training in the seminaries, secondary and college education devoted to athleticism and vocationalism, schools perceived more as agents of moral development than as creative centers of thought—all of those factors helped to produce a ghetto mentality and intellectual narrowness—if not an anti-intellectualism. Walter Ong found the source of American Catholic intellectual lethargy in a constant return to the safe past of Europe for intellectual orthodoxy. Thomas F. O'Dea discovered the source of the failure in the fact that American Catholicism was a minority tradition that found it difficult to relate its distinctive religious and cultural traditions to the rapidly "changing patterns of a dominant non-Catholic culture."[136]

These criticisms by respected Catholic intellectuals unwittingly prepared the ground for the barrage of self-criticism that would be unleashed during and after the Second Vatican Council. These criticisms and others that were taking place within neo-scholasticism also helped to break down the Thomistic synthesis that American Catholics had been trying to establish since the beginning of the 1920s.

CONCLUSION

The Neo-Thomistic synthesis was of short duration. American Catholics prior to the 1920s were almost totally unaffected by it. American Catholic history shows, if one concentrates upon the writings of its major opinion makers, that American Catholic thought prior to Vatican II cannot be put into some kind of intellectual straight jacket called Post-Tridentine Catholicism. A number of intellectual changes and shifts of emphases existed amidst the fundamental ecclesiastical, sacramental and devotional unities. By experience as well as by intellectual culture

American Catholic thinkers were not entirely out of contact with the modern world. Their intellectual world was not a ghetto world, as some would have us believe.

Although American Catholic thinkers did indeed relate their understanding of Christianity to the larger currents of Western thought during the pre-Vatican II period, they developed few intellectual centers for a more systematic examination of their Catholic tradition within American society. Seminaries and the Graduate School of Theology at the Catholic University of America had been the primary source of theological education prior to Vatican II; gradually thereafter, the universities became the primary source for the theological education of lay men and women as well as clergy. Encouraged by the conciliar developments of Vatican II, greater contact with twentieth-century European Catholic intellectual traditions, and the general mutations in American social consciousness, American Catholic thinkers began to establish graduate theological schools at their major universities (e.g., Marquette, Fordham, St. Louis, Notre Dame, Boston College).

Catholic laity and clergy, educated at these schools, the European Catholic schools of theology, and the American Protestant and secular universities began to establish or strengthen departments of theology and religious studies at various Catholic and secular universities. The diversity of professional theological education, among other things, led almost inevitably toward a pluralism in theological perspectives in American Catholicism. The story of this recent American Catholic development must be left for another volume.

NOTES

1. T. T. McAvoy, *A History of the Catholic Church in the United States* (Notre Dame: University of Notre Dame Press, 1969), pp. 75, 131; T. T. McAvoy, "The Formation of the American Catholic Minority, 1820-1860," *The Review of Politics* 10 (January, 1948), 13-34; Jay P. Dolan, *The Immigrant Church: New York's Irish and German Catholics, 1815-1865* (Baltimore: Johns Hopkins University Press, 1975), p. 88; C. R. Fish, *Rise of the Common Man* (New York, 1927), p. 195; Walter Ong, S. J., *Frontiers of American Catholicism* (New York: Macmillan, 1957), p. 44; T. F. O'Dea, *American Catholic Dilemma* (New York: Sheed and Ward, 1958), pp. 83-84; J. T. Ellis, "American Catholics and the Intellectual Life," *Thought* 30 (Autumn, 1955), 351-388.

2. Quoted in Philip Gleason, *The Conservative Reformers: German-American Catholics and the Social Order* (Notre Dame: University of Notre Dame Press, 1968), p. 21.

3. Some important shapers of Catholic opinion not included in the anthology are: John Carroll, Francis P. Kenrick, Peter R. Kenrick, John L. Spalding, James

Cardinal Gibbons, Thomas Merton, Fulton J. Sheen, John LaFarge, Gustave Weigel.

4. Ong, *Frontiers*, p. 116.

5. On this, see Sydney Ahlstrom, "The Scottish Philosophy and American Theology," *Church History* 2 (September, 1955), 257- 72; E. Brooks Holifield, *The Gentlemen Theologians: American Theology in Southern Culture 1795-1860* (Durham, N.C.: Duke University Press, 1978), pp. 110-155.

6. John Carroll's acceptance of the civil contract theory is evident in his praise of Joseph Berington's *The State and Behavior of English Catholics* and his approval of Arthur O'Leary's works on toleration. On this, see Thomas O'Brien Hanley, S.J. (ed.), *The John Carroll Papers* (3 vols.; Notre Dame: The University of Notre Dame Press, 1976), I, 148, 224-226. Hereafter JCP.

7. *United States Catholic Miscellany*, January 28, 1824, and Ignatius A. Reynolds (ed.), *The Works of the Right Reverend John England* (5 vols.; Baltimore: John Murphy and Co., 1849), IV, 208.

8. Carroll to Charles Plowden, February 24, 1790, JCP, I, 432.

9. England, *Works*, IV, 228.

10. Carroll to John Troy, July 12, 1794, JCP, II, 121.

11. JCP, I, 140.

12. Carroll to Charles Plowden, February 27, 1785, JCP, I, 168; cf. also Carroll to Andrew Nugent, July 18, 1786, JCP, I, 215.

13. England, *Works*, II, 249.

14. England, *Works*, III, 511.

15. January 24, 1786, JCP, I, 204; cf. also Peter K. Guilday, *The Life and Times of John Carroll, Archbishop of Baltimore* (2 vols.; Baltimore: Newman, 1922), I, 265, where Guilday has "representation" for "presentation."

16. Carroll to Trustees of St. Mary's, Philadelphia, August 16, 1814, JCP, III, 290; cf. also Carroll to Troy, July 12, 1794, JCP, II, 120-121.

17. Carroll to Andrew Nugent, January 17, 1786, JCP, I, 201.

18. England, *Works*, V, 91-105; cf. also Patrick Carey, *An Immigrant Bishop: John England's Adaptation of Irish Catholicism to American Republicanism* (Yonkers, New York: U.S. Catholic Historical Society, 1982), pp. 111-128; 149-160.

19. Carroll to Don Diego de Gardoqui, April 19, 1788, JCP, I, 297.

20. Carroll to Charles Plowden, September 2, 1790, JCP, I, 454.

21. John Milner (1752-1826) was Vicar Apostolic of the Midland District (1803-1826) who opposed an elective episcopate advocated by some English Catholics. Between 1787 and 1793 he became the foremost English Catholic spokesman for a non-elective ecclesiastical hierarchy as his two books during the period indicate: *The Divine Right of Episcopacy* (London: J. P. Coghlan, 1791) and *Ecclesiastical Democracy Detected* (London, 1792).

22. Carroll to Charles Plowden, December 22, 1791-91, JCP, I, 548; cf. also Carroll to Leonardo Antonelli, April 23, 1792, JCP, II, 32.

23. JCP, I, 59-63.

24. Carroll to Charles Plowden, February 20, 1782, JCP, I, 66.

25. JCP, I, 71-76.

26. Patrick Carey, "The Laity's Understanding of the Trustee System, 1785-1855," *Catholic Historical Review* 64 (July, 1978), 357-377; Patrick Carey, "Republicanism Within American Catholicism, 1785-1860," *Journal of the Early Republic* 3 (Winter, 1983), 413-438.

27. Patrick Carey, *An Immigrant Bishop*, pp. 141-148; James Hennesey, S.J., "Papacy and Episcopacy in 18th and 19th Century American Catholic Thought," *Records of the American Catholic Historical Society* 77 (1966), 175-189; Gerald P. Fogarty, S.J., "Church Councils in the United States and American Legal Institutions," *Annuarium Historiae Conciliorum* 4 (1972), 83-105.

28. England, *Works*, IV, 174, 175; cf. also JCP, I, 83.

29. England, *Works*, I, 17, 89; IV, 176.

30. Henry F. Brownson (ed.), *The Works of Orestes A. Brownson* (20 vols.; Detroit: T. Nourse, 1882-1887), XII, 466-467.

31. Ong, *Frontiers*, p. 117.

32. Descriptions of the elements of romanticism vary. I have taken some of the above characteristics of Catholic romanticism from Roger Aubert, "The Complex Revival of Religious Studies," *The Church Between Revolution and Restoration,* Vol. VII, *History of the Church*, ed. by Hubert Jedin and John Dolan (New York: Crossroad, 1981), pp. 240-257. For other descriptions of romanticism, see Sydney E. Ahlstrom, *A Religious History of the American People* (New Haven: Yale University Press, 1972), pp. 583-632; Paul Tillich, *Perspectives on 19th and 20th Century Protestant Theology* (New York: Harper and Row, Publisher, 1967), pp. 71-135; Jacques Barzun, *Classic, Romantic and Modern* (Chicago: The University of Chicago Press, 1975); Alexander Dru, *The Contribution of German Catholicism* (New York: Hawthorn Books, 1963), pp. 27-92; James Hastings Nichols, *Romanticism in American Theology: Nevin and Schaff at Mercersburg* (Chicago: University of Chicago Press, 1961); Harold P. Simonson, *Radical Discontinuities: American Romanticism and Christian Consciousness* (London and Toronto: Associated University Presses, 1983); Robert Gleckner and Gerald Enscoe (eds.), *Romanticism: Points of View* (Englewood Cliffs, New Jersey: Prentice-Hall, 1962).

33. John Hughes, *Pastoral Letter of the Right Rev. Dr. Hughes to the Clergy and Laity of the Diocese of New York* (New York: George Mitchel, 1842), p. 5.

34. Jay P. Dolan, *Catholic Revivalism: The American Experience 1830-1900* (Notre Dame, Indiana: University of Notre Dame Press, 1978), p. xvii.

35. Ann Taves, "Relocating the Sacred: Roman Catholic Devotions in Mid-Nineteenth Century America" (Unpublished Ph.D dissertation, University of Chicago, 1983); Ann Taves, " 'External' Devotions and the Interior Life: Popular Devotional Theologies in Mid-Nineteenth Century America" (Cushwa Working Paper Series, Series 13, No. 2; University of Notre Dame, Spring, 1983).

36. See, e.g., the following lectures in Lawrence Kehoe (ed.), *Complete Works of the Most Reverend John Hughes, D.D., Archbishop of New York; comprising his sermons, letters, lectures, speeches, etc.* (2 vols.; New York, 1865): "Influence of Christianity upon Civilization," I, 351-370; "The Influence of Christianity on Social Servitude," I, 371-385; "The Mixture of Civil and Ecclesiastical Power in the Middle Ages," I, 417-436; "The Importance of a Christian Basis for the Science of Political Econ-

omy," I, 513-534; "The Church and the World," II, 69-86; "The Decline of Protestantism and Its Causes," II, 87-102; "The Catholic Chapter in the History of the United States," II, 102-121.

37. Hughes, *Works*, I, 354.

38. *Ibid.*, 352-353.

39. *Ibid.*, 430.

40. *Ibid.*, 359, 362-363, 386; II, 119.

41. "The Dogma of an All-Ruling Providence Confirmed by History," *The Religious Cabinet* I (May, 1842), 257-268.

42. Hughes, *Works*, I, 513-534.

43. Leonard Gilhooley, *Contradiction and Dilemma; Orestes Brownson and the American Idea* (New York: Fordham University Press, 1972), p. 79.

44. Brownson, *Works*, V, 130.

45. *The American Republic: Its Constitution, Tendencies, and Destiny* (Detroit: H. P. Brownson, 1895), p. 67.

46. Brownson, *Works*, XII, 479.

47. *The American Republic*, pp. 47, 68, 77, 46.

48. Brownson, *Works*, XII, 101.

49. *Ibid.*, XII, 465-496.

50. For an excellent study of the influence of romanticism upon Hecker's thought, see William LeRoy Portier, "Providential Nation: An Historical-Theological Study of Isaac Hecker's Americanism" (Unpublished Ph.D. dissertation, University of St. Michael's College, Toronto, 1980).

51. Isaac T. Hecker, "Dr. Brownson's Road to the Church," *Catholic World* 66 (October, 1887), p. 6.

52. See, e.g., John England, *Cork Mercantile Chronicle*, April 18, 1814; John Carroll, "Pastoral on the Restoration of Pius VII," JCP, III, 279-284; Ambrose Maréchal, *Pastoral Letter to the Roman Catholics of Norfolk* (Baltimore, 1819), pp. 44-47; Martin J. Spalding, *The Evidences of Catholicity: A Series of Lectures, Delivered in the Cathedral of Louisville* (6th ed.; Baltimore: J. Murphy, 1876), p. 474.

53. England, *Works*, V, 96.

54. *Concilii plenarii Baltimorensis II, in ecclesia metropolitana Baltimorensi a die vii ad diem xxi octobris MCCCLXVI habiti, et a Sede Apostolica recogniti, acta et decreta* (Baltimore, 1868), p. 41.

55. England, *Works*, V, 92.

56. Peter Richard Kenrick, *Concio in Concilio Vaticano habenda et non habita* (Naples: Typis Fratrum de Angelis, 1870); English translation in Raymond J. Clancy, "American Prelates in the Vatican Council," *Historical Records and Studies* 28 (1937), 93-131.

57. Kenrick, *The Primacy of the Apostolic See Vindicated* (4th rev. ed.; Baltimore: John Murphy, 1855), pp. 230, 223.

58. M. J. Spalding, *Lectures on the Evidences of Catholicity* (4th ed.; Baltimore: John Murphy, 1870), pp. 263-268; see also Thomas Spalding, *Martin John Spalding: American Churchman* (Washington, D.C.: Catholic University of America Press, 1973), pp. 283-325, for Spalding's participation at Vatican I.

59. Brownson, "Conversations on Liberalism and the Church," *Works*, XIII, 13.

60. *Ibid.*, XII, 490-491; for Brownson's view of the papacy, see Thomas R. Ryan, "Brownson on the Papacy," *American Ecclesiastical Review* 112 (1946), 114-122.

61. Brownson's review of Kenrick's *The Primacy of the Apostolic See Vindicated* (1845) in *Brownson's Quarterly Review* 7 (April, 1845), 264.

62. Kenrick, *The Primacy* (1855), p. 19.

63. *Brownson's Quarterly Review* 7 (April, 1845), 264; cf. also Kenrick, *The Primacy*, p. 20.

64. *Brownson's Quarterly Review* 7 (April, 1845), 264.

65. Kenrick, *The Primacy*, p. 224.

66. M. J. Spalding, "Pastoral . . . on Papal Infallibility," in *General Evidences*, p. 473.

67. *Brownson's Quarterly Review* 7 (April, 1845), 266.

68. James J. Hennesey, *The First Council of the Vatican: The American Experience* (New York: Herder and Herder, 1963), pp. 281-282.

69. On this see Gerald Fogarty, S.J., "Archbishop Peter Kenrick's Submission to Papal Infallibility," *Archivum Historiae Pontificiae* 16 (1978), 205-223.

70. M. J. Spalding, *General Evidences*, pp. 450-453; cf. also Edward McGlynn, "The Bugbear of Vaticanism," *American Catholic Quarterly Review* 1 (January, 1876), 96.

71. I. T. Hecker, "An Exposition of the Church in View of Recent Difficulties and Controversies and the Present Needs of the Age," *Catholic World* 21 (April-September, 1875), 125.

72. Ong, *Frontiers*, p. 125.

73. Joseph Schroder, "Theological Minimizing and Its Latest Defender," *American Ecclesiastical Review* 5 (July, 1891), 56.

74. Salvatore Brandi, S.J., "Touchstone of Catholicity," *American Ecclesiastical Review* 6 (February, 1892), 89-90.

75. John Ireland, *The Church and Modern Society* (New York: D. H. McBride and Co., 1903), pp. vii, viii, xii, xiii, xiv.

76. *Ibid.*, pp. xxi, 149.

77. Quoted by M. V. Gannon, "Before and After Modernism: The Intellectual Isolation of the American Priest," in John T. Ellis (ed.), *The Catholic Priest in the United States: Historical Investigations* (Collegeville, Minnesota: St. John's University Press, 1971), p. 325.

78. Ireland, *The Church and Modern Society*, p. 409.

79. *Ibid.*, p. 188.

80. *Ibid.*, pp. 408-409, 165, 380, 410, 411, 151, 152, 155.

81. *Ibid.*, p. 76.

82. See Gannon, "Before and After Modernism," p. 337 and p. 376, n. 158 for a discussion of the literature on the connection between Americanism and Modernism; for a more recent favorable interpretation of the connection, see M. M. Reher, "The Church and the Kingdom of God in America: The Ecclesiology of the Americanists" (Unpublished Ph.D. dissertation, Fordham University, 1972), p. 295.

83. F. L. Cross (ed.), *The Oxford Dictionary of the Christian Church* (2nd ed., rev.; London: Oxford University Press, 1974), p. 926.

84. John A. Zahm, C.S.C., *Evolution and Dogma* (reprint of 1895 ed.; with a new introduction by Ralph E. Weber; Hicksville, New York: Regina Press, 1975), pp. 436, 435, 433, 437, 436.

85. "Seminary and University Studies," *American Ecclesiastical Review* 19 (1898), 366, n. 1.

86. William J. Kerby, "The Priesthood and the Social Movement," *Catholic University Bulletin* 6 (January, 1900), 18-28; also published in Aaron I. Abell (ed.), *American Catholic Thought on Social Questions* (New York: The Bobbs-Merrill Co., 1968), pp. 271, 273, 274.

87. Bernard Noone, F.S.C., "American Catholic Periodicals and the Biblical Question, 1893-1908," *Records of the American Catholic Historical Society* 89 (March-December, 1978), 85-109.

88. "The Study of Sacred Scripture in Theological Seminaries," *American Ecclesiastical Review* 23 (September, 1900), 234; quoted in Gannon, "Before and After Modernism," p. 331.

89. Ong, *Frontiers*, p. 125.

90. Anon., "Modernism in the Church in America," *American Ecclesiastical Review* 38 (January, 1908), 2-3, 5-6.

91. "The Encyclical Against Modernism," *North American Review* 187 (February, 1908), 199, 204.

92. "The Dogmatic Authority of the Papacy: The Encyclical on Modernism," *North American Review* 187 (April, 1908), 494.

93. Gannon, "Before and After Modernism," p. 350.

94. Hughes, *Works*, I, 515.

95. *Ibid.*, I, 513-534.

96. For Catholic opinion on slavery, see Madeleine Hooke Rice, *American Catholic Opinion in the Slavery Controversy* (New York: Columbia University Press, 1944) and James Hennesey, S.J., *American Catholics: A History of the Roman Catholic Community in the United States* (New York: Oxford University Press, 1981), pp. 143-157.

97. "View of the Labor Movement," *Catholic World* 10 (March, 1870), 784-798; excerpts reprinted in A. I. Abell (ed.), *American Catholic Thought*, pp. 72-90.

98. A. I. Abell (ed.), *American Catholic Thought*, p. xxiv.

99. Ireland, *The Church and Modern Society*, pp. 85, 95-97.

100. *Rerum Novarum: Encyclical Letter of Pope Leo XIII on the Condition of Labor*, ed. by Rev. Gerald C. Treacy, S.J. (New York: Paulist Press, 1939), pp. 5, 6, 15, 28.

101. John Ryan, *A Living Wage: Its Ethical and Economic Aspects* (New York: The Macmillan Co., 1906), p. xii.

102. John Ryan, *Distributive Justice: The Right and Wrong of Our Present Distribution of Wealth* (New York: The Macmillan Co., 1927), pp. 220-222.

103. *Ibid.*, p. 220.

104. Ryan, *A Living Wage*, pp. 43, 44, 45.

105. John T. Ellis (ed.), *Documents of American Catholic History* (Milwaukee: Bruce Publishing Company, 1962), pp. 585-603.

106. "The Coughlin Sixteen Points," *The Guildsman*, 3 (April, 1935), 10-11; reprinted in A. I. Abell (ed.), *American Catholic Thought*, pp. 407-408.

107. Will Herberg, *Protestant, Catholic, Jew: An Essay in American Religious Sociology* (New York: Doubleday Anchor Books, 1955).

108. See, e.g., Edward R. Kantowicz, "Cardinal Mundelein of Chicago and the Shaping of Twentieth-Century American Catholicism," *Journal of American History* 68 (June, 1981), 52-68; Edward R. Kantowicz, *Corporation Sole: Cardinal Mundelein and Chicago Catholicism* (Notre Dame, Indiana: University of Notre Dame Press, 1983).

109. The best historical work on Neo-Thomism in the United States from 1920 to 1940 is William M. Halsey, *The Survival of Catholic Innocence* (Notre Dame, Indiana: University of Notre Dame Press, 1980). Although I differ from some of Halsey's interpretations, I am relying upon his work in much of what follows on Neo-Thomism.

110. Gerald A. McCool, S.J., *Catholic Theology in the Nineteenth Century: The Quest for a Unitary Method* (New York: The Seabury Press, 1977), p. 238.

111. Halsey, *The Survival*, pp. 141-142.

112. The commentators' theologies were clearly distinguished from that of St. Thomas. On this, see McCool, *Catholic Theology*, pp. 243-244.

113. On the different kinds of twentieth-century Neo-Thomism, see *ibid.*, pp. 252-267, and Helen James John, S.N.D., *The Thomist Spectrum* (New York: Fordham University Press, 1966).

114. Robert J. Henle, S.J., "The New Scholasticism," *Thought* 13 (September, 1938), 475, quoted in Halsey, *The Survival*, p. 17.

115. "Everyman's Philosophy," *Proceedings of the American Catholic Philosophical Society* 11 (1935), 186-187, quoted in Halsey, *The Survival*, p. 148.

116. J. Edward Coffey, S.J., "Classroom Disease and the Scholastic Prescription," *American Ecclesiastical Review* 69 (July, 1923), p. 34.

117. George Bull, S.J., "The Function of a Catholic Graduate School," *Thought* 13 (September, 1938), 368, 378, quoted in Gannon, "Before and After Modernism," pp. 358-359.

118. "The Mission of Catholic Thought," *American Catholic Quarterly Review* 46 (1921), 662-663.

119. John A. Ryan and Moorhouse F. X. Millar, S.J., *The State and the Church* (New York: Macmillan, 1922), pp. 38, 39.

120. *The Problem of Religious Freedom* (Westminster, Maryland: The Newman Press, 1965), pp. 109, 19.

121. *Ibid.*, pp. 20, 24.

122. *We Hold These Truths: Catholic Reflections on the American Proposition* (New York: Doubleday Image Books, 1964), pp. 53, 116.

123. *Ibid.*, p. 52.

124. *Problem of Religious Freedom*, pp. 28-33.

125. *Ibid.*, p. 33.

126. For an extended examination of Weigel's views, see Patrick W. Collins, "Gustave Weigel: Ecclesiologist and Ecumenist" (Unpublished Ph.D. dissertation, Fordham University, 1972).

127. "The Rebirth of Our Liturgical Life," *American Ecclesiastical Review* 81 (July, 1929), 23.

128. "The True Christian Life," *American Ecclesiastical Review* 82 (February, 1930), 135, 132.

129. William Miller, *A Harsh and Dreadful Love: Dorothy Day and the Catholic Worker Movement* (New York: Liveright, 1973), pp. 3-4.

130. On Peter Maurin, see Marc H. Ellis, *Peter Maurin: Prophet in the Twentieth Century* (New York: Paulist Press, 1981) and Miller, *A Harsh and Dreadful Love*, pp. 17-23, 114-127, 201-216.

131. Fyodor Dostoyevsky, *The Brothers Karamazov*, trans. by Constance Garnett (New York: The Modern Library, 1950), p. 65, quoted in *Catholic Worker*, May, 1939 p. 4.

132. Miller, *A Harsh and Dreadful Love*, pp. 14-15.

133. *Thought* 30 (Autumn, 1955), 353-386.

134. *Review of Politics* 19 (July, 1957), 275-307.

135. *Thought* 30 (Autumn, 1955), 353.

136. T. O'Dea, *American Catholic Dilemma*, p. 76.

Part I

THE ENLIGHTENMENT, 1784-1842

1

John England

John England (1786-1842), first Catholic Bishop of Charleston South Carolina (1820-1842), was the most articulate and dynamic Catholic representative of the Enlightenment in the United States during the twenty-two years of his episcopate. Like Archbishop John Carroll of Baltimore, he advocated religious liberty, separation of church and state, voluntaryism, and American republicanism. Unlike Carroll, he believed that the best way to destroy prejudice against Catholics in America was to demonstrate publicly and to argue articulately in the press and pulpit the compatibility of Catholicism and American republicanism.

England was born in Cork, Ireland, to Thomas and Honora Lordan England. He studied at St. Patrick's College, Carlow, Ireland (1803-08) in preparation for the priesthood. After ordination in 1808, he served in various pastoral capacities in the cities of Cork and Bandon (1808-1820), and took an active role in the anti-veto resistance movement[1] led by Daniel O'Connell (1775-1847). Influenced by the Enlightenment writings of Rev. Arthur O'Leary (1729-1802), he became a forceful advocate of religious and civil liberty in Ireland, editing the Cork Mercantile Chronicle (1813-16), an organ of anti-vetoism. In 1820, Irish clerics in Rome nominated England for the newly-established Diocese of Charleston, South Carolina. From 1820 to 1842, he served as Bishop of Charleston, establishing the first Catholic newspaper, the United States Catholic Miscellany, demanding a conciliar form of episcopal government in the United States, modeling his diocesan government after the Federal Constitution and the convention system of the Protestant Episcopal Church, and becoming the foremost apologist for American Catholicism.

The following selection is a constitution that England framed to eliminate excessive lay control over ecclesiastical affairs, to outline the govern-

ing powers within his diocese and to show the compatibility of Catholic Church government with American republicanism.[2] The written constitution was a governing instrument that met the demands of canon law and the aspirations of England's democratic-minded people. It was a legally binding document, approved in the state legislatures, that created a voluntary corporation within the Diocese of Charleston and that outlined various rights and responsibilities in the church, balanced the powers of all members within the ecclesiastical government of the diocese, provided for lay participation in the administration of temporal ecclesiastical affairs at the parish and diocesan levels, and delineated rules for a yearly diocesan convention of elected lay and clerical representatives of the diocese.

NOTES

1. Periodically, from 1808 to 1816, a number of Irish and English politicians (Catholics as well as Protestants) tried to obtain for the British Government the right to veto the nominations to Irish and English episcopal sees. In exchange for the veto, the Catholics were to obtain emancipation and financial support for their church. Anti-vetoists resisted such attempts on the grounds that such a proposal would, among other things, unite church and state.

2. For a more extensive treatment of England's Constitution, see Patrick Carey, *An Immigrant Bishop: John England's Adaptation of Irish Catholicism to American Republicanism* (New York: United States Catholic Historical Association, 1982), pp. 111-128, 149-161, and Peter Guilday, *The Life and Times of John England* (New York: The America Press, 1927), I, 343-383; II, 480-502.

TEXT

"THE CONSTITUTION OF THE ROMAN CATHOLIC CHURCHES OF NORTH CAROLINA, SOUTH CAROLINA, AND GEORGIA: WHICH ARE COMPRISED IN THE DIOCESE OF CHARLESTON, AND PROVINCE OF BALTIMORE, U.S.A. AS FULLY AGREED TO, AND ACCEPTED, AFTER REPEATED DISCUSSION, BY THE CLERGY AND THE SEVERAL CONGREGATIONS, AND REGULARLY CONFIRMED BY THE BISHOP, AND SUBSEQUENTLY AMENDED ACCORDING TO THE FORM PRESCRIBED" [SECOND EDITION; DECEMBER 31, 1839].

Source: Ignatius A. Reynolds (ed.), *The Works of the Right Reverend John England* (5 vols.; Baltimore: John Murphy and Co., 1849), V, 91-107.

PREFACE

. . . The constitution of this diocese was formed, for the purpose of preventing in future the recurrence of evils of this description [i.e., trustee-ism] within its limits.

The portions of our church government are very like to those of the government of this Union. The entire consists of dioceses, the bishop of each of which holds his place, not as the deputy of the Pope, but as a successor to the Apostles; as the governor of each state holds his place not as the deputy of the President, but as vested therewith by the same power which vests the President with his own authority. And as all the states are bound together in one federation, of the which the President is the head, so are the dioceses collected into one church, of which the Pope is the head. Each state has power to make its own laws, provided they do not contravene the general Constitution of the United States; so in each diocess there exists the power of legislation, provided the statutes made therein be not incompatible with the faith or general discipline of the Catholic Church. The legislature of the Union is collected from all the states, and the decisions of the majority bind the individuals and the states which they represent; the general legislative body of the church is a council composed of the representatives of each diocess, and the decision of the majority binds the members and their dioceses. It is the duty of the President to have the laws of the Union executed in every state, as it is the duty of the Pope to have the general laws of the church executed in every diocess. The bishop is also bound to have them carried into execution within his own diocess, and he has power, and it is his duty to make such special regulations and laws as circumstances may render necessary for their more effectual observance, and for the spiritual benefit of his own district. As our states are subdivided, so are our dioceses: and as the laws of Congress and those of the state are binding in each subdivision, so are the general laws of the church and the laws of the diocess in each parish or district of the same; but in each subdivision, special regulations are made, each corporate city, town, or district, has its own by-laws, which would be invalid if incompatible with the laws of Congress or those of the states, otherwise they are of force; so in each parish or district by-laws which are incompatible with the general law of the church or the law of the diocess, are invalid.

With this general view, the frame of the following Constitution will be the more easily understood. The object of its formation was to lay down those general principles of law, and to show their special bearing in the most usual cases; and then upon the mode of raising, vesting, and managing church property, to fix the special manner in which the great principles that are recognized by the church should be carried into practice. This was done by consultation, discussion, and arrangement between the bishop, the clergy, and the laity, in several meetings in the several districts; and the outline of the entire, together with some of the most important of its special provisions, was laid before the Holy See, after it had been adopted, on the 25th of September, 1822. No objection having been received from that quarter, and its provisions having been more maturely examined, and tested by some experience, it is now published for the use of the members. . . .

CONSTITUTION OF THE ROMAN CATHOLIC CHURCH,
OF THE DIOCESS OF CHARLESTON.
TITLE I.
DOCTRINE.

1. Our principle is that man is bound to believe all those things, and only those things which God hath revealed. Hence we have no right to select some of those doctrines which we will believe, and others which we may reject; for the divine authority and credit is equal as to each; therefore we admit no distinction between the doctrines of revelation, so as to call some fundamental, which should be received in preference to others to be called not fundamental, as if they may be rejected; for we believe no person is at liberty to reject the testimony of God in great things or in small things.

2. We are not to reject doctrines revealed by God, because they exhibit to us matters beyond the force of our reason to discover. For the unlimited knowledge of God comprehends many things beyond the discovery of our limited reason,—and he may, if he thinks proper, reveal to us that such things do exist, though he should not manifest to us the manner of that existence, nor the reason why those things so be.

3. Faith is the belief, upon the authority of God, of all those matters which he hath revealed to us, even though they should be above or beyond the comprehension of our reason.

4. Although we be not obliged by faith to submit our understanding to our fellow-creature, as to God; yet we may have evidence, and of course certainty, that God hath made that creature his infallible witness to us. In receiving the testimony of that witness, we therefore pay our homage, not to our fellow-creature who testifies, but to the Creator, who, by that witness, reveals to us his doctrines, or gives to us his precepts.

5. We have evidence that God hath spoken frequently, in divers ways in times of old, by his prophets to the fathers, and last of all by his beloved

Son, who hath on earth established his church as the pillar and the ground of truth; and who hath commanded all persons to hear and to obey that church as the infallible witness of his doctrine and precepts; which church he hath built upon a rock, making to her a promise that the gates of hell shall not prevail against her.

6. We have evidence that, notwithstanding many persons have in several ages gone out from this church, and formed for themselves new associations, yet that Church of Christ hath subsisted in every age, and still continues to be a visible body of believers, united under one visible head, in the profession of the same faith, using the same sacraments, teaching doctrines of moral and religious observance which are confessedly holy, and which, being reduced to practice, have exhibited, at all times, men and women of eminent sanctity in the bosom of that society spread through the whole civilized world, and tracing its origin through the unbroken succession of its pastors, to the Apostles who were commissioned by the Son of God to teach all nations; and with whom and with whose successors he promised to be, all days, to the consummation of the world.

7. From this church we receive the testimony of the doctrines and precepts which God hath revealed; to which doctrines no man may add, from which doctrines no man may take away; and which precepts by the divine authority are binding upon those to whom they are given.

8. We therefore believe with a firm faith, and profess all and every one of those things which are contained in that creed which the holy Catholic (Roman) Church maketh use of, to wit: we believe in one God, the Father Almighty, maker of heaven and earth, of all things visible and invisible. And in one Lord Jesus Christ, the only begotten Son of God, and born of the Father before all ages. God of God; light of light; true God of true God; begotten, not made; consubstantial to the Father, by whom all things were made. Who for us men, and for our salvation, came down from heaven, and was incarnate by the Holy Ghost of the Virgin Mary; and was made man. Was crucified also for us under Pontius Pilate; he suffered and was buried; and the third day he arose again according to the Scriptures. He ascended into heaven; sitteth at the right hand of the Father, and is to come again with glory to judge the living and the dead; of whose kingdom there shall be no end. And in the Holy Ghost, the Lord and lifegiver; who proceedeth from the Father and the Son, who, together with the Father and the Son, is adored and glorified, who spoke by the Prophets. And we believe one, holy, Catholic and Apostolic Church. We confess one baptism for the remission of sins; and we expect the resurrection of the dead and the life of the world to come. *Amen.*

We most steadfastly admit and embrace apostolical and ecclesiastical traditions, and all other observances and constitutions of the church.

We also admit the holy Scriptures according to that sense which our holy mother, the church, hath held and doth hold, to which it belongs *to judge* of the true sense and interpretation of the Scriptures; neither will we ever take and interpret them otherwise than according to the unanimous consent of the fathers.

We also profess that there are truly and properly *Seven Sacraments* of the new law instituted by our Lord Jesus Christ, and necessary for the salvation of mankind, though not all for every one: to wit, Baptism, Confirmation, Eucharist, Penance, Extreme Unction, Order, and Matrimony; and that they confer grace: and that of these. Baptism, Confirmation, and Order cannot be reiterated without sacrilege. We also receive and admit the received and approved ceremonies of the Catholic Church in the solemn administration of all the aforesaid Sacraments.

We receive and embrace all and every one of those things which have been defined and declared in the holy Council of Trent concerning original sin, and justification.

We profess, likewise, that there is offered to God in the Mass a true, proper, and propitiatory sacrifice for the living and the dead. And that in the most holy Sacrament of the Eucharist there is truly, really, and substantially, the body and blood, together with the soul and divinity, of our Lord Jesus Christ; and that there is made a conversion of the whole substance of the bread into the body, and of the whole substance of the wine into the blood,—which conversion the Catholic Church calls Transubstantiation. We also confess that, under either kind alone, Christ is received whole and entire, a true Sacrament.

We constantly hold that there is a Purgatory, and that the souls therein detained are helped by the suffrages of the faithful.

Likewise, that the saints reigning together with Christ are to be honoured and invoked: and that they offer prayers to God for us, and that their relics are to be respected.

We most firmly assert that the images of Christ, of the Mother of God, ever Virgin, and also of other saints, may be had and retained, and that due honour and veneration is to be given to them.

We also affirm that the power of indulgences was left by Christ in the church, and that the use of them is most wholesome to Christian people.

We also acknowledge the holy Catholic Apostolic Roman Church for the mother and mistress of all other churches; and we promise true obedience to the Bishop of Rome, successor to St. Peter, prince of the Apostles and Vicar of Jesus Christ.

We likewise undoubtedly receive and profess all other things delivered, defined, and declared by the sacred canons and general councils, and particularly by the holy Council of Trent. And we condemn, reject, and anathematize all things contrary thereto, and all heresies whatsoever condemned, rejected and anathematized by the church.

This true catholic faith, without which none can be saved,* we do at this present, freely profess and sincerely hold, and we promise most constantly to retain and confess the same entire and unviolate, with God's holy assistance, to the end of our lives.

TITLE II.

GOVERNMENT.

SECTION 1.

The Church of Christ on earth, of which we here treat, is the visible body of true believers under its proper government. (See Tit. I. cl. 6.)

1. The government of the church is not of human invention, nor established by the agreement of men; but it is the positive institution of God; and is subject only to the administration of those persons whom he hath commissioned to regulate and carry it on.

2. It is not in the power of men by any convention or law, or act of authority, or of force, to change the nature of that government which our Lord Jesus Christ hath established for his church.

3. We do not believe that our Lord Jesus Christ gave to the civil or temporal governments of states, empires, kingdoms, or nations, any authority in or over spiritual or ecclesiastical concerns.

4. We do not believe that our Lord Jesus Christ gave to the rulers of his church, as such, any authority in or over the civil or temporal concerns of states, empires, kingdoms, or nations.

5. We do not believe that our Lord Jesus Christ hath appointed any special or particular mode of civil or temporal government for mankind, so that men should be bound by the divine law to adopt or to prefer one mode of civil or temporal government to any other.

6. We believe that as Church government and temporal government

---

*The following declaration of the bishops of the Irish Church gives the exact meaning of this too often misrepresented tenet of exclusive salvation. John, Bp. of Ch.

"Catholics hold, that, in order to attain salvation, it is necessary to belong to the true church, and that heresy, or a wilful and obstinate opposition to revealed truth, as taught in the Church of Christ, excludes from the kingdom of God. They are not, however, obliged to believe, that all those are wilfully and obstinately attached to error, who, having been seduced into it by others, or who, having imbibed it from their parents, seek the truth with a cautious solicitude, disposed to embrace it when sufficiently proposed to them; but leaving such persons to the righteous judgment of a merciful God, they feel themselves bound to discharge towards them, as well as towards all mankind, the duties of charity and a social life."

are not necessarily united the one to the other, nor dependent the one upon the other; the one unchangeable mode of Church government may therefore continue for ever to subsist, as it hath, during all ages of Christianity, subsisted, in the several nations which have had different modes of temporal government; and that the several members of that one Church may still continue in their respective nations, as they have hitherto been, faithful and meritorious citizens of republics, and loyal subjects of limited or of absolute monarchs. Nor does, therefore, the difference of temporal government in their several nations require or make lawful any change in Church government, so as to assimilate the same to the temporal governments of those several nations.

7. We do not believe that our Lord Jesus Christ gave to the faithful at large the government of the Church, nor any power to regulate spiritual or ecclesiastical concerns; neither do we believe that he gave to the laity nor to any part of the laity such government nor such power, nor any portion of such government or of such power.

8. We believe that our Lord Jesus Christ hath appointed his Apostles the governors of his Church; to be witnesses of his doctrine in Jerusalem and all Judea, and Samaria, and to the very ends of the earth; his ministers the dispensers of the mysteries of God, the Sacraments instituted by our blessed Redeemer; and bishops placed by the Holy Ghost to govern the Church of God, by establishing and preserving wholesome discipline therein.

9. We believe that for the purpose of preserving his Church in unity and in that peace which the world could not give, and of making it one as he and his heavenly Father are one, the Saviour Jesus Christ did establish one chief ruler amongst his Apostles, with a primacy of honour and of jurisdiction: to which supreme ruler every member of the Church ought to pay the reverence and the obedience justly due to a person placed by the divine authority in so eminent a station.

10. We believe that this supremacy in and over the universal church was promised by our blessed Redeemer to Simon the son of Jonas, when the Saviour changed the name of that Apostle to Peter, and that it was conferred upon him principally when our blessed Lord told him that he had prayed for him that his faith should not fail, and exhorted him when he should be converted, to confirm his brethren; and again, when after his resurrection the Saviour having required from him a declaration of greater love, gave to him more extensive authority; to feed his lambs and to feed his sheep: we behold in his subsequent acts, evidence of his exercise of this power, and the same doctrine is testified to us by the Church.

11. We are taught, and do believe that this office of supreme ruler was ordained by our Lord Jesus Christ to remain in the Church during its

existence: and we find undoubted evidence that St. Peter, the chief Apostle, did finally establish his seat of authority in the city of Rome, near to which he and the Apostle St. Paul were put to death, and that the power with which he was invested by our blessed Redeemer was thus caused to descend to the Bishops of that Holy See.

12. We also find that the Christian Churches from the beginning did receive and hold this doctrine of the supremacy of one see, and did recognize and acknowledge the fact, that it was vested in the Bishops of Rome, who have at all times by divine appointment exercised the power thereof, and to which power those churches that did continue in the primitive communion have at all times willingly submitted.

13. We therefore acknowledge the primacy of honour and of spiritual jurisdiction throughout the whole world to be, of divine right, in the Pope or Bishop of Rome, duly and properly appointed; and we pay to him the reverence and the obedience justly due to his eminent station, and we feel it necessary to adhere to his communion and to be subject to his spiritual and ecclesiastical authority.

14. We are not required by our faith to believe that the Pope is infallible, nor do we believe that he is impeccable, for it is not a consequence of his being vested with great authority that he should be exempt from the frailties of human nature; but we do not believe that his authority would be diminished, nor the institutions of our blessed Saviour destroyed, even if the Pope were to be guilty of criminal actions.

15. We do not believe that by virtue of this spiritual or ecclesiastical authority, the Pope hath any power or right to interfere with the allegiance that we owe to our state; nor to interfere in or with the concerns of the civil policy or the temporal government thereof, or of the United States of America.

16. We believe and acknowledge the majority of the bishops of the church, who are the successors of the apostles, in union with their head aforesaid, to be an ecclesiastical tribunal appointed by our Lord Jesus Christ to decide by his authority, with infallible certainty of truth, in all controversies of doctrine, and to testify truly to us those things which have been revealed by God to man. We also recognize and acknowledge in that same tribunal full power and authority, by the same divine institution, to regulate and to ordain the general ecclesiastical discipline of the whole Church of Christ.

17. We believe and acknowledge that in the several diocesses, bishops are placed by the Holy Ghost to govern the Church of God. And we acknowledge the bishop regularly appointed, according to the usages of the church, and in due time consecrated according to the form of the same, and holding communion with the Pope, to be the ordinary lawful governor

and ecclesiastical legislator of the church of this diocess: to whom we are bound to pay reverence and obedience in all spiritual and ecclesiastical concerns, according to the divine institution and the canons and usages of the church.

18. During the absence of the bishop, we acknowledge the power of governing the church of this diocess in conjunction with him, to be in the vicar whom he may appoint. And even when the bishop may be present, we acknowledge the vicar appointed by him to be vested with such spiritual and ecclesiastical authority as the bishop may specify, and that such vicar is to be respected and obeyed accordingly.

19. During the vacancy of the see, we acknowledge the power of governing the church of this diocess to be in the vicar who may be regularly appointed by the proper ecclesiastical authority; and that such vicar is to be respected and obeyed accordingly.

20. We acknowledge the priests of the church to be, in subordination to the bishop, the preachers of the doctrine of Christ, the ministers of the sacraments, and, when duly appointed, the local rulers of ecclesiastical districts, and that they ought to be respected and obeyed accordingly.

21. As in the church there are other orders of clergymen, who may occasionally receive from the bishop authority to perform those duties of which they are capable: we acknowledge the existence of the orders of deacon and sub-deacon and minor clerks. And according to divine and apostolical institutions, canons, and ancient usages, we will yield due obedience to the authority with which they may be invested, and we will respect themselves, their orders and their offices.

22. As our religion was not invented by men, but revealed by God, and as the government of the church was not framed by human convention, nor by human authority, but by the institution and by the authority of our Lord Jesus Christ; we acknowledge its source to be divine; we therefore disavow and disclaim any right or power, under any pretext, in the laity to subject the ministry of the church to their control, or to interfere in the regulation of its sacred duties, this being the exclusive province of those persons whom the Holy Ghost hath placed bishops to govern the Church of God. . . .

[Ed. Title III of this constitution delineates the ownership, collection and distribution of property. Title IV outlines the qualifications for membership within the corporation created by the constitution. Only baptized males who were twenty-one years of age, were free from ecclesiastical censures and who had assented to the constitution were considered qualified members of this voluntary corporation.]

TITLE V.

DISTRICT CHURCHES.

SECTION I.

How created and regulated.

1. The power of creating a separate church, by the formation of a parochial or other district, belongs to the bishop.

2. When the bishop shall create a separate church, he will give due public notice for a meeting of the members thereof, to be held at some convenient time and place, for the necessary purposes consequent upon such creation, at which meeting he or his deputy will preside.

3. At this meeting the members will, by a majority of votes, determine what are to be the special qualifications, if any, in addition to membership for voters in that district, and for vestrymen therein; also how many lay members shall serve in the vestry. They shall then proceed to elect by ballot so many discreet, well-conducted men, having a regard for religion, and if possible, persons who are in the habit of receiving the sacrament of the holy Eucharist; and those laymen, together with the clergyman or clergymen of that district, shall be the vestry of the same, and shall continue in office during one year, and after the expiration of the same until the second Sunday in January next succeeding, or until their successors shall be chosen.

4. Those special qualifications for voters and for vestrymen in any district, and also the number of laymen to serve in the vestry thereof, may be altered by the majority of voters, at a general meeting of the members of that district, specially convened for that purpose after at least ten days' public notice; but such alteration shall not be of force until it shall have been approved of by the bishop or vicar.

5. The members qualified to vote in each district shall, on the first Sunday in January, in each year, at twelve o'clock, assemble in the church, or usual place of meeting, and there by ballot elect the proper number of qualified laymen—who, together with the clergy, shall be the vestry thereof, from the second Sunday in January to the second Sunday in January of the next year, or until their successors shall be elected and admitted into office. But should the election, by any cause, not have been held on the first Sunday in January, it shall be held as soon as possible thereafter, upon public notice of at least one week, which the clergyman shall give.

6. The laymen elected to serve upon the vestry shall, before entering into office, subscribe in presence of the clergyman, if he be in the district, and of the congregation, the proper declaration and promise.

7. No person elected to serve upon the vestry can, during the year of his office, be removed therefrom, except by 1. His voluntary resignation. 2. His refusal or neglect during one month to qualify; or 3. His loss of membership.

8. Should there be a vacancy in the vestry by reason of death, removal from the district, or either of the causes in the foregoing clause, the same shall as soon as possible be filled up by an election to be held for that special purpose after a public notice of at least one week from the clergyman.

9. When the clergyman is present, the elections shall be conducted under his regulations; in his absence, they will be conducted by the secretary and the wardens then in office.

Each separate church thus formed shall have power to make by-laws for its own special regulation in the following manner, provided they be not inconsistent with this constitution: 1. Such by-law must be an act of vestry. 2. It must be confirmed by a majority of the members of that church who may be present at a public meeting to be held for that special purpose, after at least one week's sufficient notice; and 3. It must be approved of by the bishop or vicar. And no by-law of any separate church shall be altered or repealed, except in the same manner as a new by-law might be made.

SECTION II.

Mode of proceeding, power and duty of the vestry.

1. In the meetings of the vestry, the principal clergyman who may be present is to be president; and in order to proceed to business, the presence of one clergyman and of three laymen shall be necessary. But if there be no clergyman resident in the district, the laymen may proceed to business, and procure the subsequent confirmation of their acts by the proper clergyman.

2. For the validity of an act of vestry there will be required the assent of a majority of the lay-members who may be present, and of the proper clergyman,—or in case of the refusal of the clergyman, the assent of the bishop or of the vicar.

3. But in making contracts or agreements for the performance of any work or duty which shall have been directed by an act of vestry, and in all elections and appointments to be made by the vestry, no clergyman shall have a negative power, but shall only possess his right of precedence and his right of vote.

4. At all meetings of the vestry, the president, or, in his absence from the district, the layman who may take the chair, shall, in case of an equality of votes, have a second or casting vote, so as to enable the meeting to

decide. But it is strongly recommended that all things be done in peace, harmony, and good will; and in any cases of importance, or where the feelings of opposed parties appear to be deeply interested, it would be better that an adjournment should take place, to afford time for calmness and reflection, than that a hasty decision should be made, and jealousy and ill-will be excited.

5. When the vestry assembles without the clergyman, the chair shall be taken by one of the wardens, according to the precedence of the name upon the entry of their appointment; and if the wardens be absent, by that vestryman whose name stands first upon the list of their appointment.

6. It shall be the duty of the vestry to exert themselves to procure for the bishop and the clergymen of their own district decent and comfortable support; to have the church and other buildings kept in good order and repair, and to provide all the necessaries therefor, according to the means which they shall be able to procure; to provide and to keep in order a burial ground for the interment of members in the communion of the church according to the canons of the same; and to see that the church property intrusted to their care be well preserved and improved, and faithfully administered.

7. The vestry have the right of electing the organist, the clerk, the sexton, and the other lay-officers or servants of the church; also they have the appointment of their own secretary and treasurer, and of the church wardens of their district, and of the collector of the general fund within the same. The church wardens shall be chosen from amongst the lay-members of the vestry. The treasurer, the secretary, and the collector for the general fund may be chosen by the vestry either from amongst their own body, or from the other members of the church.

8. The bishop or the clergyman of the district has a right and power, whenever he may see a cause to suspend the organist, the clerk, the sexton, or any other lay-officer or servant of the church. But the church warden, the secretary, or treasurer of the vestry, or the collector for the general fund, are only removable by an act of vestry. Any officer or servant so removed or suspended is ineligible to the same or to any other office or place of the church for one year, unless with the written consent of the bishop or of the clergyman of the district.

9. The vestry shall every year lay a fair and correct statement of their accounts and of the situation of the church before the congregation, and another such statement before the bishop previous to the first Sunday in January. And they shall also furnish and exhibit their accounts at any other time to the bishop, and to the congregation when called upon by either of them to do so.

10. Should the vestry of the district be displeased with the conduct or

the proceedings of the clergyman of the same, they shall have power, upon sufficient notice from the secretary, who must issue such notice upon the requisition in writing of two vestrymen, signed by them, to assemble without the clergyman, for the sole purpose of conferring together upon their cause of complaint and of embodying the same in writing; to be immediately transmitted to the bishop or vicar for his judgment thereupon; but which complaint they shall not publish in any other way without the leave, in writing, of the bishop or vicar first had and obtained therefor. But no person shall upon such occasion take the chair, nor shall any business be done, unless there be and continue present, a majority of the lay-members of the vestry.

11. Should the vestry of any district lodge a regular complaint in the manner prescribed against the clergyman of the same, the bishop or vicar will, as soon as possible, diligently inquire into the same; and as soon as may be, give his judgment and decision to the best of his ability for the benefit of religion and according to the canons and usages of the church: and the vestry will support and accede to such decision, unless they shall see cause for making their appeal to a superior ecclesiastical tribunal; in which case they shall abide by the said decision, until it shall have been set aside by such competent superior ecclesiastical tribunal; and in case such tribunal shall not set aside such decision, it shall be considered final and conclusive.

SECTION III.

Duties and Powers of Officers.

1. The duty of the secretary shall be to summon and to attend at all meetings of the vestry; to keep a fair record of their acts and appointments and resolutions, and when necessary to publish or to furnish extracts of the same; to sign their orders upon the treasurer when duly passed; to inform the bishop or vicar, when by him duly required, of their proceedings; to make out such report of their proceedings as may be required by the convention of the church of the diocess, or by the delegates of the district; and to notify to the vestry or to the church of the district such directions or information as may be conveyed to him for that purpose by the general trustees, or by the convention of the church, or by the bishop or vicar, or by the See of Rome.

2. The duty of the treasurer shall be, to keep fair and plain accounts of the income, and expenditure, and of the property of the church of that district; to collect the money payable to its use or due thereto; when necessary, to sue for the same; to have charge of the money and other valuable

property of the church; except the sacred vessels and vestments, of which the clergyman shall have charge, and for which he shall be accountable to the proper ecclesiastical persons; to pay, as far as the funds in his hands will allow, all orders of the vestry signed by the secretary and approved by the proper clergyman; to render an exact and fair statement of all his accounts on the first day of January in each year to the bishop, and another to the vestry at the same time, and also to the bishop and to the vestry when so required by either of them.

3. The duty of the church wardens shall be, to superintend the execution of any work ordered or contracted for by the vestry; to preserve in decency and repair the buildings and other property of the church; to aid the clergyman in preserving order and decency in the church, to remove therefrom all disturbers or nuisances.

TITLE VI.

THE CONVENTION.

SECTION I.

Composition, and mode of assembling.

1. There shall be held yearly in some convenient part of the diocess, to be designated by the bishop or vicar, and at the time by him appointed, a convention of this church, which shall consist of the following portions, which shall hold their sessions separately, viz.:

1. The bishop, or in his absence the vicar.

2. The clergy having spiritual jurisdiction in the diocess and not claiming any exemption from the bishop's ordinary jurisdiction, nor any special privileges except such as may arise from the special act of the bishop, or from statutes of the diocess.

3. The lay-delegates from the districts of the diocess.

2. The bishop, or in his absence, the vicar, will give at least two months' public notice of the time and place of holding the convention, as well by one or more public advertisements in the newspapers, as also by special letter to each clergyman who is entitled to a seat; the clergymen shall also publish the same to their respective flocks.

3. Upon the creation of a new district the bishop will specify how many lay delegates shall be elected therefrom to the next convention, which number shall be elected and admitted accordingly.

4. The delegates of the laity to the convention from each district shall be men having the qualifications which, in that district, are required for members of the vestry, and they shall be chosen by the voters of that district, upon due notice to be given by the vestry of the time and place for

holding the election, within six weeks preceding the day for holding the convention, the election to be conducted in the same manner as that for electing the vestry.

5. The districts of the diocess shall be ranked from time to time by the house of lay delegates according to the Catholic population, as of the first, second, and third rank; districts of the first rank shall, during their being so classed, send four delegates to the convention; districts of the second rank, two delegates; and districts of the third rank, one delegate; and each district will contribute its proportion to defray the expense of the Convention.

The bishop or vicar will judge of the qualifications of the clergy; the house of lay delegates will judge of the qualifications of its own members.

SECTION II.

Order of proceeding.

1. The clergyman highest in dignity, and if there be no precedence in dignity, the clergyman senior in ordination shall be president of the house of the clergy.

2. The house of the laity will choose its own president.

3. Each house shall appoint its own officers and servants, and regulate the internal order of its own proceedings.

4. When a majority of both houses shall have met, and the presidents have been ascertained, they will inform the bishop of the same, and he will appoint the time when the convention will be opened.

5. The convention will be opened with a solemn mass, at which it is recommended that the members of each house do go to communion. At this mass there will be a sermon, and if the bishop shall think proper to add a charge or exhortation. Before the blessing, the presidents of both houses shall, standing in presence of the bishop, hear and sign the proper declaration and promise, after which each president will read or cause to be read for the members of his house the same declaration and promise, which each member shall subscribe.

6. After mass each house shall meet apart for business, and the bishop will cause to be laid before them the treasurer's account, the report of the general trustees, and any other documents and communications which may be necessary.

7. Neither house shall adjourn, except from one period to another of the same day, or from day to day, before the third day of business, unless with the consent of the bishop. And after the dissolution of the convention,

neither house shall meet, except it be specially convened for some particular purpose by the bishop or vicar.

SECTION III.

Powers.

1. The convention has no power or authority to interfere respecting any of the following subjects, viz.:

1. The doctrine of the church.
2. The discipline of the church.
3. The administration of sacraments.
4. The ceremonies of the church.
5. Spiritual jurisdiction.
6. Ecclesiastical appointments.
7. Ordinations.
8. The superintendence of the clergy.

2. The convention is not to be considered as a portion of the ecclesiastical government of the church; but the two houses are to be considered rather as a body of sage, prudent, and religious counsellors to aid the proper ecclesiastical governor of the church in the discharge of his duty, by their advice and exertions in obtaining and applying the necessary pecuniary means to those purposes which will be most beneficial, and in superintending the several persons who have charge thereof; to see that the money be honestly and beneficially expended; wherefore the convention has the following powers, viz.:

1. To dispose of the general fund of the church in the way that it may deem most advantageous.

2. To examine into, and to control the expenditures made by its own order or by that of a former convention.

3. To examine into, regulate and control, with the exception of their spiritual concerns, all establishments of its own creation; or which being otherwise created may be regularly subjected to its control.

4. To appoint the lay-officers and servants of such establishments.

5. The house of the clergy has power to examine into the ecclesiastical concerns of such establishments, and to make its private report thereon to the bishop or vicar, together with its opinion and

advice, but such report of advice shall not be published in any other way, without the consent of the bishop or vicar first had and obtained in writing under his hand and seal.

3. In those cases where the convention has no authority to act, should either house feel itself called upon by any peculiar circumstances to submit advice, or to present a request to the bishop, he will bestow upon the same the best consideration at the earliest opportunity; and as far as his conscientious obligations will permit, and the welfare of the church will allow, and the honour and glory of Almighty God, in his judgment require, he will endeavour to follow such advice or to agree to such request.

4. No act shall be considered a valid act of the convention except it shall have been passed by a majority of the clergy and by a majority of the house of the laity, and been assented to by the bishop or vicar.

5. In all elections to trust, or places or offices, the decision will be made by a majority of the clergy and laity voting conjointly, and their choice assented to by the bishop, except when in any instance a different mode of election shall have been specially provided for. . . .

TITLE VII.

AMENDMENT OF CONSTITUTION.

SECTION I.

What parts may not be altered.

1. There are parts of this Constitution which are of the doctrine of the Holy Roman Catholic and Apostolic Church—of course they are part of the revelation of God; they are unchangeable, for we have no power to add to the revelation of God, nor to take from it. Those parts may be known by the decision of the bishop, or in case of an appeal from his decision, by the testimony and decision of the See of Rome; which decision shall be final and conclusive.

2. There are parts of this Constitution which are matter of divine institution, they are unchangeable; for no human power has authority to change the institutions of God. Those parts which are of divine institution may be known in the same manner as those parts which are of doctrine.

3. There are parts of this Constitution which are of the general discipline of the Holy Roman Catholic and Apostolic Church: those parts, so far as regards our power are unchangeable; because the Church of the diocess of Charleston, being only a very small portion of the Universal Church, is bound by the general laws of the same, and hath not authority to alter the enactments of the supreme legislature of that body, of which it is so small a particle: neither hath it power to withdraw itself from the

observance of the general discipline of the Universal Church, without thereby separating from its communion, and thus incurring the guilt of schism. Those parts which are of such general discipline may be known in the same manner as those which are of doctrine, or those parts which are of divine institution.

SECTION II.

What part the Bishop may change.

1. There are parts of this Constitution which are part of the special ecclesiastical discipline of the diocess of Charleston, and which are enacted by the bishop, who by divine institution is the proper and competent ecclesiastical legislator thereof: those parts are distinguished from the former as they relate only to this diocess, and from the parts recited in Sect. III., and may be known by the bishop's testimony and decision, which in that case is final and conclusive.

2. Those parts of this Constitution which are of the special ecclesiastical discipline of the diocess of Charleston, may by the bishop of the diocess, be altered and amended as he may see cause; especially after he shall have advised with the diocesan synod thereupon, according to the canons and usages of the church; but such consultation, though useful, is not essential.

3. But the said special discipline of the diocess of Charleston, and its alterations and amendments, must be not in opposition to, but in conformity with the doctrine and general discipline of the church, and the divine institutions; upon all which matters, in case of doubt, or of appeal, the supreme See of Rome is to judge and determine; and such judgment and determination shall be final and conclusive.

SECTION III.

What parts many be amended by the Convention, and how.

1. The parts of this Constitution, which regard the collection and regulation of property, the appointment of trustees, and lay-officers, and servants; the qualifications for lay-delegates, and vestrymen, and voters, and generally all the parts thereof which are not of, or belonging to the divine institution, or the doctrine or general discipline of the church, or the special diocess of Charleston, may be altered and amended in the following manner only, viz.:

1. A copy of the proposed alteration, addition, or amendment shall be laid before the bishop with a request to know whether the

same is compatible with the doctrine and the general discipline of the church, and with the special discipline of this diocese, and with the divine institutions.

2. Should the bishop answer that he judges such alteration, &c., to be so compatible, the said propositions, in the same words in which they shall have been returned by the bishop, shall be submitted to the two houses of the convention, and if a majority of each house should concur in their support, they shall be submitted to the bishop for his approbation.

3. Should the bishop approve the alterations so concurred in, he will send copies thereof to the several vestries of the diocese, who will, as soon as may be, signify their assent or dissent to the bishop.

4. Should two-thirds in number of the vestries approve of the propositions so sent to them, and the bishop continue of the same judgment as before, he will at the next convention signify the same to both houses, and the said proposed alterations, or additions, or amendments shall then be finally submitted to the decision of those houses, and should a majority in each house be in favour of the same, they shall then be part of this Constitution.

2. But should a majority of both houses differ from the bishop respecting the nature of the said proposed alterations, as to their compatibility with the doctrine and general discipline of the church, or the divine institution, they may of course appeal from his judgment to the See of Rome, but pending the appeal they must conform to his judgment.

3. And should the judgment of the bishop be set aside upon such appeal, he shall not thereby lose his power of assent or dissent which he possesses as one branch of the convention. . . .

A SELECTED BIBLIOGRAPHY

PRIMARY SOURCES:

Sebastian G. Messmer (ed.), *The Works of the Right Reverend John England* (7 vols.; Cleveland: The Arthur Clark Co., 1908).

Ignatius A. Reynolds (ed.), *The Works of the Right Reverend John England* (5 vols.; Baltimore: John Murphy & Co., 1849).

United States Catholic Miscellany, 1822-42.

SECONDARY SOURCES:

Patrick Carey, *An Immigrant Bishop: John England's Adaptation of Irish Catholicism to American Republicanism* (New York: United States Catholic Historical Society, 1982).

_____, "John England," *Biographical Dictionary of Modern British Radicals Since 1770: 1770-1832*, eds., J. O. Baylen and N. J. Gossman (New Jersey: The Harvester Press, 1978).

Peter Clarke, *A Free Church in a Free Society: The Ecclesiology of John England, Bishop of Charleston, 1820-1842. A Nineteenth Century Missionary Bishop in the United States* (Hartsville, South Carolina: Center for John England Studies, 1982).

Peter Guilday, *The Life and Times of John England* (2 vols.; New York: The America Press, 1927).

Virginia Lee Kaib, S.S.J., "The Ecclesiology of John England, The First Bishop of Charleston, South Carolina 1821-1842" (unpublished Marquette University Ph.D. dissertation, 1968).

Richard W. Rousseau, S.J., "Bishop John England and American Church-State Theory" (unpublished Saint Paul University Ph.D. dissertation, Ottawa, Canada, 1969).

_____, "The Greatness of John England," *The American Ecclesiastical Review* 168 (March, 1974), 196-206.

Part II

ROMANTIC CATHOLICISM, 1830-1888

Orestes A. Brownson

Orestes A. Brownson (1803-1876), a convert to Catholicism, was the foremost American Catholic lay theologian of the nineteenth century. He called his own philosophy and theology "synthetic"[1] because they attempted to reconcile the polar opposites subject and object, grace and nature, without destroying the distinction between them. Although his positions developed and changed in the course of his life, he never totally abandoned his attempt to synthesize the polarities that constituted life itself.

Orestes Brownson was born to Sylvester and Relief Metcalf Brownson in Stockbridge, Vermont. Throughout his life he was an active religious pilgrim. He was born to a Presbyterian father and a Universalist mother, but was raised in a relative's Calvinist-Congregationalist home from the age of six to fifteen, when he had a Methodist-Arminian evangelical conversion experience. In 1822, after this experience, be became a Presbyterian and in late 1823 he rejoined his mother's Universalist religion, becoming a Universalist minister in 1825. Throughout the years 1826 to 1831, he edited three different journals of theological and social concerns and contributed articles to numerous other periodicals. He rejected Universalism in 1829, became a member of the Workingmen's Party, and for a brief period disassociated himself from all organized religion. In 1832, influenced by the liberal Christianity of William Ellery Channing, he became a Unitarian minister and from 1838 to 1842 edited the prestigious Boston Quarterly Review.

Brownson's fluctuating religious positions did not cease after his conversion to Catholicism in 1844. Most historians, in fact, have noted three distinct periods during his Catholic years. From 1845 to 1855, he became a militant apologist for American Catholicism, using the traditional historical apologetics of post-Tridentine scholasticism. During the

97

years 1856 to 1864, he revealed more liberal views on the accommodations of Catholicism to modern society, and he demonstrated a more optimistic view of the world. After the publication of Pope Pius IX's Quanta cura and the Syllabus errorum on December 8, 1864, however, he became the unquestioning champion of Roman Catholic orthodoxy, repeatedly denouncing liberalism and accommodation to nineteenth-century values. During most of his Catholic years he edited Brownson's Quarterly Review (1843-65; 1873-75), one of the foremost journals of mid-nineteenth-century Catholic thought. Brownson had very little formal education; he was a self-taught philosopher and theologian influenced by the various currents of thought in early nineteenth-century New England, by the French philosophers Claude Henri de Saint-Simon, Benjamin Constant, Victor Cousin, and Pierre Leroux, and by post-Tridentine Catholic apologetics. He was a creative eclectic whose own religious quest made his theology an independent reflection upon what he read and what he experienced in American society.

The following selection comes from the period just prior to Brownson's conversion to Catholicism and reflects his fundamental doctrine of Life by Communion.[2] That doctrine tried to establish, against the positions of Theodore Parker and Benjamin Constant, that the origin and ground of religion was not to be found in a natural and therefore universal human religious sentiment but in the relation of Creator and creature which was made known to humans by God himself. Religion originated and was grounded in the infusion, through communion, of a supernatural life into natural human life.

Brownson placed primary emphasis upon the church's mediatorial role in the process of salvation. Communion with Christ, he argued, is possible only through communion with the church—the living organism and medium through which the Son of God practically redeems humankind. This doctrine, which Brownson articulated in a Unitarian paper, was partially republished and favorably commented upon by the New York Freeman's Journal (May 6, 1843, p. 358; May 20, 1843, p. 374) and other Catholic papers. The articles clearly placed Brownson outside the Unitarian communion to which he then belonged and revealed a logical trajectory toward Catholicism. The fact that Catholic journals copied his articles made Brownson aware for the first time of the possible termination of his thought in Catholicism.[3]

NOTES

1. "The Synthetic Philosophy," *The Works of Orestes A. Brownson,* ed. by Henry F. Brownson (20 vols.; Detroit: T. Nourse, 1882-1887), I, 58-129; "The Synthetic Theology," *Works,* III, 536-564.

2. For other sources of Brownson's view of life by communion see, e.g., "The Mediatorial Life of Jesus," *Works,* IV, 140-172; *The Convert, or Leaves From My Experience* (New York: Sadlier & Co., 1857): *The American Republic* (New York: P. O'Shea, 1866).

3. *The Convert,* p. 265.

TEXT

"THE CHURCH AND ITS MISSION"

Source: The Christian World, Vol. I, February 4, 1843;
February 11, 1843; February 18, 1843.

We proceed now to answer briefly, but still as satisfactorily as we can within our limits, the two questions proposed in our last, namely,

1. What is the Church?
2. What is its connexion with the salvation of the sinner?

We mean in this discussion, by the Church, the Lord's Church, not man's; the Church of Christ, not a human institution, which men may make or unmake. The definition sometimes proposed of the Christian Church, that it is "a voluntary association of believers for religious purposes," does not, embrace what we understand by the Church. In this sense, it would be impossible to make any distinction between the Church and Bible, Missionary, Tract, or even Temperance Societies, for these, in fact, are principally composed of believers who have associated for religious purposes. In this sense also, the Church would be a mere human institution, the creature of the individuals who form it by their associating together, and therefore, subject to their control; and to be altered, preserved, dissolved, abolished, at their pleasure.

We mean, moreover, by the Church, an outward, visible, organized body; not an internal mystical body, like the Church of our Quaker and Transcendental friends. There are those among us, and they not a few, who say that the Church is in the soul, and not only in the soul of those who have been renewed through the Spirit, but in the soul of every man, of the sinner as of the saint; and therefore, all that we have to do to find it, is to "look within," and all to be united to it, and saved through it, is to "enter into ourselves." But the Church, in this mystical sense, is identical with the great principles of Truth, Justice, and Love, and is rather Christ himself, than the Church of Christ. Unquestionably, the kingdom of God is within, and consists not in "meat and drink, but in righteousness and peace, and joy in the Holy Ghost." [Rom. xiv. 17] But within *whom*? Does God, Christ, Truth, Justice, Love, reign in the heart of the sinner? Can Christ be in a man, and that man still be a sinner? Can the Light be in us, and we still be in darkness? The Truth dwell in us, and we be in error? The Life, the true Eternal Life, live in us, and we be dead in trespasses and sins? The Church, in this mystical sense, in which sense it is Christ himself, rather than the Church of Christ, can be in none except those who, through Christ, have been redeemed and united to God. It is, in this sense, the end that we are in pursuit of, and not the means of obtaining the end. How shall that end be obtained?

These mystics, for whom we have great respect, for they are in general a very pure-minded, and well-meaning race, fall into the mistake of confounding the Church, as a means appointed by Divine Grace for the salvation of the sinner, with the salvation itself, or the great, eternal, and immutable principles, in the possession of which, the salvation consists. They see very clearly, this great truth, a truth never to be lost sight of, that religion, regarded not as the means, but the end, consists in the union of the soul, through Christ, with God, and is what our old Divines call "the Life of God in the Soul." For this, they also see, that no hand-writing of ordinances, no outward Churches, Temples, Sanctuaries, External Services, or Forms of Worship, of any kind whatsoever, can be any the least substitute. All this is well enough; but, unfortunately, they fix their eyes so exclusively on this, that they forget that the sinner is alienated from God, and cannot come into this union with God, without a mediator, a medium. Unquestionably, he who is so united to God, has all that he needs, all that God demands of him, and is, therefore, saved, and safe. But what is this to me, who am not so united to God? Will you say, Be united to God? Alas, my brother, this is my very difficulty; I am alienated from God, and have no power in myself to become one with him. I need a Church to bring me into your Church. Your Church takes me not, where I am, a sinner, but takes me only when I have already become redeemed and sanctified. I want a Church, that shall take me, a sinner, all polluted as I am, and bring me into union with Jesus, and through him, into union with God. The

Church that proposes to do this, not the Church that takes me only after this has been done, is what we now understand by the Church of Christ.

The Church of Christ is the outward, visible, organized Body of our Lord, bearing the same relation to Jesus, as our ever-present Saviour, as did the body in which he was crucified, to him as Son of Mary. It is the real body of Christ in which he now lives, and through which, he carries on his mediatorial work. It is not only his body, his living body, but the individual men and women, who are members of it, are literally joined to it as living members, and bear a relation to it, analogous to that borne by the hand, the foot, the eye, or the ear, to our bodies. This we learn from Paul, in a manner so clear and explicit as to leave no room to doubt. "For us we have many members in one body, and all the members have not the same office; so we, being many, are ONE BODY IN CHRIST and every one members one of another." [Rom. xii. 4, 5]. So again: "For as the body is one, and hath many members, and all the members of that one body, being many, are one body, so also is Christ. For by one Spirit, are we all baptized into ONE BODY whether we be Jews or Gentiles, whether we be bond or free; and all have been made to drink into one Spirit. For the body is not one member, but many. If the foot shall say, Because I am not the hand, I am not of the body; is it, therefore, not of the body? And if the ear shall say, Because I am not the eye, I am not of the body; is it, therefore, not of the body? . . . God hath tempered the body together, having given more abundant honor unto that part which lacked, that there should be no schism in the body, but that the members should have the same care one for another. And whether one member suffer, all the members suffer with it, or one member be honored, all the members rejoice with it. Now YE ARE THE BODY OF CHRIST, AND MEMBERS IN PARTICULAR." 1 Cor. xxi. 12-27.

That Paul here means to assert expressly that the Church is the body of Christ, is evident from Ephesians i. 23. "And hath put all things under his feet, and gave him to be the head over all things to *the Church, which is his body*;" and Colossians, i. 24. "Who now rejoice in my sufferings for you, and fill up that which is behind of the afflictions of Christ, in my flesh, *for his body's sake, which is the Church*." Nothing can be plainer, or more express to our purpose than this. The Church, then, we may assume as settled, is the BODY OF CHRIST.

This body has many members, and these members are, unquestionably, individual men and women. What is the relation of these members to the body? What is the relation of them one to another? The relation of the members to the body is, we have said, that of the hand or the foot to the human body. "We are," says Saint Paul, Ephesians, v.

30, "members of his body, of his flesh, and of his bones." The relation of member to member, is that of living members of one and the same body. "We are," says Saint Paul, again, in the passage already quoted from Romans, "one body in Christ, and *every one members one of another.*" So that if one member suffer, all the members suffer with it, and if one member be honored, all the members rejoice with it.

According to this view, the Church as the body of Christ, is not an *Association*, but an *Organism.* Without individual members, there would, of course, be no actual Church, as there would be no actual body, if all the members were taken away; but do the members make the body? The life of the body,—understanding now by the word life, the principle of life, or power to live,—the life of the body, is it in the parts? or is the life of the parts in the body? If the life of the body were in the members, the members would have a separate and independent life, and be able to live as well, when severed from the body, as when united to it. In such case it would excite no surprise, to see feet severed from the body, walking about, hands working, ears hearing, and eyes seeing. But we know that in the human body, this is not true; for the members have no life, but in their union with the body, in which is the one common principle of their vitality. Herein is the distinction between an association and an organism. In the association, the body has no life but the aggregate life of the members, and therefore, none but what they impart to it; in the organism, it is precisely the reverse, the life of the members is in the body, and they have none but what they receive from it, through their intimate union with it. If the Church were a mere association, although an association of saints, for the holiest purposes, it would receive all its life from its members, just as if the body were to receive its life from the hand, the foot, the ear, and the eye. The members of the association would receive no increase of life from their union with it. They might be severed from it, and it dissolved, abolished, with no loss of life to themselves, or to the world. This would be reducing our low-Churchism, to no-Churchism, with a vengeance. But now is the Church of Christ, not an association, but a body, an ORGANISM, and therefore, does not receive its life from its members, but imparts in them their life; and they can live only in their intimate union with it. Hence the significance of Excommunication.

In declaring the Church to be the body of Christ, we necessarily declare that Christ is the *life* of the Church, as the Spirit is the life of the body. If he is the life of the Church, then he lives in the Church, and, then, is the Church his body, his embodyment in time and space, and the medium of communion with him, as the body of a man is the medium of communion with the spirit of a man.

How Christ can or does literally live in the Church is not by any means difficult to be explained to those who comprehend the doctrine we established in our third Essay on the Mission of Jesus,[1] which Essay we pray our readers to read over again, and as many times as they find necessary, in order to comprehend the Law of Life, expressed by the term Communion, which we have there insisted upon. This Law is, that the Life of the object with which we commune, to the full extent of the communion, becomes literally an indissoluble portion of our life, so that what we call our life is always the resultant, so to speak, of two factors, of which I am one, and that with which I commune, but which is not I, is the other.—This law, is profound, and is co-extensive with all dependent beings.

Now, represent to your minds Jesus, who lives by intimate but supernatural communion with God, so that in his life, he is at once indissolubly human and Divine, as incarnated, that is, dwelling like us in a body of flesh, amongst our brethren. He becomes in this case an object of communion. They who commune with him are his Disciples. Through communion, his life, called in the New Testament, sometimes the Life, and sometimes the Spirit, passes into these disciples, and thus he lives in them, and they in him. While in the flesh his body served as the medium through which, by this Law of Life, he could and would naturally communicate the Life, the Spirit, to those who communed with him personally; but when he personally ascended into heaven, to be seated at the right hand of the Father, men could no longer commune with him through the medium of that body; and of course he would have been lost to the world had he not continued to live embodied in these very disciples, friends to whom he had through communion communicated himself, on whom he had breathed, saying, "Receive my Spirit."—But as he could, as he naturally would, and as we are assured that he did, so continue to live in them, these would constitute his body, through which others might have access to him, and through him to the Father.

Jesus, then could live in his Disciples by virtue of this Law of life, which we express by the word Communion, and began so to live through personal communion with them while he was with them in the flesh. It was necessary, nay, absolutely necessary that he should come in the flesh, for in no other way could the life be communicated, without changing or violating the laws of human nature, which would have been tantamount to the annihilation of humanity. Hence, John assures us that they who confess not that Jesus Christ has come in the flesh, are deceivers and Anti-christs. He must also have been Divine, the Son of God, or his coming in the flesh, and becoming the life of his Disciples, would have amounted to nothing. Hence again, "he is an Anti-christ that denied the Father and the Son," [1 Jn. ii. 22] that is, that the Father is to us by and through the Son, or that the Son is the Revelation of the Father; so that he who hath the Son, may truly say that he hath the Father—"He that hath seen me, hath seen the Father." [Jn. xiv. 9]

The Life, the Spirit, by which Jesus lives in his Disciples, is one life, one spirit, and therefore would, as we have seen, unite all those in whom he lived into one body. These at first were his personal disciples, those with whom he lived while in the flesh, and who through personal communion received him. They must from the nature of the case, have been all those, and could have been only those. These then constituted, not the *first* Church as we sometimes say, but the Church, and the whole Church in the beginning. They were all who had the Life, the unity of the Spirit with its diversity of operations.

The Life, the Spirit, being the life, the spirit of Jesus, was a Divine Life, the Spirit not of man, but of God. Jesus was the Way, the Truth, and the Life. Consequently, he, continuing to live in the Church, in the life of his followers, is in them the Truth and the Life.—Hence, Jesus living in the Church, becomes identical with the Holy Ghost, the Comforter, the Spirit of Truth, that should lead into all truth. The Holy Ghost the Church has always affirmed to be God, but God proceeding forth from the Father through the Son, which is precisely the view here given.

Jesus, through communion of his Disciples with him, lives in them. This answers the question, How can Jesus literally live in the Church? This Life, or the Spirit is one, and therefore, necessarily unites into one body, and, as it is *life*, into one living organism, all in whom Jesus through the Spirit lives. This establishes the UNITY of the Church. The indwelling Jesus, being identical with the spirit of Truth, the Comforter, the Holy Ghost, the body in which he dwells must be an inspired body. Jesus was not a mere man. The whole Gospel is a mere farce on the supposition of what is called his simple Humanity. He is the Son of God, and in a sense, in which no man is naturally a Son of God. He is then supernatural, and then the life that from him goes out into his Disciples, into the Church, is a supernatural life, a life transcending the generic power, which is what we must mean by the natural power, of man to live. Hence, the life of the Church is a supernatural life, and not only supernatural, but is the life of God. Here is seen the ABILITY of the Church. The Church is competent to instruct us, for the Holy Ghost is its life, for the Spirit of Truth lives in it. It is competent to discipline us, because it has within itself the ability to know, and from the nature of the case, the disposition to do, whatever is necessary for our spiritual welfare.

But if the Church be constituted, as it must be, according to what we have said, by the indwelling Jesus, by the Holy Ghost being in it, its unity, its teacher, and its life, or power to live, then it must not only be an inspired body, not only a body competent to the work of salvation, but must be an *authoritative* body. What has the right to command us, if not the Spirit of Truth, of Jesus, of God? Is not God the Sovereign? Is not Jesus his Son, his revelation, speaking in the name, that is to say, with the authority of his Father? If, then, the Church be the body of Jesus, through which he speaks, is not the voice of the Church, the highest expression of the Law that we have, or can have? The Church speaks by the authority of the Spirit, and as the Spirit is the Holy Ghost, one in the last analysis with God, where is there, or can there be, for us any higher authority? Question this authority, you question that Jesus lives in the Church; therefore, that he lives at all for us; and therefore again, that there is for us any medium of communion with God.

If we confine our remarks to the Church when it consisted solely of those who personally communed with Jesus, we presume none who profess to believe in him, in the Gospel, will question our statements, in regard either to the unity of universality, either to the inspiration or the authority, of the Church. We all admit, nay, all contend, that at that moment, the Church was composed of these disciples, and of all who had, the Spirit, and of none others; and that these were literally the body of Christ. Or, in other words, that Christ literally lived in them; that it was this fact of his living in them, that made them the Church, his body; that by virtue of his living in them, they were inspired, were possessed of a supernatural life, and competent to the work of mediating between Christ and the sinner; and finally, that by virtue of the Holy Ghost, shed abroad in their hearts, they could, and did speak with authority. This is precisely, what all those believe, who assert the authority and sufficiency of the Scriptures; for it is on their authority that Christians assert the inspiration of the Old Testament; and the New Testament is nothing but a record, more or less full, of the life of this very Church of the Disciples. Here, then, in the very fact that we affirm the inspiration and authority of the Scriptures, do we necessarily affirm that the Church in its origin was one, catholic, inspired and authoritative. God did, then, "set some in the Church; first, apostles; secondarily, prophets; thirdly, teachers; after that, miracles; then gifts of healings, helps, governments, diversities of tongues." 1 Cor. xii. 28.

Well, will any one tell us when this constitution of the Church was altered, and by whose authority? Has the original Church, the Church of Christ, passed away? Have sin and Satan triumphed and crushed and obliterated the works of the Son of God? Or has God altered his modes of dealing with men, changed the Christian dispensation; or given us a new dispensation? Answer, we beseech you, ye wise ones of the earth, who revolt at an inspired, authoritative Church. Say, has the Church failed? Has Christ ceased to dwell with man? Has he abandoned Humanity in despair, and acknowledged himself vanquished? Or have we grown so good, so holy, so wise, so all-sufficient for ourselves, that there is no longer any work for the Saviour to do, in bringing us to God? If not, why contend that the Church is not now precisely what it was in its origin? Did not Jesus promise his disciples, saying, "Lo! I am with you, unto the end of the world"? [Mt. xxviii. 20] Did he mean any thing by this promise, or did he not? Has he kept this promise, or has he broken it? We demand of those who contend that the Church is a differently constituted body now, from what it was when it was the Church of the Disciples, that they bring us the proofs of the fact they allege. We would know when the alteration took place? In what it consists? And by whose authority it was made? You all admit there was a Church of God once on the earth, which was all that we allege the Church is; for you receive and acknowledge the inspiration, sufficiency and authority of the Scriptures, which were its production. Well, is there, or is there not, such a Church still on the earth? When has the Apostolic Church ceased?

The fact is, we cannot assert that there was an Apostolic Church, without asserting that it still continues, and has never for a moment ceased. Whence did the Disciples receive Jesus? Was it not by communion? Well, they did receive him, and he lived in them, and they were filled with the Holy Ghost. Then they had power to impart life. They who should come into communion with them, would, by the very law of communion, receive the very same Spirit, which they had received through personal communion with Jesus. Now, either show that the succession has been broken: that the continuity of the Church, from that time to this, has been interrupted, and that there have been, in time, chasms so broad that the Spirit could not leap across them, or else admit that the Church has continued the one, catholic, inspired, authoritative body, it was in its apostolic origin.

The Church may have been nay, it no doubt has been, in the world, as leaven hidden in three measures of meal; and it has not all at once succeeded in leavening the whole lump. The great Dragon, or the principle of evil, working in the hearts of the rebellious, may have at times seemed to have swallowed her up with the floods of iniquity, and she have been forced to be a Church of the Captivity, hanging her harps upon the willow, and sitting down in a strange land, by the rivers of Babylon, and weeping as she remembers the days of her glory. She may have become, as we believe she now is, the Church in the Wilderness; but ever has she been the true Church, battling with sin and Satan, and showing forth the grace and mercy of God, in the face of the armies of his enemies. Nay, and she shall return from her captivity; nay, she shall come up out of the wilderness, leaning on the arm of her beloved, beautiful as the morning, mild as the evening, but terrible as an army with banners. God will arise. Why did the heathen rage? and the people imagine a vain thing? The Lord's hand is not shortened, that he cannot save; nor his ear heavy, that he cannot hear.

We answer, therefore, to the question, What is the Church? that it is the living body of Christ, composed of all those men and women who are by the unity of the Spirit united to it as living members; that it is a one, catholic, inspired, authoritative body. Whether it is identical with this or that one of the extant organizations, calling themselves Christian Churches, is an inquiry into which we do not enter at present. All we say is, that the true Church of Christ is an outward body, formed by the indwelling of his Spirit and that it still exists in time and space, unchanged in spirit, capacity, disposition, or authority, from what it was in the Apostolic age.

The connexion of this Church with the salvation of the sinner, the second question we asked, we will answer in our next; which we shall follow by the attempt to answer the question, How does the Church accomplish its Mission in the salvation of the sinner? That is, By what agencies does it take the sinner, all defiled with sin, and bring him to God?

"THE CHURCH AND ITS MISSION" [FEBRUARY 11, 1843]

Having ascertained what the Church is, we now proceed to consider the connection with the salvation of the sinner.

Is the Church absolutely essential to salvation? Is it competent to mediate between the sinner and Christ, and therefore between the sinner and God. . . .

We do not wish to dissemble that this conclusion [i.e., that the Church is absolutely necessary for salvation], from which for the life of us we see no escape, will not be acceptable to our liberal brethren. We are aware that many among us, who would shrink with horror from the bare thought of denying the Lord that brought us, do not regard the

Church as by any means indispensable to salvation. They even go so far as to believe that men can be saved by the "light of nature," if they follow it, without even stopping to ask if men without Christ, have the power to follow the "light of nature" which after all is an exceedingly dim and uncertain light. But, have they reflected, that in so believing, they believe men can be saved without the mediation of Christ? If men can be saved without the mediation of Christ, if the heathen, for instance, can be saved by the light of nature, then, what need of his mediation? But is not Christ the door? Is there any way of coming to God, but through him? Assuredly not. For he himself says expressly, John xiv. 6, "I am the Way, the Truth, and the Life; NO MAN COMETH TO THE FATHER BUT BY ME." To affirm that we can come to God in any other way than through the mediation of Jesus, is in fact to deny the authority of Jesus, and the necessity of his mediation.

But if we can come to God, that is, be saved, only through the mediation of Jesus, then, comes up our old question, how shall that mediation be made effectual in the actual salvation of the sinner? *Immediately*, that is, miraculously? We have refuted this notion already, for it would be to declare that there was no occasion for his coming in the flesh. It also virtually declares that no mediator between God and men is necessary, for God at any time, might by a miracle have brought the sinner to himself: that is, he could have as well done it without the Mission of Jesus, as with it, providing that the Mission leaves the necessity for a resort to miracle still standing.

Moreover, this way of bringing men to Christ by a miracle,— which, by the by, is no way at all, for *a way* is a medium,—is very far from meeting the wants of the sinner. The sinner, it is true, cannot be regenerated, saved, without the intervention of supernatural power; that is, a power which transcends man's *generic* power, or simple power as a human being; but the mode in which this power intervenes and operates in transforming the sinner must be *natural*, that is, in perfect harmony with the principles of human nature; or, as we have already shown, its intervention, instead of saving a man, would annihilate him, by changing him into a being of a different kind. In order to meet this necessity, the supernatural power must intervene, in a regular, certain, and fixed manner. If it do not so intervene, then is there no regular, fixed, and certain way of salvation. Then is all in the Economy of Grace, left, so to speak, at loose ends. We are, as sinners, poor invalids, gathering around the pool of Bethesda, obtaining and able to obtain no relief, till the angel of the Lord comes down and troubles the waters, and even then, able to obtain no help for cur infirmities, unless we chance to be the first assisted to step in. Has Jesus left his work thus unfinished? Did he not come expressly for the purpose of establishing a regular, fixed, and certain way of salvation? Is all then still uncertain, and must we continue to wander up and down the earth crying out continually, "who will show us any good?"—If so, O Jesus, why didst thou come? In vain hast thou lived, preached, suffered, died, and risen again; in vain hast thou sent forth Apostles, founded thy Church, declared that the gates of hell shall not prevail against it, and given unto it the keys of the kingdom of heaven, and asserted that whatsoever it should bind on earth should be bound in heaven, and whatsoever it should loose on earth should be loosed in heaven. In vain hast thou founded the kingdom of Grace, and provided the means of redemption and sanctification, if still the way is uncertain, and men can come to thee only through the intervention of a miracle!

This notion of immediate, or miraculous communion with Jesus, must be abandoned. The Church which asserts that it is still necessary to resort to a miracle, denies that Jesus has opened the way of salvation, nay, that there is any fixed and certain way of salvation, and proclaims its own weakness and utter insufficiency as a Church of Christ.

Some of our brethren have tried to make a distinction between Christ and Christianity, and have alleged that it is possible to have a very sufficient Christianity, without any Christ at all. If there be any truth in the principles we have laid down, no separation, in fact no *distinction*, can be made between Christ and Christianity. Christ does not teach Christianity, does not make it: HE IS IT, and there is no Christianity but Christ. Hence, the Evangelists tell us to believe in Christ Jesus, to embrace him, never Christianity. Now, we have shown that Christ himself must be received, not what he taught: and that he can be received only where he is.—He is only in the Church. That is his body. There he lives, if one may so say, dwells. He can live nowhere else, for he can live only in the lives of those who are united to him by the unity of the Spirit, or the Life, and his living in them, a one life, constitutes them the Church. Then it is as impossible to make any distinction between Christianity and the Church, as between Christ and Christianity. There is no Christianity, but Christ, and no Christ for us, but the Church, that is to say, the informing life of the Church, of which all partake who come into communion with the Church. Go out of the Church, there is no Christianity, no Christ, and therefore, no medium of access to the Father.

Here we are controverted. "What! do you mean to say that all who die without the pale of the Christian Church, die without hope?" Whence, we ask in turn, comes the hope of the sinner? Do you mean to tell us that a man can be saved without receiving the very life of Jesus into his life, so that Christ does literally become to him "the Lord our righteousness?" If not, how is this life to be received, but by communion with it where it is, that is to say, in the Church where we have proved that he lives? If the reverse, then you deny all necessity for the mediation of Christ, and are to be met as infidels, not as Christian believers.

But, we are told again, that we reason upon a false assumption. "This notion of yours about receiving the life of Jesus is all moonshine. Jesus came merely to set us an example in his own life of what we should be and do. This life may be lived by those who never heard of Jesus or saw his example, as there were many who were virtuous before Socrates defined virtue." Admirable, my brother! only thou forgottest that, on this ground, the Gospel is no such mighty affair as some people think it, and especially, that admitting Jesus set this example, through sin thou hast lost thy power to follow it, and for this eighteen hundred years no one, notwithstanding the most strenuous efforts, has been able to follow it. O my brother! do not deceive thyself. Jesus, as an example merely, is as good as no Jesus at all; for what thou wantest is not so much to perceive what thy duty is, as inward power to do it. O do not mock the sinner, who is all helpless, and cannot through the destruction he has brought upon himself, take one single step towards heaven, and who is lost forever unless sovereign Grace comes to his rescue,—O do not mock him with a Jesus who is only the Way, and not also the Truth, and the LIFE! Where shall the sinner obtain the power to walk in the way, to follow this example of Jesus?—My brother, thou forgettest this question, which after all is the main question.

But we are controverted again, and this time from the other side of the house. "We are saved, it is true," say these voices from the *extreme right*, "by the righteousness of Christ, but not as you suppose, by its being *imparted* to us, so that it becomes literally ours; but by its being *imputed* to us, adjudged ours by the Father, for and in consideration of the great merits of his Son; as if I, to show my regard for Peter, should forgive his brother James the debt he owes me. Christ saves us by his DEATH. He died for us on the cross. By that death he opened the door of salvation, made it possible, or consistent, for God to forgive the sinner; and so now all obstacles being removed, God *imputes* the righteousness of his Son to whomsoever he will, and makes that one practically holy through the sovereign workings of his Spirit. Now, as salvation, or rather redemption, comes by the death of Christ, which of course was not through the mediation of the Church, and as justification unto life is by the free gift of God *imputing* to whom he wills, the righteousness of his Son, and owning them in reward of the merits of his Son, where is or can be this absolute necessity of the Church for which you contend?"

This objection is urged against us in consequence of a misappre-hension of the scheme of Divine Grace for the salvation of men.—This whole scheme is the work, unquestionably, of Sovereign Grace. Man had no agency in devising it, and none in providing or establishing the means for carrying it into effect.—But we totally and fatally misappre-hend the Gospel, if we suppose that the life and death of Jesus save us any further than they operate as means of making us personally holy. The simple fact that Christ died, viewed as isolated from the virtue which went out from it, and which converts the souls of men, saves nobody, as is evident from the fact, that notwithstanding it, we are sin-ners and under the wrath of God, till we are personally renewed, till the blood of the atonement has been personally applied.

The old doctrine of *imputed* righteousness had a deeper significance than its partisans perceived. They saw very clearly that the sinner could not save himself; that he could never *merit* heaven as a reward; and that God could not consistently with his moral government, receive him to heaven while a sinner, nay, that heaven could be no heaven to the sin-ner. Thus far all was right. They saw also that the only righteousness in which the sinner could appear before God in an acceptable light, was the righteousness of Christ.—But how establish an actual relation between the sinner and this righteousness of Christ, so that the sinner should be actually clothed with it? This was the question. The old Divines answered by *imputation*. But after all, what did they really mean? What lay at the bottom of their thought? Assuredly, that the righteousness of Christ must become the righteousness of the sinner, before the sinner could be acceptable to his Maker. How it could become so, they did not precisely see, and therefore said, by *imputation*. We accept their thought, which is true, but reject their philosophy, which is defective.

But even the advocates of the doctrine of imputation, also held that no one could be saved, without what they called, a *"personal application of the blood of the atonement."* This, if it mean any thing, must mean actually clothing us with the righteousness of Christ; or literally *imparting* to us his life; so that he becomes truly, without a figure, the life of our life. God is just, and can justify none till they are just. Hence, the righteous-ness of Christ must not only be *putatively* ours, but actually ours.— Then, the work of saving the sinner was not completed by the death of Jesus on the Cross. That is to say, we are not, after all, saved by the Christ that *was*, but by the Christ that *is*, for we can receive the life of Christ only by personal communion with him where he lives. The moment we substitute *imparted* for *imputed* righteousness, a living Sav-iour becomes necessary, and a body through which we may receive him.

Jesus must be imparted to us, must be received into us, and assimilated to us, as the sole condition of our acceptance with God. "Except ye eat my flesh and drink my blood, ye have no life in you." [Jn. vi. 53] We can receive him only by communion, and since he is embodied only in the Church, it is only in and through the Church that we can commune with him. Hence, again, the indispensableness of the Church.

But a new class of objectors springs up "We admit your premises. We admit that we come to God only through Jesus Christ, and that we can come to him only through a medium; but this medium is not the Church, but FAITH. 'If thou shalt confess with thy mouth, that Jesus is Lord, and believe in thine heart that God hath raised him up from the dead, thou shalt be saved.' " Admit, my brother, that we commune with Jesus through faith, does this answer every question? Is there no question back of this? Admit we come to Jesus by faith, pray how do we come to faith? That is how or by what agencies do we obtain this saving faith in the Lord Jesus? Paul shall answer for us. Rom. x. 13-15: "For whosoever shall call upon the name of the Lord shall be saved. How then shall they call on him in whom they have not believed? and how shall they believe in him of whom they have not heard? and how shall they hear without a preacher? and how shall they preach except they be sent?" Faith, then, it would seem, can be obtained only through the medium of the Church, and in point of fact, except where the witness and the instructions of the Church are found, faith in the Lord Jesus is not found. But after all, to speak accurately, faith is the communion with Jesus, or the immediate effect of communion with him, rather than the medium through which we obtain access to him.

But we are told once more, that "if this be conceded, still you are wrong in asserting that the mediation of the Church is indispensable to communion with Jesus. For we commune with him, and, in fact, even with the Father, through PRAYER." Thou art fertile in objections, my brother; but I would that thou wouldest look a little deeper. We admit that prayer is a medium, not of communion with Jesus in the sense in which we now consider communion with him, but of communion with God; but what then? Our prayers to be acceptable must be in faith. "He that cometh to God must believe that he is, and that he is a rewarder of them that diligently seek him." "So then without faith it is impossible to please God." [Heb. xi. 6] Thus, in order to commune with God through prayer, we must have faith; and to the production of faith, we have seen that the Church is indispensable. Nor is this all. We are commanded to pray *in the name of Jesus,* and the promise is only to those who meet together in his *name,* or pray in his *name.* By this we must understand, that to pray acceptably, we must pray in the *Spirit* of

Jesus. The prayers of the wicked do not reach to heaven; they are an abomination in the sight of God. We must, then, receive of the life of Jesus,—be to some extent filled with his Spirit, before even we can pray. Here comes up again our old question, How receive the life of Jesus, or come into communion with him? This brings us back to the Church as the depositary of his life, and the agency by which we are brought into communion with him.

But there is still another objection to our doctrine behind, and the one on which they who do not accept our doctrine, rely more than on any other which can be urged. "We admit," say they who urge it, "all you say about the necessity of Christ as the Mediator between God and men,—all that you say about the necessity of a regular, fixed and certain method of communion with Jesus,—of some agency to give us faith in Christ, and to teach us, and enable us to pray; but all this, which you find in the Church, we find in the Bible. The Bible is alone sufficient to bring us into communion with Jesus, and to make us wise unto salvation."

This objection deserves a serious and full answer, and a fuller answer than we now have room to give it. We will therefore adjourn its consideration till our next, when we will take it up at length.

"THE CHURCH AND ITS MISSION" [FEBRUARY 18, 1843]
SUFFICIENCY OF THE SCRIPTURES

They who reject the doctrine that Jesus mediates between us and the Father, only through the medium of his body, the Church and allege, in opposition thereto, the sufficiency of the Holy Scriptures, proceed on the ground that Christianity is distinguishable from Christ, and assume that the immediate object of Christian faith, is not Christ but Christianity, that salvation is the effect not of receiving Christ himself, but Christ's teachings, and that the sinner is able, uninstructed by the Church, from the Bible alone, to find out what Jesus really taught, and to conform to it in his life. This is the only ground, so far as we can see, on which men can even pretend to assert the sufficiency of the Scriptures.

But this ground is very far from being tenable. There is no distinction possible between Christ and Christianity. There are not certain eternal and immutable truths, or Divine purposes, which we may call Christianity, and which must be believed; and a Jesus Christ, separate or distinguishable from these, who reveals them, illustrates and confirms them by the beauty and authority of his miraculous life. In this abstract

sense there is no Christianity. Jesus does not teach the Truth, imperson-
ate, or symbolize the Truth; HE IS IT, and there is no Truth for us, no
Christianity, but the living Son of man, who is also, and at the same
time, the Son of God. The *object* of Christian faith, is not then what
Jesus taught, whether by precept or example, nor indeed what he was
or did, but simply and solely HIMSELF. It is an error then to assume that
salvation is the effect of faith in his teachings. We are not saved by
believing in any doctrine whatever; neither in the Unity nor the Trinity;
neither in the Divinity, nor in the Humanity of Jesus; neither in God's
sovereignty, nor in man's agency; neither in justification by faith alone,
nor in justification by works; neither in justification by having the righteousness of Christ *imputed* to us, nor in justification by having the righteousness of Christ *communicated* to us. We are saved, as we have already
proved over and over again, not by believing what Christ taught, but by
receiving and assimilating to our spiritual life Christ himself, so that we
may say truly, without a figure, that he lives in us, and we live in him.

Assume now, what indeed we shall soon proceed to question, that
the Bible alone is sufficient to instruct us in all the mysteries of the
Christian faith, to tell us exactly who and what Jesus was, and in a
word, to make us acquainted with the whole scheme of Gospel salvation, all the details of the economy of Divine Grace, it will not follow
that the Scriptures alone are sufficient to make the sinner wise unto salvation. We may know and believe all the facts and doctrines of the Gospel, in the ordinary sense of knowing and believing, and in the ordinary
sense of facts and doctrines, and be still in the "bonds of iniquity and
the gall of bitterness." Even believing that we ought to receive and
assimilate the Divine Life, who is Christ the Lord, the *living* God, as we
do the bread that we eat and which sustains our mortal bodies, avails
us, as we have seen, nothing, nothing at all; but the literal reception of
Christ himself into us, the life of our life, so that we are united to him
by one spirit, as the branch to the vine. Now, the most the Bible can do,
is to give us a correct view of the truth as it is in Jesus. It cannot give us
Christ himself, a living, personal, ever-present, indwelling Saviour. It
therefore is not, and cannot be alone sufficient, as all must see and own
the moment that they understand that we are saved by receiving Christ
himself, not merely by a knowledge of, and faith in what he taught. The
Holy Scriptures themselves, whose authority we admit to the fullest
extent, declare their own insufficiency, when they declare that it is the
Son himself, not instruction concerning the Son, that frees us from the
bondage of sin and death.

Nor is this all. We deny the ability of the sinner to find out from
the Bible alone, what it was that Jesus really taught; and therefore, we

deny that the Bible alone would be sufficient, even in case saving faith were faith in the teachings of Jesus, and not, as we have seen, the literal, actual, but spiritual reception of Jesus himself. We who are born in Christian lands, do breathe from the first the atmosphere of the Church, and long before we have become able to read the Bible, are instructed, directly or indirectly, as to what we are to find in it, when we do read it. We are, therefore, never in a condition to rely on the Bible alone. We never go to it wholly devoid of preliminary instructions, and therefore, of prepossessions. Hence it turns out, that for the most part, when we do come to study the Bible, we find little else in it than the faith, we have brought to it, so that we may be said to put our faith into the Bible, not to obtain our faith from it. Hence it is Episcopal children find the New Testament full of Episcopacy; Congregational children full of Congregationalism; Trinitarian children full of Trinitarianism; Unitarian children full of Unitarianism, &c. Our prepossessions determine, even with the best intentions on our part, the meaning we attach to the words we read.

Suppose we could come to the Bible without these prepossessions, divested of all the religious instruction we have received prior to reading it, so that our minds on approaching it were a perfect blank, we should not help the matter; for in such case the pages of the book would be as blank as our minds. It is not possible for us to come so to the Bible, and it would avail us nothing if we could. We should be obliged to inquire into the meaning of the words, and to do this we should need to resort to the grammars, dictionaries, glossaries, and commentaries which have been made by students of the Bible, who had brought to the study of it their prepossessions, and had explained the words and sentences according to the understanding of them which they had been previously taught. There is no getting over this. Take the Bible to a heathen land, and translate it into the language of a heathen people. If this people have no notion of God, how will you translate into their language the Hebrew, Greek, or English word for God? If they have some notion of God, they will have a word for God, and you must use, in translating, that word to express the Christian conception of God. But that word conveys to them their own previous conception of God, and how will you, without the discipline of the missionary, prevent them from substituting that conception for the Christian conception?

But we go a step further; we affirm that all ecclesiastical history goes to prove the insufficiency of the Scriptures, when taken alone, without the authoritative interpretation of the Church. Have men, left to themselves and the Bible alone, ever agreed as to its precise import? Nay, with all the aids they could receive from erudition, science, the study of ecclesiastical history and philosophy, have they been able to come to any tolerable agreement as to its doctrines? Protestantism starts with the right of private judgment and the sufficiency of the Scriptures. It assumes the Bible as the authoritative rule in faith and practice, and that private judgment is competent, from the study of the Bible alone, to find out and apply this rule. This rule, we have a right to assume, is one. There is but one way to heaven. There is but one God, and one Mediator between God and men. Well, have our Protestant sects, left free to study the Bible, and to interpret it by their private judgment, come to any thing like an agreement as to what this one rule is? Is there a single point on which the Protestant world has departed from the Catholic faith, and the Catholic interpretation of the Bible, on which Protestant sects are not divided, and concerning which they are not, as it were, at sword's points? The disputes between Protestant sects, let it be understood, are not about trifles; they extend to the very essentials of the Christian faith. The Gospel, according to John Calvin, is fundamentally different from the Gospel, according to Joseph Priestley;[2] and we confess that the Gospel we are ourselves advocating, seems to us to be totally another Gospel from that set forth by Belsham, and the English Unitarians as that contended for by the German Rationalists, whether of the school of Paulus, or of the school of Strauss.[3] How then, say, the Scriptures are alone sufficient? What private judgment has, from the study of them alone, nay, with all the helps of science and erudition, been able to determine, even in essentials, what it is they teach?

Nor will we stop here. We allege the inability of the *sinner* to know and believe in the truth as it is in Jesus. One ground of the condemnation of the sinner, as well as his need of help, is, in the fact, that while a sinner, unrenewed, he is unable to discover the truth, and still more unable to embrace it as truth. If the sinner were able, in and of himself, to know and believe the truth, he would be able, in and of himself, to work out his own salvation. We must not forget that they are the pure in heart only who see God. Sin blunts intellectual as well as moral perceptions. "The natural man receiveth not the things of the Spirit of God: for they are foolishness unto him; neither can he know them, because they are spiritually discerned." [1 Cor. ii. 14] We must have spiritual discernment before we can know and receive the doctrine of Jesus; but can we have spiritual discernment without receiving Christ himself? In other words, faith, instead of being as some contend, the medium of salvation, is the effect of salvation. The regenerating influences of the Spirit do not come to us through our faith in the truth, but precede that faith, and are its indispensable condition. As Paul says to Timothy, "God will have all men to be saved, and to come to the knowledge of the truth." [1 Tim. ii. 4] He does not say,—God will have all men come to the knowledge of the truth, and be saved. The salvation must precede the knowing, as its condition. Assuming, then, that a man who is saved, who has been enlightened by the indwelling of the Spirit, is able from the Bible alone, to become acquainted with the truth, this would not prove the sufficiency of the Scriptures to make the sinner wise unto salvation, which is the point to be made out. A man must receive Christ, before he can understand the Bible; but when he has received Christ, he is saved. Now will reading the Bible without understanding it, give us Christ, and unite us to him by one spirit? Then, if not, we need some other medium than the Bible, through which to come into communion with the Saviour. Understanding of and faith in the Gospel, in what may be termed the philosophy of religion, are not the preliminary conditions of salvation, for they presuppose no small degree of spiritual illumination; but they are among the means by which we grow in grace; that is to say, come into closer and fuller communion with Jesus; a communion which with the saint will be eternally becoming more intimate and complete.

But waiving even this, assuming that the sinner has the ability to see and comprehend and believe the truth, and that seeing and believing of it will be sufficient as the means of his redemption and sanctification, the difficulty is now removed; for no sinner, unless, as it were, compelled by some outward authority, will read the Bible, or if reading it, so read as to profit by it. The Bible, for the most part, is not only unintelligible to the sinner, but it is offensive to his taste and feelings. He finds no pleasure in it; and finding no pleasure in it, he will not study it. If he do not study it, we presume it will not be contended that it will make him wise. We presume no Protestant idolator of the Bible will go so far as to suppose that there is virtue in merely having the printed volume in our possession, and that virtue goes out from it to those who comprehend nothing of what it contains. Is not the Church necessary, then, to enjoin the reading of the Bible, and to discipline us into the reading it? "But this work may be done by the parents." No matter. It is a work that is necessary to be done, before the Bible can be at all effectual as a means of our instruction; and therefore a work to which the Bible is not itself sufficient.

Furthermore, even admitting that the sinner needs no disciplining to bring him to read the Bible, and no divine illumination of the Spirit, in order to enable him to understand and believe what it teaches, still, the *ability* to *conform* to what it teaches is unprovided for. We have seen that the sinner is not able to do what is demanded of him. How shall this disability be removed? "But we deny," says the reader, "this disability of which you speak. The sinner, knowing his duty, can do it if he will." Very well; suppose he will not. Is *will* not less a disability to be overcome than *cannot*? Granted, that the difficulty, the whole difficulty, on the side of the sinner is, that he *will* not; this strikes us as by no means lessening the difficulty. It requires a foreign power to overcome *will* not, as much as it does to overcome *cannot*. This power, we presume all will concede us, is the Grace of God. Well, will reading of the Bible, with this strong *will* not, become to us the medium of this Grace? Who so infatuated as to pretend it?

Nay, our brethren who contend for the sufficiency of the Scriptures, do themselves deny that sufficiency in stronger terms than we do. They contend as well as we, to point of fact, that the sinner must be regenerated, and regenerated by a supernatural influence, too. Well, do they believe that reading the Bible alone is the medium, or a sufficient medium through which this supernatural influence is or may be regularly and certainly obtained? If so, why do they build churches? Why do they have teachers and pastors, preaching, praying, singing, exhorting, parochial visitings, baptisms, and love-feasts? Nay, why these revival meetings, these inquiry meetings, protracted meetings, anxious seats and revival preachers, and all the ordinary and extraordinary ministrations of the Word? If the Bible alone is sufficient to make us wise unto salvation, why not leave us to that alone? Why adopt these other means of coming into communion with the Spirit? Where would be the harm, if these people who contend for the sufficiency of the Scriptures should put their faith in practice? Why, instead of sending out missionaries to the heathen, do they not content themselves with merely sending a copy of the Holy Scriptures?

Far be it from us to say one word against the inspiration or the authority of the Scriptures; but we insist upon it, that without the interpretation of the Spirit, which is in the Church and nowhere else, they are to us not only a sealed book, but a dangerous book, which men may and do wrest to their own destruction. There is no use in concealing this fact. They who have been engaged for years in the effort to instruct their congregations in the sacred mysteries of our faith, do know that the greatest obstacle they have to contend with is in the almost universal perversion of the Scriptures. Men who are unacquainted with the simplest elements of the Christian faith, and who know nothing of the divine significance of the Holy Scriptures,—who indeed can hardly read them, set up to be oracles, and reject with proud disdain the words of the Gospel as uttered by its humble minded and pious ministers. Is there an appeal made from the pulpit? the veriest stripling in the assembly is ready to resist it, by alleging that it is founded upon a false interpretation of Scripture. Is there a sin rebuked? the sinner turns aside the edge of the rebuke, by entering into a dispute with you about the meaning of some text, or the true nature of some abstract dogma of faith. All our congregations are too wise to be taught; and, instead of listening to the preacher as an ambassador from God, to learn their duty, and to be admonished of their short-comings, assume the judgment-seat, place the minister on trial, and acquit or condemn him, as he does or does not countenance their own crude speculations. All teachableness is lost, and our people no longer comprehend that, unless they become as little children, they shall in no wise enter into the kingdom of heaven. We are all prophets, all teachers; and the more ignorant we are, the more dogmatical; and the less we have of the graces of the Spirit, the more competent we feel ourselves to instruct. A worse state of things cannot well be conceived of. The preacher has become a lecturer; the minister of Jesus has become little more than a rhetorician. And whence? Simply from our constant exhortations to our people to read the Bible, and our constantly ringing it in their ears that they are, no matter how ignorant, abundantly able, sinners, or not, to read and understand the word for themselves; because instead of *preaching* to men, we *discourse* to them; and instead of speaking to their consciences, and rebuking them in the name of God, we discuss with them from the pulpit the various points of Christian theology. We would hinder no one from teaching who is competent to teach; but we deny the competency of individuals to teach till they have shown a willingness to be taught,—and we think it more important that the people should be made to feel that they would be wiser and more modest, if they would distrust their competency to instruct their teachers, than they are by assuming as they now do, their ability to decide off-hand, because they can quote Scripture, the knottiest points of Christian faith. Nothing has tended more to foster heresy, and to spread infidelity, and through these to introduce a general laxity of moral principle, than this feeling cherished in our congregations of their ability, without the aid of the Church, to interpret the word for themselves. Religion loses its hold upon us; we sink into doubt, skepticism, indifferency to all that is spiritual; become cold, calculating, worldly-minded, with no god but our bellies, with no faith but in Mammon, and no reverence but for the ledger. We know what will be said of this statement, but we must be faithful to our Master, and at the risk of offending human pride, say that the Bible is a book which may be perverted to the worst ends, and is so perverted when placed in the hands of the ignorant, the impure, the proud, and the self-willed. We should feel that our ability to read and understand the word of God, is not innate, born with us, a portion of our natural inheritance, but comes solely from our union with Christ, and the illuminations which we receive from him through the medium which he himself has instituted.

But waiving all this, admitting that through the Bible we could even become united to the spirit of Jesus, and therefore members of his body, it could be only to the Christ that *was*; for it is only the Christ that was, that is in the Bible. But we are saved not by a Christ that was, but by the Christ that *is*. We need a personal Christ as much as did those among whom Jesus tabernacled as Son of Mary. The Savior must be a *living* Savior; but the Savior in the Bible is not a living Savior; it is but the echo of the Savior, bearing about the same relation to Jesus as the living Savior, that a fact of memory bears to a fact of consciousness,—a joy remembered to a joy which is present. But we not only need a present Savior, but we are promised one; for Jesus says to the Apostolic Church, "Lo! I am with you always unto the end of the world."

The Bible again, and this follows from the necessity of a present Savior, is too inflexible to be received as the authoritative rule, unless there be a co-ordinate authority to interpret and apply it. Paul evidently teaches passive obedience, and forbids resistance in any case whatever to civil government. Suppose that we take the Bible alone as our rule, what will be the result? Civil governments, we know, nay, we are told from the Bible itself, do often oppress; but we must not resist them, and therefore oppression can never be ended. The Bible in this case would be a glorious book for tyrants, and we are not surprised that civil rulers have always been very willing to have it circulate among their subjects.

But may not tyranny be ever lawfully resisted? Not by the individual, unless you surrender the very possibility of legitimate authority. The individual is called upon to obey not to sit in judgment on the authority that commands. It is nonsense to pretend that I am bound to obey an authority which I have the right to judge. I am bound to obey, and the command of the sovereign is to me my only rule of right. Therefore I, as an individual, as one of the people, have not, and never can have, the right to resist the magistrate whatever he commands. This is Paul's doctrine, and it is sound, the only doctrine compatible with any civil government at all.

What, then, shall tyranny be perpetual? Certainly it must be, if you have no authority, beyond the State, beside the Bible and private judgment. Here is where we are reduced by Protestantism. Protestantism has raised the State over the Church, and, therefore, reduced us either to no government at all, or to absolute submission to the civil ruler. There is no escape from this, but by assuming an authority, ever present, capable of interpreting and applying the *dicta* of the New Testament writers. Give us an authoritative Church; it will command the subject to submit to the magistrate, and forbid him ever to resist it, however oppressive, on his own authority; for that would be to put an end to the State at once; but it will admonish the civil ruler of his duty, point out to him the wrong he does, and command him to redress it. If he refuse, it declares him a tyrant, and legitimates resistance, by absolving the subject from his allegiance. This the Church formerly did, and through it, peaceably, without anarchy or rebellion, the poor and downtrodden could be protected against the civil tyrant. But now, alas! we are obliged to submit to the grossest wrongs, or else become rebels, or anarchists.

But we shall be told, "common sense will interpret these rules of the Bible aright, so that the authority of the Church is not needed to tell us their meaning and application. The common sense of whom? Of the unregenerate, and the unenlightened? Or of the regenerate, and enlightened, that is to say, of the Church? If of the last, shall it be the common sense of the Church formally or informally expressed. If the first, then all we contend for is conceded; for then there must be a regular, official way, of declaring the sense of the Church, and when so declared, it is authoritative.

But in conclusion, the Bible, we have already seen, is the production of the Church, and has been received on the authority of the Church. The simple question then, in regard to its sufficiency, is, whether the Church that produced the Bible, was all the Church needed, and that now, since the Bible is produced, there is no longer any necessity of the Church? None are willing to say that the Church is no longer necessary. Will someone, then, tell us, wherein consists its necessity, if the Bible alone be sufficient?

P.S. In consequence of the conductors of the Christian World, having expressed their unwillingness to hold themselves responsible for the views of the writer of this series of articles, and as the writer wishes to implicate no one but himself, in his views, he will simply say that they are published on his own responsibility; and he here adds his initials, which he will do to whatever else he may contribute to this Journal. O. A. B.

NOTES

1. "The Mission of Jesus," *The Christian World*, January 21, 1843. Growth in Christ's life, Brownson says, "is not by development, but by assimiliation." "Something more is always needed than the mere tempting forth of what is already within." Growth and progress, for Brownson, is dependent upon the influence of or

communion with an object outside the self that is superior to the self and, therefore, can raise the self above its own inherent qualities. A teacher, for example, communicates and imparts, whether by precept or example, a portion of his own life to the student, and the student actively, not passively, receives this communication. In this process of communion "the influence and the influenced, so far as the influence extends, do literally become one, living one and the same life." The Law of Life is a result of the interaction of the subject and the object with which the subject communes. All life, therefore, is simultaneously subjective and objective. Life, in a word, is the result of the synthesis of the subject's and the object's joint activity. Jesus imparts his life, which is a redeeming life because it is above the life of any human being, to humankind by virtue of this law of life.

  2. [Ed. Joseph Priestley (1733-1804), scientist and theologian, was a founder of the Unitarian movement in England and had an influence upon its development in the United States where he lived after 1794. DAB, 15, 223-26.]

  3. [Ed. Thomas Belsham (1750-1829) was Joseph Priestley's fellow Unitarian at Hackney College in Hackney, England. Belsham wrote frequently in defense of Unitarianism and accepted Priestley's Unitarian pulpit at Hackney when Priestley moved to the United States. DNB, 2, 202. Heinrich Eberhard Gottlob Paulus (1761-1851), German orientalist and theologian at the Universities of Jena and Heidelberg, tried to reconcile belief in the substantial accuracy of the Gospel narrative with disbelief in the miracles and the supernatural. David Friedrich Strauss (1808-1874), German theologian at the University of Tübingen, wrote a *Life of Jesus* (1835-1836) that pointed to mythical elements in the Gospels and denied the historical foundation of all supernatural elements in them.]

A SELECTED BIBLIOGRAPHY

PRIMARY SOURCES:

  The Works of Orestes A. Brownson, ed. by Henry F. Brownson, 20 vols. (Detroit: Thorndike Nourse, 1882-1887).

  "The Brownson Papers" (19 microfilm rolls; and *A Guide to the Microfilm Edition of the Orestes A. Brownson Papers*, ed. by Thomas T. McAvoy, C.S.C. and Lawrence J. Bradley (Notre Dame, Indiana: University of Notre Dame Press, 1966).

  The Brownson-Hecker Correspondence, ed. and intro. by Joseph F. Gower and Richard M. Leliaert (Notre Dame, Indiana: University of Notre Dame Press, 1979).

  Boston Quarterly Review, 1838-42.

  Brownson's Quarterly Review, 1844-64; 1873-75.

SECONDARY SOURCES:

  Spencer Clare Bennett, "Orestes Brownson: On Civil Religion, Conflicts in the Evolution of a Concept of National Faith," Ph.D. dissertation, Case Western Reserve University, 1973.

Henry F. Brownson, *Life of Orestes Brownson* 3 vols. (Detroit: Henry F. Brownson, 1898-1900).

Dennis Joseph Deare, "The Theological Influence of Orestes Brownson and Isaac Hecker on John Ireland's Americanist Ecclesiology," Ph.D. dissertation, Catholic University of America, 1978.

Leonard Gilhooley, C.F.X., *Contradiction and Dilemma: Orestes Brownson and the American Idea* (New York: Fordham University Press, 1972).

William James Gilmore, "Orestes Brownson and New England Religious Culture, 1803-1827," Ph.D. dissertation, University of Virginia, 1971.

Robert Emerson Ireland, "The Concept of Providence in the Thought of William Ellery Channing, Ralph Waldo Emerson, Theodore Parker, and Orestes A. Brownson. A Study in Mid-Nineteenth-Century American Intellectual History," Ph.D. dissertation, University of Maine, 1972.

Americo D. Lapati, *Orestes A. Brownson* (New Haven, Connecticut; College and University Press, 1965).

Richard Maurice Leliaert, "Orestes A. Brownson (1803-1876): Theological Perspectives on His Search for the Meaning of God, Christology, and the Development of Doctrine," Ph.D. dissertation, Graduate Theological Union, 1974.

————, "The Religious Significance of Democracy in the Thought of Orestes A. Brownson," *The Review of Politics* XXXVIII (January, 1976) 3-26.

————, "Brownson's Approach to God: The Catholic Period," *The Thomist* XL (October, 1976) 571-607.

George K. Malone, *The True Church: A Study in the Apologetics of Orestes Brownson* (St. Mary's of the Lake Seminary, Mundelein, Illinois, 1957).

Theodore Maynard, *Orestes Brownson: Yankee, Radical Catholic* (New York: Macmillan Co., 1943).

Hugh Marshall, S.T., *Orestes Brownson and the American Republic: An Historical Perspective* (Washington D.C.: The Catholic University of America Press, 1971).

Thomas R. Ryan, *Orestes A. Brownson, A Definitive Biography* (Huntington, Indiana: Our Sunday Visitor Press, 1975).

Arthur M. Schlesinger, Jr., *Orestes A. Brownson, A Pilgrim's Progress* (Boston: Little, Brown, and Co., 1939).

Per Sveino, *Orestes A. Brownson's Road to Catholicism* (New York: Humanities Press, 1970).

3

Isaac Thomas Hecker

Isaac Thomas Hecker (1819-1888), convert to Catholicism and founder of the Congregation of St. Paul, Missionary Priests of the Apostle (i.e., Paulists), was another American Catholic representative of the Romantic mood in the United States. Influenced by the transcendentalist movement, American revivalism, Orestes Brownson, and the theology of Johann Adam Möhler, Hecker developed his own method of apologetics. Rather than using what Brownson called the apologetics of external authority, Hecker tried to demonstrate that the basic drives of the human heart and of the nineteenth century could be fully satisfied only by Catholicism. The starting point of his theological reflection was human and cultural interiority (i.e., "the wants of the heart," the "Questions of the Soul," the "Aspirations of Nature," "The Church, in view of the Needs of the Age"), and not external authority, motives of credibility, or reason. From this starting point, Hecker developed a style of apologetics for Catholicism that tried to correlate the interior questions and needs of man and his age with the external answers and workings of the Catholic Church. The Holy Spirit, working within man and his world, therefore, harmonized with the Holy Spirit's activity within the institutional church. In fact, the external ministries of the institutional church were the sacramentalizations of human and cultural aspirations.

Hecker was born in New York City to John and Susan Friend Hecker, immigrants from Germany. As a young man, Isaac was loosely associated with his mother's Methodist Church. He received very little formal education, attending a public school in New York City for five years. After leaving school, he worked in various jobs before joining his two older brothers in establishing a bakery and flour mill in the late 1830s. After meeting Orestes A. Brownson in the early 1840s, Hecker began to become acquainted with the intellectual movements of the day, journeying to the Transcendentalist stronghold in Massachusetts. In 1844, after some years of religious searching, he converted to Catholicism. In 1845, he joined the Congregation of the Most Holy Redeemer (Redemptorists), going to the novitiate of St. Trond, Belgium and to Witten, Holland to receive his education for the priesthood. After ordination in London in 1849, he served the next seven years as a Redemptorist missionary in New York and other American cities. In 1858, he was released from the Redemptorist vows and established the Paulists, as a religious order dedicated to the conversion of American Protestants. He served as superior of that order until his death in 1888. As a Paulist he established and edited the Catholic World, a periodical of religious thought for American Catholics.

In 1874 and 1875, while visiting Europe, Hecker wrote "An Exposition" of his plan for the future direction of the church. The "Exposition" was to be "nothing less than a general outline of a movement from without to within."[1] In the essay, Hecker called for greater Catholic emphasis upon the role of the Holy Spirit in personal and ecclesiastical regeneration. He envisioned an effusion of the Holy Spirit in the present age and urged the Catholic Church to complement its stress upon the Holy Spirit's activities in the church's external structures by a corresponding emphasis upon its activities in the individual soul. Such an emphasis would, in his estimate, bring about the renewal of religion which in turn would revitalize society. Divine Providence, which had guided the church to defend its external authority during the post-Tridentine era, was now guiding it to reassert the power of the Holy Spirit within the individual person.

NOTE

1. Quoted in John Farina, *An American Experience of God: The Spirituality of Isaac Hecker* (New York: Paulist Press, 1981), p. 154.

TEXT

"AN EXPOSITION OF THE CHURCH
IN VIEW OF RECENT DIFFICULTIES AND CONTROVERSIES
AND THE PRESENT NEEDS OF THE AGE"

Source: Catholic World 21
(April-September, 1875), 117-138.

"These are not the times to sit with folded arms, while all the enemies of God are occupied in overthrowing every thing worthy of respect."—Pius IX., Jan. 13, 1873.

"Yes, this change, this triumph, will come. I know not whether it will come during my life, during the life of this poor Vicar of Jesus Christ; but that it must come, I know. The resurrection will take place and we shall see the end of all impiety."—Pius IX., Anniversary of the Roman Plebiscite, 1872.

I. THE QUESTION STATED.

The Catholic Church throughout the world, beginning at Rome, is in a suffering state. There is scarcely a spot on the earth where she is not assailed by injustice, oppression, or violent persecution. Like her divine Author in his Passion, every member has its own trial of pain to endure. All the gates of hell have been opened, and every species of attack, as by general conspiracy, has been let loose at once upon the church.

Countries in which Catholics out-number all other Christians put together, as France, Austria, Italy, Spain, Bavaria, Baden, South America, Brazil, and, until recently, Belgium, are for the most part controlled and governed by hostile minorities, and in some instances the minority is very small.

Her adversaries, with the finger of derision, point out these facts and proclaim them to the world. Look, they say, at Poland, Ireland, Portugal, Spain, Bavaria, Austria, Italy, France, and what do you see? Countries subjugated, or enervated, or agitated by the internal throes of revolution. Everywhere among Catholic nations weakness only and incapacity are to be discerned. This is the result of the priestly domination and hierarchical influence of Rome!

Heresy and schism, false philosophy, false science, and false art, cunning diplomacy, infidelity, and atheism, one and all boldly raise up their heads and attack the church in the face; while secret societies of world-wide organization are stealthily engaged in undermining her strength with the people. Even the Sick man—the Turk—who lives at the beck of the so-called Christian nations, impudently kicks the church of Christ, knowing full well there is no longer in Europe any power which will openly raise a voice in her defence.

How many souls, on account of this dreadful war waged against the church, are now suffering in secret a bitter agony! How many are hesitating, knowing not what to do, and looking for guidance! How many are wavering between hope and fear! Alas! too many have already lost the faith.

Culpable is the silence and base the fear which would restrain one's voice at a period when God, the church, and religion are everywhere either openly denied, boldly attacked, or fiercely persecuted. In such trying times as these silence or fear is betrayal.

The hand of God is certainly in these events, and it is no less certain that the light of divine faith ought to discern it. Through these clouds which now obscure the church the light of divine hope ought to pierce, enabling us to perceive a better and a brighter future; for this is what is in store for the church and the world. That love which embraces at once the greatest glory of God and the highest happiness of man should outweigh all fear of misinterpretations, and urge one to make God's hand clear to those who are willing to see, and point out to them the way to that happier and fairer future.

What, then, has brought about this most deplorable state of things? How can we account for this apparent lack of faith and strength on the part of Catholics? Can it be true, as their enemies assert, that Catholicity, wherever it has full sway, deteriorates society? Or is it contrary to the spirit of Christianity that Christians should strive with all their might to overcome evil in this world? Perhaps the Catholic Church has grown old, as others imagine, and has accomplished her task, and is no longer competent to unite together the conflicting interests of modern society, and direct it towards its true destination?

These questions are most serious ones. Their answers must be fraught with most weighty lessons. Only a meagre outline of the course of argument can be here given in so vast a field of investigation.

II. REMOTE CAUSE OF PRESENT DIFFICULTIES.

One of the chief features of the history of the church for these last three centuries has been its conflict with the religious revolution of the XVIth century, properly called Protestantism. The nature of Protestantism may be defined as the exaggerated development of personal independence, directed to the negation of the divine authority of the church, and chiefly aiming at its overthrow in the person of its supreme representative, the Pope.

It is a fixed law, founded in the very nature of the church, that every serious and persistent denial of a divinely-revealed truth necessitates its vigorous defence, calls out its greater development, and ends, finally, in its dogmatic definition.

The history of the church is replete with instances of this fact. One must suffice. When Arius denied the divinity of Christ, which was always held as a divinely-revealed truth, at once the doctors of the church and the faithful were aroused in its defence. A general council was called at Nice, and there this truth was defined and fixed for ever as a dogma of the Catholic faith. The law has always been, from the first Council at Jerusalem to that of the Vatican, that the negation of a revealed truth calls out its fuller development and its explicit dogmatic definition.

The Council of Trent refuted and condemned the errors of Protestantism at the time of their birth, and defined the truths against which they were directed; but, for wise and sufficient reasons, abstained from touching the objective point of attack, which was, necessarily, the divine authority of the church. For there was no standing ground whatever for a protest against the church, except in its denial. It would have been the height of absurdity to admit an authority, and that divine, and at the same time to refuse to obey its decisions. It was as well known then as to-day that the keystone of the whole structure of the church was its head. To overthrow the Papacy was to conquer the church.

The supreme power of the church for a long period of years was the centre around which the battle raged between the adversaries and the champions of the faith.

The denial of the Papal authority in the church necessarily occasioned its fuller development. For as long as this hostile movement was aggressive in its assaults, so long was the church constrained to strengthen her defence, and make a stricter and more detailed application of her authority in every sphere of her action, in her hierarchy, in her general discipline, and in the personal acts of her children. Every new denial was met with a new defence and a fresh application. The danger was on the side of revolt, the safety was on that of submission. The poison was an exaggerated spiritual independence, the antidote was increased obedience to a divine external authority.

The chief occupation of the church for the last three centuries was the maintenance of that authority conferred by Christ on S. Peter and his successors, in opposition to the efforts of Protestantism for its over-throw; and the contest was terminated for ever in the dogmatic defini-tion of Papal Infallibility, by the church assembled in council in the Vatican. Luther declared the pope Antichrist. The Catholic Church affirmed the pope to be the Vicar of Christ. Luther stigmatized the See of Rome as the seat of error. The council of the church defined the See of Rome, the chair of S. Peter, to be the infallible interpreter of divinely-revealed truth. This definition closed the controversy. . . .

III. PROXIMATE CAUSE.

The church, while resisting Protestantism, had to give her principal attention and apply her main strength to those points which were attacked. Like a wise strategist, she drew off her forces from the places which were secure, and directed them to those posts where danger threatened. As she was most of all engaged in the defence of her exter-nal authority and organization, the faithful, in view of this defence, as well as in regard to the dangers of the period, were specially guided to the practice of the virtue of obedience. It is a matter of surprise that the character of the virtues developed was more passive than active? The weight of authority was placed on the side of restraining rather than of developing personal independent action.

The exaggeration of personal authority on the part of Protestants brought about in the church its greater restraint, in order that her divine authority might have its legitimate exercise and exert its salutary influence. The errors and evils of the times sprang from an unbridled personal independence, which could be only counteracted by habits of increased personal dependence. *Contraria contrariis curantur.* The defense of the church and the salvation of the soul were ordinarily secured at the expense, necessarily, of those virtues which properly go to make up the strength of Christian manhood.

The gain was the maintenance and victory of divine truth and the salvation of the soul. The loss was a certain falling off in energy, result-ing in decreased action in the natural order. The former was a perma-nent and inestimable gain. The latter was a temporary, and not irreparable, loss. There was no room for a choice. The faithful were placed in a position in which it became their unqualified duty to put into practice the precept of our Lord when he said: *It is better for thee to enter into life maimed or lame, than, having two hands or two feet, to be cast into everlasting fire.* (Mt. 18:8)

In the principles above briefly stated may in a great measure be found the explanation why fifty millions of Protestants have had generally a controlling influence, for a long period, over two hundred millions of Catholics, in directing the movements and destinies of nations. To the same source may be attributed the fact that Catholic nations, when the need was felt of a man of great personal energy at the head of their affairs, seldom hesitated to choose for prime minister an indifferent Catholic, or a Protestant, or even an infidel. These principles explain also why Austria, France, Bavaria, Spain, Italy, and other Catholic countries have yielded to a handful of active and determined radicals, infidels, Jews, or atheists, and have been compelled to violate or annul their concordats with the Holy See, and to change their political institutions in a direction hostile to the interests of the Catholic religion. Finally, herein lies the secret why Catholics are at this moment almost everywhere oppressed and persecuted by very inferior numbers. In the natural order the feebler are always made to serve the stronger. Evident weakness on one side, in spite of superiority of numbers, provokes on the other, where there is consciousness of power, subjugation and oppression.

IV. IS THERE A WAY OUT?

Is divine grace given only at the cost of natural strength? Is a true Christian life possible only through the sacrifice of a successful natural career? Are things to remain as they are at present?

The general history of the Catholic religion in the past condemns these suppositions as the grossest errors and falsest calumnies. Behold the small numbers of the faithful and their final triumph over the great colossal Roman Empire! Look at the subjugation of the countless and victorious hordes of the Northern barbarians! Witness, again, the prowess of the knights of the church, who were her champions in repulsing the threatening Mussulman; every one of whom, by the rule of their order, were bound not to flinch before two Turks! Call to mind the great discoveries made in all branches of science, and the eminence in art, displayed by the children of the church, and which underlie—if there were only honesty enough to acknowledge it—most of our modern progress and civilization! Long before Protestantism was dreamed of Catholic states in Italy had reached a degree of wealth, power, and glory which no Protestant nation—it is the confession of one of their own historians——has since attained.

There is, then, no reason in the nature of things why the existing condition of Catholics throughout the world should remain as it is. The blood that courses through our veins, the graces given in our baptism, the light of our faith, the divine life-giving Bread we receive, are all the same gifts and privileges which we have in common with our great ancestors. We are the children of the same mighty mother, ever fruitful of heroes and great men. The present state of things is neither fatal nor final, but only one of the many episodes in the grand history of the church of God.

V. WHICH IS THE WAY OUT?

No better evidence is needed of the truth of the statements just made than the fact that all Catholics throughout the world are ill at ease with things as they are. The world at large is agitated, as it never has been before, with problems which enter into the essence of religion or are closely connected therewith. Many serious minds are occupied with the question of the renewal of religion and the regeneration of society. The aspects in which questions of this nature are viewed are as various as the remedies proposed are numerous. Here are a few of the more important ones.

One class of men would begin by laboring for the reconciliation of all Christian denominations, and would endeavor to establish unity in Christendom as the way to universal restoration. Another class starts with the idea that the remedy would be found in giving a more thorough and religious education to youth in schools, colleges, and universities. Some would renew the church by translating her liturgies into the vulgar tongues, by reducing the number of her forms of devotion, and by giving to her worship greater simplicity. Others, again, propose to alter the constitution of the church by the practice of universal elections in the hierarchy, by giving the lay element a larger share in the direction of ecclesiastical matters, and by establishing national churches. There are those who hope for a better state of things by placing Henry V on the throne of France, and Don Carlos on that of Spain. Others, contrariwise, having lost all confidence in princes, look forward with great expectations to a baptized democracy, a holy Roman democracy, just as formerly there was a Holy Roman Empire. Not a few are occupied with the idea of reconciling capital with labor, of changing the tenure of property, and abolishing standing armies. Others propose a restoration of international law, a congress of nations, and a renewed and more strict observance of the Decalogue. According to another school, theological motives have lost their hold on the people, the task of directing society has devolved upon science, and its apostolate has begun. There are those, moreover, who hold that society can only be cured by an immense catastrophe, and one hardly knows what great cataclysm is to happen and save the human race. Finally, we are told that the reign of Antichrist has begun, that signs of it are everywhere, and that we are on the eve of the end of the world.

These are only a few of the projects, plans, and remedies which are discussed, and which more or less occupy and agitate the public mind. How much truth or error, how much good or bad, each or all of these theories contain, would require a lifetime to find out.

The remedy for our evils must be got at, to be practical, in another way. If a new life be imparted to the root of a tree, its effects will soon be seen in all its branches, twigs, and leaves. Is it not possible to get at the root of all our evils, and with a radical remedy renew at once the whole face of things? Universal evils are not cured by specifics.

VI. THE WAY OUT.

All things are to be viewed and valued as they bear on the destiny of man. Religion is the solution of the problem of man's destiny. Religion, therefore, lies at the root of everything which concerns man's true interest.

Religion means Christianity, to all men, or to nearly all, who hold to any religion among European nations. Christianity, intelligibly understood, signifies the church, the Catholic Church. The church is God acting through a visible organization directly on men, and, through men, on society.

The church is the sum of all problems, and the most potent fact in the whole wide universe. It is therefore illogical to look elsewhere for the radical remedy of all our evils. It is equally unworthy of a Catholic to look elsewhere for the renewal of religion.

The meditation of these great truths is the source from which the inspiration must come, if society is to be regenerated and the human race directed to its true destination. He who looks to any other quarter for a radical and adequate remedy and for true guidance is doomed to failure and disappointment.

VII. MISSION OF THE HOLY SPIRIT.

It cannot be too deeply and firmly impressed on the mind that the church is actuated by the instinct of the Holy Spirit; and to discern clearly its action, and to co-operate with it effectually, is the highest employment of our faculties, and at the same time the primary source of the greatest good to society.

Did we clearly see and understand the divine action of the Holy Spirit in the successive steps of the history of the church we would fully comprehend the law of all true progress. If in this later period more stress was laid on the necessity of obedience to the external authority of the church than in former days, it was, as has been shown, owing to the peculiar dangers to which the faithful were exposed. It would be an inexcusable mistake to suppose for a moment that the holy church, at any period of her existence, was ignorant or forgetful of the mission and office of the Holy Spirit. The Holy Spirit established the church, and can he forget his own mission? It is true that he has to guide and govern through men, but he is the Sovereign of men, and especially of those whom he has chosen as his immediate instruments.

The essential and universal principle which saves and sanctifies souls is the Holy Spirit. He it was who called, inspired, and sanctified the patriarchs, the prophets and saints of the old dispensation. The same divine Spirit inspired and sanctified the apostles, the martyrs, and the saints of the new dispensation. The actual and habitual guidance of the soul by the Holy Spirit is the essential principle of all divine life. "I have taught the prophets from the beginning, and even till now I cease not to speak at all."[1] Christ's mission was to give the Holy Spirit more abundantly.

No one who reads the Holy Scriptures can fail to be struck with the repeated injunctions to turn our eyes inward, to walk in the divine presence, to see and taste and listen to God in the soul. These exhortations run all through the inspired books, beginning with that of Genesis, and ending with the Revelations of S. John. "I am the Almighty God, walk before me, and be perfect" (Gen 17:11) was the lesson which God gave to the patriarch Abraham. "Be still and see that I am God." (Ps 45:2) "O taste, and see that the Lord is sweet; blessed is the man that hopeth in him." (Ps 33:9) God is the guide, the light of the living, and our strength. "God's kingdom is within you," said the divine Master. "Know you not that you are the temple of God, and that the Spirit of God dwelleth in you?" (I Cor 3:16) "For it is God who worketh in you both to will and to accomplish, according to his will." (Phil 2:13) The object of divine revelation was to make known and to establish within the souls of men, and through them upon the earth, the kingdom of God.

In accordance with the Sacred Scriptures, the Catholic Church teaches that the Holy Spirit is infused, with all his gifts, into our souls by the sacrament of baptism, and that, without his actual prompting or inspiration and aid, no thought or act, or even wish, tending directly towards our true destiny, is possible.

The whole aim of the science of Christian perfection is to instruct men how to remove the hindrances in the way of the action of the Holy Spirit, and how to cultivate those virtues which are most favorable to his solicitations and inspirations. Thus the sum of Spiritual life consists in observing and fortifying the ways and movements of the Spirit of God in our soul, employing for this purpose all the exercises of prayer, spiritual reading, sacraments, the practice of virtues, and good works.

That divine action which is the immediate and principal cause of the salvation and perfection of the soul claims by right its direct and main attention. From this source within the soul there will gradually come to birth the consciousness of the indwelling presence of the Holy Spirit, out of which will spring a force surpassing all human strength, a courage higher than all human heroism, a sense of dignity excelling all human greatness. The light the age requires for its renewal can come only from the same source. The renewal of the age depends on the renewal of religion. The renewal of religion depends upon a greater effusion of the creative and renewing power of the Holy Spirit. The greater effusion of the Holy Spirit depends on the giving of increased attention to his movements and inspirations in the soul. The radical and adequate remedy for all the evils of our age, and the source of all true progress, consist in increased attention and fidelity to the action of the Holy Spirit in the soul. "Thou shalt send forth thy Spirit, and they shall be created: and thou shalt renew the face of the earth." (Ps. 103:30)

VIII. THE MEN THE AGE DEMANDS.

This truth will be better seen by looking at the matter a little more in detail. The age, we are told, calls for men worthy of that name. Who are those worthy to be called men? Men, assuredly, whose intelligences and wills are divinely illuminated and fortified. This is precisely what is produced by the gifts of the Holy Spirit; they enlarge all the faculties of the soul at once.

The age is superficial; it needs the gift of wisdom, which enables the soul to contemplate the truth in its ultimate causes. The age is materialistic; it needs the gift of intelligence, by the light of which the intellect penetrates into the essence of things. The age is captivated by a false and one-sided science; it needs the gift of science, by the light of which is seen each order of truth in its true relations to other orders and in a divine unity. The age is in disorder, and is ignorant of the way to true progress; it needs the gift of counsel, which teaches how to choose the proper means to attain an object. The age is impious; it needs the gift of piety, which leads the soul to look up to God as the Heavenly Father, and to adore him with feelings of filial affection and love. The age is sensual and effeminate; it needs the gift of force, which imparts to the will the strength to endure the greatest burdens and to prosecute the greatest enterprises with ease and heroism. The age has lost and almost forgotten God; it needs the gift of fear, to bring the soul again to God, and make it feel conscious of its great responsibility and of its destiny.

Men endowed with these gifts are the men for whom—if it but knew it—the age calls: men whose minds are enlightened and whose wills are strengthened by an increased action of the Holy Spirit; men whose souls are actuated by the gifts of the Holy Spirit; men whose countenances are lit up with a heavenly joy, who breathe an air of inward peace, and act with a holy liberty and an unaccountable energy. One such soul does more to advance the kingdom of God than tens of thousands without such gifts. These are the men and this is the way—if the age could only be made to see and believe it—to universal restoration, universal reconciliation, and universal progress.

IX. THE CHURCH HAS ENTERED ON THIS WAY.

The men the age and its needs demand depend on a greater infusion of the Holy Spirit in the souls of the faithful; and the church has been already prepared for this event.

Can one suppose for a moment that so long, so severe, a contest, as that of the three centuries just passed, which, moreover, has cost so dearly, has not been fraught with the greatest utility to the church? Does God ever allow his church to suffer loss in the struggle to accomplish her divine mission?

It is true that the powerful and persistent assaults of the errors of the XVIth century against the church forced her, so to speak, out of the usual orbit of her movement; but having completed her defence from all danger on that side, she is returning to her normal course with increased agencies—thanks to that contest—and is entering upon a new and fresh phase of life, and upon a more vigorous action in every sphere of her existence. The chiefest of these agencies, and the highest in importance, was that of the definition concerning the nature of papal authority. For the definition of the Vatican Council, having rendered the supreme authority of the church, which is the unerring interpreter and criterion of divinely-revealed truth, more explicit and complete, has prepared the way for the faithful to follow, with greater safety and liberty, the inspirations of the Holy Spirit. The dogmatic papal definition of the Vatican Council is, therefore, the axis on which turn the new course of the church, the renewal of religion, and the entire restoration of society.

O blessed fruit! purchased at the price of so hard a struggle, but which has gained for the faithful an increased divine illumination and force, and thereby the renewal of the whole face of the world. . . .

What is the meaning of these many pilgrimages to holy places, to the shrines of great saints, the multiplication of Novenas and new associations of prayer? Are they not evidence of increased action of the Holy Spirit on the faithful? Why, moreover, these cruel persecutions, vexatious fines, and numerous imprisonments of the bishops, clergy, and laity of the church? What is the secret of this stripping the church of her temporal possessions and authority? These things have taken place by the divine permission. Have not all these inflictions increased greatly devotion to prayer, cemented more closely the unity of the faithful, and turned the attention of all members of the church, from the highest to the lowest, to look for aid from whence it alone can come—from God?

These trials and sufferings of the faithful are the first steps towards a better state of things. They detach from earthly things and purify the human side of the church. From them will proceed light and strength and victory. *Per crucem ad lucem.* "If the Lord wishes that other persecutions should be sown, the church feels no alarm; on the contrary, persecutions purify her and confer upon her a fresh force and a new beauty. There are, in truth, in the church certain things which need purification, and for this purpose those persecutions answer best which are launched against her by great politicians." Such is the language of Pius IX.[2]

These are only some of the movements, which are public. But how many souls in secret suffer sorely in seeing the church in such tribulations, and pray for her deliverance with a fervor almost amounting to agony! Are not all these but so many preparatory steps to a Pentecostal effusion of the Holy Spirit on the church—an effusion, if not equal in intensity to that of apostolic days, at least greater than it in universality? "If at no epoch of the evangelical ages the reign of Satan was so generally welcome as in this our day, the action of the Holy Spirit will have to clothe itself with the characteristics of an exceptional extension and force. The axioms of geometry do not appear to us more rigorously exact than this proposition. A certain indefinable presentiment of this necessity of a new effusion of the Holy Spirit for the actual world exists, and of this presentiment the importance ought not to be exaggerated; but yet it would seem rash to make it of no account."[3]

Is not this the meaning of the presentiment of Pius IX., when he said: "Since we have nothing, or next to nothing, to expect from men, let us place our confidence more and more in God, whose heart is preparing, as it seems to me, to accomplish, in the moment chosen by himself, a great prodigy, which will fill the whole earth with astonishment"?[4]

Was not the same presentiment before the mind of De Maistre when he penned the following lines: "We are on the eve of the greatest of religious epochs; . . . it appears to me that every true philosopher must choose between these two hypotheses: either that a new religion is about to be formed, or that Christianity will be renewed in some extraordinary manner"?[5]

X. TWOFOLD ACTION OF THE HOLY SPIRIT.

Before further investigation of this new phase of the church, it would perhaps be well to set aside a doubt which might arise in the minds of some, namely, whether there is not danger in turning the attention of the faithful in a greater degree in the direction contemplated?

The enlargement of the field of action for the soul, without a true knowledge of the end and scope of the external authority of the church, would only open the door to delusions, errors, and heresies of every description, and would be in effect merely another form of Protestantism.

On the other hand, the exclusive view of the external authority of the church, without a proper understanding of the nature and work of the Holy Spirit in the soul, would render the practice of religion formal, obedience servile, and the church sterile.

The action of the Holy Spirit embodied visibly in the authority of the church, and the action of the Holy Spirit dwelling invisibly in the soul, form one inseparable synthesis; and he who has not a clear conception of this twofold action of the Holy Spirit is in danger of running into one or the other, and sometimes into both, of these extremes, either of which is destructive of the end of the church.

The Holy Spirit, in the external authority of the church, acts as the infallible interpreter and criterion of divine revelation. The Holy Spirit in the soul acts as the divine Life-Giver and Sanctifier. It is of the highest importance that these two distinct offices of the Holy Spirit should not be confounded.

The supposition that there can be any opposition or contradiction between the action of the Holy Spirit in the supreme decisions, of the authority of the church, and the inspirations of the Holy Spirit in the soul, can never enter the mind of an enlightened and sincere Christian. The same Spirit which through the authority of the church teaches divine truth, is the same Spirit which prompts the soul to receive the divine truths which he teaches. The measure of our love for the Holy Spirit is the measure of our obedience to the authority of the church; and the measure of our obedience to the authority of the church is the measure of our love for the Holy Spirit. Hence the sentence of S. Augustine: *"Quantum quisque amat ecclesiam Dei, tantum habet Spiritum Sanctum."* There is one Spirit, which acts in two different offices concurring to the same end—the regeneration and sanctification of the soul.

In case of obscurity or doubt concerning what is the divinely-revealed truth, or whether what prompts the soul is or is not an inspiration of the Holy Spirit, recourse must be had to the divine teacher or criterion, the authority of the church. For it must be borne in mind that to the church, as represented in the first instance by S. Peter, and subsequently by his successors, was made the promise of her divine Founder that "the gates of hell should never prevail against her." (Mt 16:18) No such promise was ever made by Christ to each individual believer. "The church of the living God is the pillar and ground of truth." (2 Tim 3:15) The test, therefore, of a truly enlightened and sincere Christian, will be, in case of uncertainty, the promptitude of his obedience to the voice of the church.

From the above plain truths the following practical rule of conduct may be drawn: The Holy Spirit is the immediate guide of the soul in the way of salvation and sanctification; and the criterion or test that the soul is guided by the Holy Spirit is its ready obedience to the authority of the church. This rule removes all danger whatever, and with it the soul can walk, run, or fly, if it chooses, in the greatest safety and with perfect liberty, in the ways of sanctity.

XI. NEW PHASE OF THE CHURCH.

There are signs which indicate that the members of the church have not only entered upon a deeper and more spiritual life, but that from the same source has arisen a new phase of their intellectual activity.

The notes of the divine institution of the church—and the credibility of divine revelation—with her constitution and organization, having been in the main completed on the external side, the notes which now require special attention and study are those respecting her divine character, which lie on the internal side.

The mind of the church has been turned in this direction for some time past. One has but to read the several Encyclical letters of the present reigning Supreme Pontiff, and the decrees of the Vatican Council, to be fully convinced of this fact.

No pontiff has so strenuously upheld the value and rights of human reason as Pius IX.; and no council has treated so fully of the relations of the natural with the supernatural as that of the Vatican. It must be remembered the work of both is not yet concluded. Great mission that, to fix for ever those truths so long held in dispute, and to open the door to the fuller knowledge of other and still greater verities!

It is the divine action of the Holy Spirit in and through the church which gives her external organization the reason for its existence. And it is the fuller explanation of the divine side of the church and its relations with her human side, giving always to the former its due accentuation, that will contribute to the increase of the interior life of the faithful, and aid powerfully to remove the blindness of those—whose number is much larger than is commonly supposed—who only see the church on her human side.

As an indication of these studies, the following mere suggestions, concerning the relations of the internal with the external side of the church, are here given.

The practical aim of all true religion is to bring each individual soul under the immediate guidance of the divine Spirit. The divine Spirit communicates himself to the soul by means of the sacraments of the church. The divine Spirit acts as the interpreter and criterion of revealed truth by the authority of the church. The divine Spirit acts as the principle of regeneration and sanctification in each Christian soul. The same Spirit clothes with suitable ceremonies and words the truths of religion and the interior life of the soul in the liturgy and devotions of the church. The divine Spirit acts as the safeguard of the life of the soul and of the household of God in the discipline of the church. The divine Spirit established the church as the practical and perfect means of bringing all souls under his own immediate guidance and into complete union with God. This is the realization of the aim of all true religion. Thus all religions, viewed in the aspect of a divine life, find their common centre in the Catholic Church.

The greater part of the intellectual errors of the age arise from a lack of knowledge of the essential relations of the light of faith with the light of reason; of the connection between the mysteries and truths of divine revelation and those discovered and attainable by human reason; of the action of divine grace and the action of the human will.

The early Greek and Latin fathers of the church largely cultivated this field. The scholastics greatly increased the riches received from their predecessors. And had not the attention of the church been turned aside from its course by the errors of the XVIth century, the demonstration of Christianity on its intrinsic side would ere this have received its finishing strokes. The time has come to take up this work, continue it where it was interrupted, and bring it to completion. Thanks to the Encyclicals of Pius IX, and the decisions of the Vatican Council, this task will not now be so difficult.

Many, if not most, of the distinguished apologists of Christianity, theologians, philosophers, and preachers, either by their writings or eloquence, have already entered upon this path. The recently-published volumes, and those issuing day by day from the press, in exposition, or defence, or apology of Christianity, are engaged in this work.

This explanation of the internal life and constitution of the church, and of the intelligible side of the mysteries of faith and the intrinsic reasons for the truths of divine revelation, giving to them their due emphasis, combined with the external notes of credibility, would complete the demonstration of Christianity. Such an exposition of Christianity, the union of the internal with the external notes of credibility, is calculated to produce a more enlightened and intense conviction of its divine truth in the faithful, to stimulate them to a more energetic personal action; and, what is more, it would open the door to many straying, but not altogether lost, children, for their return to the fold of the church.

The increased action of the Holy Spirit, with a more vigorous cooperation on the part of the faithful, which is in process of realization, will elevate the human personality to an intensity of force and grandeur productive of a new era to the church and to society—an era difficult for the imagination to grasp, and still more difficult to describe in words, unless we have recourse to the prophetic language of the inspired Scriptures.

Is not such a demonstration of Christianity and its results anticipated in the following words?

"We are about to see," said [Frederick von] Schlegel, "a new exposition of Christianity, which will reunite all Christians, and even bring back the infidels themselves." "This reunion between science and faith," says the Protestant historian [Leopold von] Ranke, "will be more important in its spiritual results than was the discovery of a new hemisphere three hundred years ago, or even than that of the true system of the world, or than any other discovery of any kind whatever."

XII. MISSION OF RACES.

Pursuing our study of the action of the Holy Spirit, we shall perceive that a deeper and more explicit exposition of the divine side of the church, in view of the characteristic gifts of different races, is the way or means of realizing the hopes above expressed.

God is the author of the differing races of men. He, for his own good reasons, has stamped upon them their characteristics, and appointed them from the beginning their places which they are to fill in his church.

In a matter where there are so many tender susceptibilities, it is highly important not to overrate the peculiar gifts of any race, nor, on the other hand, to underrate them or exaggerate their vices or defects. Besides, the different races in modern Europe have been brought so closely together, and have been mingled to such an extent, that their differences can only be detected in certain broad and leading features.

It would be also a grave mistake, in speaking of the providential mission of the races, to suppose that they imposed their characteristics on religion, Christianity, or the church whereas on the contrary it is their Author who has employed in the church their several gifts for the expression and development of those truths for which he specially created them. The church is God acting through the different races of men for their highest development, together with their present and future greatest happiness and his own greatest glory. "God directs the nations upon the earth." (Ps. 66:5)

Every leading race of men, or great nation, fills a large space in the general history of the world. It is an observation of S. Augustine that God gave the empire of the world to the Romans as a reward for their civic virtues. But it is a matter of surprise how large and important a part divine Providence has appointed special races to take in the history of religion. It is here sufficient merely to mention the Israelites.

One cannot help being struck with the mission of the Latin and Celtic races during the greater period of the history of Christianity. What brought them together in the first instance was the transference of the chair of S. Peter, the centre of the church, to Rome, the centre of the Latin race. Rome, then, was the embodied expression of a perfectly-organized, world-wide power. Rome was the political, and, by its great roads, the geographical, centre of the world.

What greatly contributed to the predominance of the Latin race, and subsequently of the Celts in union with the Latins, was the abandonment of the church by the Greeks by schism, and the loss of the larger portion of the Saxons by the errors and revolt of the XVIth century. The faithful, in consequence, were almost exclusively composed of Latin-Celts.

The absence of the Greeks and of so large a portion of the Saxons, whose tendencies and prejudices in many points are similar, left a freer course and an easier task to the church, through her ordinary channels of action, as well as through her extraordinary ones—the Councils, namely, of Trent and the Vatican—to complete her authority and external constitution. For the Latin-Celtic races are characterized by hierarchical, traditional, and emotional tendencies.

These were the human elements which furnished the church with the means of developing and completing her supreme authority, her divine and ecclesiastical traditions, her discipline, her devotions, and, in general, her aesthetics. . . .

XVI. MIXED SAXONS RETURNING.

Christ blamed the Jews, who were skillful in detecting the signs of change in the weather, for their want of skill in discerning the signs of the times. There are evidences, and where we should first expect to meet them—namely, among the mixed Saxon races, the people of England and the United States—of this return to the true church.

The mixture of the Anglo-Saxons with the blood of the Celts in former days caused them to retain, at the time of the so-called Reformation, more of the doctrines, worship, and organization of the Catholic Church than did the thorough Saxons of Germany. It is for the same reason that among them are manifested the first unmistakable symptoms of their entrance once more into the bosom of the church.

At different epochs movements in this direction have taken place, but never so serious and general as at the present time. The character and the number of the converts from Anglicanism to the Catholic Church gave, in the beginning, a great alarm to the English nation. But now it has become reconciled to the movement, which continues and takes its course among the more intelligent and influential classes,. and that notwithstanding the spasmodic cry of alarm of Lord John Russell and the more spiteful attack of the Right Hon. William E. Gladstone, M.P., late prime minister.

It is clear to those who have eyes to see such things that God is bestowing special graces upon the English people in our day, and that the hope is not without solid foundation which looks forward to the time when England shall again take rank among the Catholic nations.

The evidences of a movement towards the Catholic Church are still clearer and more general in the United States. There is less prejudice and hostility against the church in the United States than in England, and hence her progress is much greater.

The Catholics, in the beginning of this century, stood as one to every two hundred of the whole population of the American Republic. The ratio of Catholics now is one to six or seven of the inhabitants. The Catholics will outnumber, before the close of this century, all other believers in Christianity put together in the republic.

This is no fanciful statement, but one based on a careful study of statistics, and the estimate is moderate. Even should emigration from Catholic countries to the United States cease altogether—which it will not—or even should it greatly diminish, the supposed loss or diminution, in this source of augmentation, will be fully compensated by the relative increase of births among the Catholics, as compared with that among other portions of the population.

The spirit, the tendencies, and the form of political government inherited by the people of the United States are strongly and distinctively Saxon; yet there are no more patriotic or better citizens in the republic than the Roman Catholics, and no more intelligent, practical, and devoted Catholics in the church than the seven millions of Catholics in this same young and vigorous republic. The Catholic faith is the only persistently progressive religious element, compared with the increase of population, in the United States. A striking proof that the Catholic Church flourishes wherever there is honest freedom wherever human nature has its full share of liberty! Give the Catholic Church equal rights and fair play, and she will again win Europe, and with Europe the world.

Now, who will venture to assert that these two mixed Saxon nations, of England and the United States, are not, in the order of divine Providence, the appointed leaders of the great movement of the return of all the Saxons to the Holy Catholic Church?

The sun, in his early dawn, first touches the brightest mountaintops, and, advancing in his course, floods the deepest valleys with his glorious light; and so the Sun of divine grace has begun to enlighten the minds in the highest stations in life in England, in the United States, and in Germany; and what human power will impede the extension of its holy light to the souls of the whole population of these countries?

XVII. TRANSITION OF THE LATIN-CELTS.

Strange action of divine Providence in ruling the nations of this earth! While the Saxons are about to pass from a natural to a supernatural career, the Latin-Celts are impatient for, and have already entered upon, a natural one. What does this mean? Are these races to change their relative positions before the face of the world?

The present movement of transition began on the part of the Latin-Celtic nations in the last century among the French people, who of all these nations stand geographically the nearest, and whose blood is most mingled with that of the Saxons. That transition began in violence, because it was provoked to a premature birth by the circumstance that the control exercised by the church as the natural moderator of the Christian republic of Europe was set aside by Protestantism, particularly so in France, in consequence of a diluted dose of the same Protestantism under the name of Gallicanism. Exempt from this salutary control, kings and the aristocracy oppressed the people at their own will and pleasure; and the people, in turn, wildly rose up in their might, and cut off, at their own will and pleasure, the heads of the kings and aristocrats. Louis XIV., in his pride, said, "L'Etat c'est moi!" The people replied, in their passion, "L'Etat c'est nous!"

Under the guidance of the church the transformation from feudalism to all that is included under the title of modern citizenship was effected with order, peace, and benefit to all classes concerned. Apart from this aid, society pendulates from despotism to anarchy, and from anarchy to despotism. The French people at the present moment are groping about, and earnestly seeking after the true path of progress, which they lost some time back by their departure from the Christian order of society.

The true movement of Christian progress was turned aside into destructive channels, and this movement, becoming revolutionary, has passed in our day to the Italian and Spanish nations.

Looking at things in their broad features, Christianity is at this moment exposed to the danger, on the one hand, of being exterminated by the persecutions of the Saxon races, and, on the other, of being denied by the apostasy of the Latin-Celts. This is the great tribulation of the present hour of the church. She feels the painful struggle. The destructive work of crushing out Christianity by means of these hostile tendencies has already begun. If, as some imagine, the Christian faith be only possible at the sacrifice of human nature, and if a natural career be only possible at the sacrifice of the Christian faith, it requires no prophetic eye to foresee the sad results to the Christian religion at no distant future.

But it is not so. The principles already laid down and proclaimed to the world by the church answer satisfactorily these difficulties. What the age demands, what society is seeking for, rightly interpreted, is the knowledge of these principles and their practical application to its present needs.

For God is no less the author of nature than of grace, of reason than of faith, of this earth than of heaven.

The Word by which all things were made that were made, and the Word which was made flesh, is one and the same Word. The light which enlighteneth every man that cometh into this world, and the light of Christian faith, are, although differing in degree, the same light. "There is therefore nothing so foolish or so absurd," to use the words of Pius IX. on the same subject, "as to suppose there can be any opposition between them."[6] Their connection is intimate, their relation is primary; they are, in essence, one. For what else did Christ become man than to establish the kingdom of God on earth, as the way to the kingdom of God in heaven?

It cannot be too often repeated to the men of this generation, so many of whom are trying to banish and forget God, that God, and God alone, is the Creator and Renewer of the world. The same God who made all things, and who became man, and began the work of regeneration, is the same who really acts in the church now upon men and society, and who has pledged his word to continue to do so until the end of the world. To be guided by God's church is to be guided by God. It is in vain to look elsewhere. "Society," as the present pontiff has observed, "has been enclosed in a labyrinth, out of which it will never issue save by the hand of God."[7] The hand of God is the church. It is the hand he is extending, in a more distinctive and attractive form, to this present generation. Blessed generation, if it can only be led to see this outstretched hand, and to follow the path of all true progress, which it so clearly points out!

XVIII. PERSPECTIVE OF THE FUTURE.

During the last three centuries, from the nature of the work the church had to do, the weight of her influence had to be mainly exerted on the side of restraining human activity. Her present and future influence, due to the completion of her external organization, will be exerted on the side of soliciting increased action. The first was necessarily repressive and unpopular; the second will be, on the contrary, expansive and popular. The one excited antagonism; the other will attract sympathy and cheerful co-operation. The former restraint was exercised, not against human activity, but against the exaggeration of that activity. The future will be the solicitation of the same activity towards its elevation and divine expansion, enhancing its fruitfulness and glory.

These different races of Europe and the United States, constituting the body of the most civilized nations of the world, united in an intelligent appreciation of the divine character of the church, with their varied capacities and the great agencies at their disposal, would be the providential means of rapidly spreading the light of faith over the whole world, and of constituting a more Christian state of society.

In this way would be reached a more perfect realization of the prediction of the prophets, of the promises and prayers of Christ, and of the true aspiration of all noble souls.

This is what the age is calling for, if rightly understood, in its countless theories and projects of reform.

NOTES

1. *The Imitation of Christ*, Thomas à Kempis, book iii. c. 3.
2. January 15, 1872. This, and the subsequent quotations of the words of Pius IX, are taken from *Actes et Paroles de Pius IX*. Par Auguste Roussel. Paris: Palmé, 1874.
3. *Traite du S. Esprit,* par Mgr. Gaume, 1864.
4. January 22, 1871.
5. De Maistre, *Soirée de St. Petersburg*. Xe Soirée.
6. Encyclical to the German bishops, 1854.
7. January 24, 1872.

A SELECTED BIBLIOGRAPHY

PRIMARY SOURCES:

Questions of the Soul (New York: D. Appleton & Co., 1855).

Aspirations of Nature (New York: J.B. Kirker, 1855).

The Church and the Age (New York: Catholic Publication Society, 1887).

The Catholic World, 1865-1888.

Archives of the Paulist Fathers, New York City.

The Brownson-Hecker Correspondence ed. and intro. by Joseph Gower and Richard Leliaert (Notre Dame, Indiana: Notre Dame University Press, 1979).

SECONDARY SOURCES:

Walter Elliott, C.S.P., *The Life of Father Hecker* (New York: Columbus Press, 1891).

John Farina, *An American Experience of God: The Spirituality of Isaac Hecker* (New York: Paulist Press, 1981).

John Farina (ed.), *Hecker Studies: Essays on the Thought of Isaac Hecker* (New York: Paulist Press, 1983).

Joseph F. Gower, "The 'New Apologetics' of Isaac Thomas Hecker (1819-1888): Catholicity and American Culture" (Ph.D. dissertation, University of Notre Dame, 1978).

————, "Democracy as a Theological Problem in Isaac Hecker's Apologetics," in Thomas M. McFadden, ed., *American in Theological Perspective* (New York: Seabury Press, 1976), 37-55.

————, "A 'Test-Question' for Religious Liberty: Isaac Hecker on Education," *Notre Dame Journal of Education* 7 (Spring, 1976), 28-43.

Vincent F. Holden, C.S.P., *The Early Years of Isaac Thomas Hecker, 1819-1844* (Washington, D.C.: The Catholic University of America Press, 1939).

————, *The Yankee Paul: Isaac Thomas Hecker* (Milwaukee: Bruce Publishing Co., 1958).

Le Père Hecker. Fondateur des "Paulists" Americans 1819-1888 . . . Introduction par Mgr. Ireland. Préface par 1' abbé Felix Klein (Paris 1897).

Joseph McSorley, C.S.P., *Father Hecker and His Friends* (St. Louis: P. Herder Book Co., 1952).

Charles Maignen, *Etudes sur 1'Americanisme: Pere Hecker, est'il un Saint?* (Paris: V. Retaux, 1898).

William L. Portier, "Providential Nation: An Historical-Theological Study of Isaac Hecker's Americanism." Unpublished Ph.D. dissertation, University of St. Michael's College, 1980.

Part III

VATICAN I AND PAPAL AUTHORITY,
1869-1870

4

Martin John Spalding

Martin John Spalding (1810-1871), Bishop of Louisville and Archbishop of Baltimore, as already indicated in the introduction, asserted prior to the First Vatican Council that papal infallibility was a theological opinion that he favored. During the Council he was on the side of the advocates of infallibility, but once the definition was promulgated he was careful to show the limits of papal infallibility and to explain how this definition fostered the primacy of the spiritual in Christian life and how it could be interpreted as a benefit for the modern world.

Martin Spalding was born in Rolling Fork, Kentucky to Richard and Henrietta Hamilton Spalding, descendants of seventeenth-century Pomar Catholic Marylanders. Martin received his elementary education at St. Mary's College in Lebanon, Kentucky (1821-1826) under Fr. William Byrne and his education for the priesthood at St. Thomas Seminary, Bardstown, Kentucky (1826-29) under Bishop Benedict J. Flaget, Fathers F. Kenrick and J. B. David. Like Kenrick, he then went to the Urban College in Rome (1830-34) where he received a doctorate in theology. From 1835 to 1848 he served various pastoral functions in the Diocese of Louisville. In 1848, he was consecrated Bishop of Louisville and served in that capacity until 1864 when he was made Archbishop of Baltimore (1864-1871).

The following selection on papal infallibility was written in Rome, one day after the First Vatican Council voted in favor of the definition. Spalding had been in favor of the definition throughout the council's debates over the issue. This document represents Spalding's attempts to explain and justify the doctrine to the Catholics of his Archdiocese. With a sensitivity to American constitutional values, he is quick to point out not only the meaning of the powers the pope has been declared to possess, but also the limitations of papal authority. He also argues,

151

against some opponents of the teaching, that papal infallibility is no new doctrine, that it should not shock Protestants, that it was no threat to civil government, and that the council fathers had complete freedom of debate during the council before the definition was voted upon.

TEXT

"PASTORAL LETTER OF THE MOST REVEREND MARTIN JOHN SPALDING, D.D.,
ARCHBISHOP OF BALTIMORE, TO THE CLERGY AND LAITY OF THE
ARCHDIOCESE, ON THE PAPAL INFALLIBILITY." (JULY 19, 1870)

Source: *The Evidences of Catholicity* (6th ed.; Baltimore:
John Murphy and Co., 1876),
pp. 441-445; 448-458; 460-477

VENERABLE BRETHREN OF THE CLERGY:
BELOVED BRETHREN OF THE LAITY:—

Nine months have elapsed since We left you, in obedience to the voice of the Supreme Pontiff summoning all the Bishops of Christendom to the great Vatican Council. During this period We have been busily employed, but We have not failed daily to remember our dear flock and to pour forth to the throne of grace our poor prayers in their behalf. "For you are in our hearts, to die together and to live together." (2 Cor. 7:3) And We have been comforted with the confident belief, that you too have not failed and will not fail to offer up your fervent supplications for us and for the success of the Council, whose deliberations may still be protracted for more than a year. . . .

The Vatican Council is composed of Bishops from all the quarters of the globe—from Europe, Asia, America, Africa, Australia, and the Islands of the Sea; they speak many languages, but they are all of one faith, and, in one sense, they are all of one tongue. The Latin language is still that of the Church, and her far-seeing wisdom and world-wide view are strikingly exhibited in the fact, that all the business of the Council is transacted, and all the orations are delivered in this language, which on this very spot, more than eighteen centuries ago, was spoken with so much grace and dignity by Cicero and Ennius—another striking historical coincidence, in which we find extremes meeting.

A Council means debate. Discussion is the characteristic of all deliberative assemblies, of which the oldest and best models have been the Councils of the Catholic Church. From that of Jerusalem, presided over by Peter, to that of the Vatican, presided over by his successor Pius IX., there has always been first "much disputing," and then later, after the matter had been discussed, and Peter or his successor had pronounced sentence, a great silence and peace. (Acts 15:12)

Never has there been a Council in which there has existed fuller latitude or greater freedom for discussion, or one in which greater decorum and dignity have been observed. Every subject, or *Schema*, has been thoroughly examined in its most minute details and in all its possible bearings. The regulations provided for a triple discussion; the first in writing, the other two by word of mouth. After the distribution of the *Schema*, the Fathers were invited to hand in, in writing, within a specified period, their objections or modifications, to the appropriate Deputation or Committee, which thereupon instituted a searching examination, and reported back the result of their deliberations in the shape of a revised and reprinted *Schema*. Then the oral discussion began, first in general, or on the general matter and form of the *Schema;* and next in particular, on each chapter and even on each phrase and word, the speakers at the same time presenting in writing the amendments which they deemed opportune. These amendments were printed and distributed among the Fathers, who were advised of the day assigned for voting on them. The vote taken, such of the amendments as were adopted were embodied in the reprinted *Schema*, and then the Fathers were called upon to vote first on each separate part or chapter of the revised text, and next on the whole. The last vote was most solemn; it was taken by calling separately all the members of the Council, each of whom might answer in one of three ways: either by *Placet*, or yea; by *Non Placet*, or nay; or by *Placet juxta modum*, or yea with a modification. These modifications, handed in, in writing, were printed and sent back to the Deputation for examination, and on their Report to the Council, the final preparatory vote was taken in the general Congregation, preliminary to the solemn and conclusive vote in the public Session.

The great mass of these debates regarded the forms of expression rather than the substance of the things themselves, though some of them, especially on the last Constitution, to which We will soon refer, touched to a greater or less extent the substance itself, for at least the opportuneness of the definition. Every sentence, every phrase, every word, every comma even,[1] was searchingly examined; and with a triple discussion and a triple preparatory vote, even humanely speaking, there could scarcely be room for a mistake. The judgments of the Church on matters of faith and morals when confirmed by the Roman Pontiff—as they necessarily must be—being irreversible and infallible, and regarding all time as well as all nations, all these precautions are wisely taken as a preliminary to the promised presence and assistance of the Holy Ghost, who then puts the seal of His infallible truth on the results of human research and industry. These are not only not excluded by the divine promises, but they are regarded not indeed as a condition of Infallibility, but as a moral duty of the assembled Fathers, who are bound to search the Scriptures and the Traditions of the Church before rendering their decision.

After these general remarks on the Council and its mode of procedure, We come now, Venerable and Beloved Brethren, to a subject which has excited much attention and interest throughout Christendom, and has provoked much discussion both in and outside the Council Hall. We refer to the Constitution just passed by an overwhelming majority of the Council,[2] on the Primacy and the Infallible Teaching of the Roman Pontiff, when he speaks *ex Cathedra*—that is, as Universal Pastor and Doctor, deciding for the whole Church a doctrine in matters of faith and morals. It is our duty officially to promulgate this Constitution, and to explain especially that portion of it which regards the Infallible official Teaching of the Pontiff. . . .

A brief analysis of this doctrinal exposition and definition will show us, Venerable and Beloved Brethren, how clear and comprehensive is the former and how carefully guarded in all its expressions is the latter.

The exposition begins with the declaration, that the supreme power of teaching is embraced in the Apostolic Primacy, which was instituted in the person of Peter and his successors by Christ our Lord for the good of the Church, that all His followers might be preserved in the truth and thereby in the unity of the faith, by being all alike fed not with poisonous food of error but with the wholesome aliment of sound doctrine. It then proceeds to enforce this teaching by the testimony of general Councils of the Church, particularly of those in which the East and the West came together for the purpose of re-establishing unity of faith and charity, interrupted by schism. These general Councils are three in number: the eighth, or fourth of Constantinople in the ninth century, the second of Lyons in the thirteenth, and that of Florence in the fifteenth. In these great assizes of the Church the subject of the Primacy of the Roman Pontiff, with its essential prerogatives, was specially discussed, and fully settled by general consent. The following principles were unanimously proclaimed, as clearly derived from the institution promises of Christ: first, that in the Apostolic or Roman See the Catholic faith has always been preserved immaculate, with the true and entire solidity of the Christian Religion, and that in consequence all are bound to be in communion with that See; second, that the Roman Pontiff, having received in the Blessed Peter the Primacy, with the plenitude of power, is bound above all others to defend the truth of the faith, and that all questions which may arise in matters of faith must be defined, or finally settled, by his judgment; and third, that he is the true Vicar of Christ upon earth, the Head of the whole Church, and the Father and Teacher of all Christians; and that in the Blessed Peter full power was given to him by our Lord Jesus Christ to feed, rule, and govern the universal Church.

The doctrinal exposition then proceeds to illustrate these principles by three great historical facts, which no one can gainsay, which meet your eye on almost every page of the ecclesiastical records, and which clearly prove that those principles were not merely theoretical but eminently practical, intimately connected with the practical working and the very life of the Church. The first fact is, that, in accordance with long custom and the ancient canonical rule, the Bishops of the Church were in the habit of constantly referring to the Holy See all ecclesiastical questions, especially those in which the faith was involved or might be endangered, in order, as St. Bernard says, that the damages to faith might be there repaired where the faith could not fail. The second fact is, that the Roman Pontiffs, on receiving such appeals, carefully studied the questions referred to them for final decision, availing themselves of all the means placed in their power, sometimes convoking general Councils, or enquiring into the belief of the Church dispersed, sometimes assembling particular Synods, or employing such other aids as divine Providence afforded; and after this careful preliminary study, they defined what they had ascertained to be conformable in the premises to the Holy Scriptures and Apostolical Tradition. Finally, the third fact is, that in all cases their decisions thus delivered were willingly accepted and adhered to by the Venerable Fathers and orthodox doctors of the whole Church, who were deeply persuaded that they could contain nothing but the truth, as the See of Peter could not but be preserved free from all error in virtue of the promise made by the Lord our Saviour to the Prince of His disciples: I have prayed for thee, that thy faith fail not. (St. Luke xxii. 32.)

After this doctrinal exposition comes the definition of the Pontifical Infallibility itself, as based upon and derived from the institution and promises of Christ, and as illustrated by the facts and principles just set forth, clearly showing the verdict of the Church of Christ for eighteen centuries on that divine institution and those divine promises. And lest any one should be led into error as to the nature and extent of this Pontifical Infallibility, and lest the enemies of the Church should take occasion from the definition to misrepresent and calumniate us, We deem it

Our duty, in officially promulgating the doctrine, to explain first what this Infallibility is not, and secondly what it is. In doing this, We shall not have occasion to depart from the tenor of the Record itself, which either plainly expresses or clearly implies all that We shall have occasion to state in illustration or explanation.

I.—WHAT THE PAPAL INFALLIBILITY IS NOT.

1. It is not impeccability or immunity from sin. The Pope regularly confesses his sins to the priest of Christ, like all other good Christians, and by the divine law, he is bound to do so as much as any other. Every day, before ascending the holy altar, he proclaims himself a sinner before God, before saints, angels, and men, and he thrice strikes his breast saying *mea culpa*—through my fault, through my fault, through my exceeding great fault. He makes the offertory for "his innumerable sins, offenses, and negligences," and before the communion he again strikes his breast thrice, uttering the words of the centurion: "Lord I am not worthy that Thou shouldst enter under my roof." He spends whole hours every day in prayer for himself and for the whole flock of Christ divinely committed to his care, with a deep feeling of the fearful responsibility resting upon him to answer before the Great Shepherd, whose Vicar he is, for their salvation. Though the Roman Pontiffs are and freely acknowledge themselves to be sinful men, yet it is a remarkable evidence of the divine guardianship watching over them, that nearly all of them have been men of edifying conduct and holy life, that about one-third of them have been martyrs or canonized saints, and that in the whole line of succession stretching through eighteen centuries, not more than five or six, out of two hundred and sixty, can be pointed to, even by the finger of enmity, as not having been much better in their private moral conduct than the average of contemporary worldly sovereigns; and of these few no one can say with truth that they ever attempted to change anything in the doctrines of the Church.

2. Infallibility does not attach to the Pope as a private person, nor as a temporal sovereign, nor as a private doctor writing or stating his own theological opinions; nor even as Pope delivering decisions in particular judicial cases depending for their merits on the testimony of men, much less in the words and acts of his ordinary life, outside the spiritual domain of faith and morals, of Church discipline and government.

3. The Papal Infallibility is not *inspiration*, such as was possessed by the Prophets and Apostles; nor is it a new *revelation* making known a new

doctrine; but it is only a divine *assistance*, by which, though naturally of themselves weak and fallible, the Pontiffs are divinely enabled "holily to preserve and faithfully to expound the revelation or deposit of the faith delivered through the Apostles."

4. Hence, it is manifest, that the Pontiffs cannot define any new doctrine not contained either expressly or impliedly in the original Deposit of the faith, much less can they define merely according to their own will or caprice, as their enemies are not ashamed sometimes to assert. As we have already shown, from the doctrinal exposition itself, they have always diligently used every means at their command to ascertain what is conformable to the Holy Scriptures and Apostolic Traditions before deciding on any question of faith or morals, and they will certainly continue to do so in the future; for nowhere is precedent more rigidly adhered to, or regarded as more sacred, than in the Roman Church, as every one knows.

II.—WHAT THE PAPAL INFALLIBILITY IS.

1. The Pontiff is infallible, not in his private, but in his official character, when he speaks *ex cathedra*—from his official magisterial or teaching Chair—as the Father and Teacher of all Christians, and when thus speaking, he defines, by his supreme Apostolic authority, a doctrine on faith or morals to be held by the universal Church; and this Infallibility derives, not from any personal wisdom or other quality in himself, but from the divine assistance promised to him in the Blessed Peter. The end for which it was bestowed is the good of the Church, that the flock of Christ may be always preserved in sound faith and guarded from fatal error and heresy, and that thus the purpose of Christ in establishing His Church may not be thwarted, but faithfully carried out and realized to the consummation of the world.

From this it follows: First, that the Papal Infallibility, in the strict sense of the definition, is confined to the domain of doctrine on faith and morals; secondly, that the Pontiff must *define*, or finally settle a doctrine, not merely declare more or less strongly a belief; thirdly, that the definition must contain a doctrine to be held by the whole Church; and fourthly, that the definition must be *official* or *ex cathedra*, according to the meaning attached to the word, as above stated.

2. The formula of the definition further declares, that, under these circumstances, the Pontiff "is endowed with the same Infallibility with which the divine Redeemer wished His Church to be invested while defining a doctrine on faith or morals." This portion of the definition

makes the official Papal Infallibility identical in its objects and limits, in its extent and certitude, with that of the Church itself; and as the latter is well known to all theologians and to all well instructed Catholics, the former, being the same, is thus easily ascertained by all who sincerely wish to know the truth.

3. To prescribe the error of those who pretend that the official Infallibility of the Pontiff is not derived from the promises of Christ made directly to Peter and his successors but from the consent of the Church, a clause is added to the definition of the effect, "that such definitions (as above) of the Roman Pontiff are irreformable, or irreversible, *of themselves*, and not from the consent of the Church." We shall have occasion to refer to this branch of the subject more at length further on.

All this is in full conformity with what the Angel of the Schools— St. Thomas Aquinas—wrote six hundred years ago, proclaiming the universal faith of the Church before and in the thirteenth century. He says: "The faith of the whole Church should be one, according to that of St. Paul (1 Corinth.), 'Let all say the same thing, nor let schisms exist among you;' which could not be observed, unless a question of faith which might arise should be finally settled by him who presides over the whole Church, that thus his decision may be held by the whole Church. Therefore it belongs to the authority of the Roman Pontiff alone to issue a new edition of the Symbol, (or Confession of faith,) as likewise to do all other things which concern the whole Church."[3]

In order to illustrate more fully this important subject, We will endeavor, Venerable and Beloved Brethren, to establish the three following propositions: . . .

I. *In defining the* PUBLIC *and* OFFICIAL *Infallibility of the Roman Pontiff in his solemn judgments and final decisions of matters of faith and morals for the guidance of the whole Church, the Vatican Council has set up no new doctrine, but has merely proclaimed in a more solemn manner a truth which was handed down from the beginning, and which, in all its essential principles, has been for centuries generally and practically accepted and acted upon by the Holy Catholic Church.*

We must view this subject from the Catholic standpoint, which is the Infallibility of the Church in her teaching concerning matters of faith and morals. Now we maintain, that given the Infallibility of the Church, that of the Pontiff follows as a logical and necessary consequence. For according to Catholic doctrine, the Pope, in the person of St. Peter, whose successor he is, was appointed by Jesus Christ the Rock upon which the Church is firmly built as upon a solid foundation, with the solemn promise made by Him who could not deceive, that the gates of hell shall not prevail against it (St. Math. xvi. 18); he is the divinely constituted Confirmer of his brethren, with the clearly implied promise, as a necessary consequence of the special prayer of Christ, that his faith shall not fail, while discharging the important office of confirming his brethren (St. Luke xxii. 32); he is the great chief shepherd of the one fold, with the office solemnly committed to him by Christ to feed the lambs and the sheep—the entire flock (St. John xxi. 15-17); finally, he is the visible head of the Church, Christ Jesus being the great invisible Head who purchased it with His blood, and who has by His solemn promises guaranteed its stability and purity of faith by His presence and assistance all days even to the consummation of the world.—(St. Math. xxviii. 20.) Heaven and earth will pass away, but His word shall not pass away.—(St. Math. xxiv. 35.)

Now this being the Catholic doctrine, how is it possible to conceive that the Roman Pontiff, so intimately and indissolubly connected with the indestructible and infallible Church by divine appointment, can be himself fallible in his public and official teaching for the whole Church? Can we logically conceive of an infallible and indestructible edifice built upon a fallible and tottering foundation? Can we imagine an infallible body of brethren confirmed, or strengthened in the faith, by a fallible Confirmer? Can we suppose that an infallible sheepfold can be guided, governed, and nurtured with the food of sound doctrine by a fallible chief shepherd? Finally, can we conceive of an infallible body directed by a fallible head? All these suppositions are plainly inconsistent and illogical; they are clearly unworthy of the wisdom of Christ and irreconcilable with His solemn and reiterated promises in behalf of His Church. In willing the indefectibility and the infallibility of His Church, He clearly adopted means adequate to this great end; and no matter how seemingly weak or imperfect these means might appear, His wisdom and His power could and would supply all deficiencies and infallibly secure the end contemplated. Evidently, in comformity with His plan and promise, the infallibility of the Church and that of its visible head are indissolubly associated; they stand and fall together; they are one.

Accordingly we find, Venerable and Beloved Brethren, that this great principle has been recognized and acted on by the Church from the very beginning. The Church has invariably and in all ages received and adhered to the solemn decisions of its visible head and supreme judge in matters of faith and morals; there is clearly no exception to this great fact of Church History.[4] Partial, even violent opposition there may have been, and there occasionally was, for a time, against such decisions; but in the end, the papal decision carried the day and won the general assent of the Church. . . .

For, the general fact of adhesion just stated reaching back to the earliest ages of the Church, there are two practical principles which have been clearly settled and generally acted on by the Church for centuries, especially for about two hundred years, since the rise of Jansenism and the controversies excited by Gallicanism. These are: 1st, that all Christians are bound to yield not only *external* respect, but also *internal* assent to the solemn decisions of the Roman Pontiff; 2d, that no appeal can be lawfully made from such decisions to a general Council—the only other tribunal in the Church to which an appeal could possibly be made. . . .

If all Catholics are bound to yield full and cordial assent to the official judgments of the Pontiff, and if no appeal lies from his decisions, is it not plain that if the Pontiff should err in such decisions the whole Church would necessarily be led into fatal error, the whole work of Christ for the salvation of men would be marred, and the infallibility of the Church would be at an end. The conclusion then is obvious: that to be consistent, a Catholic must either believe in the official infallibility of the Pope, or reject the infallibility of the Church. There is clearly no alternative.

You will naturally ask Us, Beloved Brethren, if the matter was already practically settled, why did the Vatican Council issue its solemn definition on the subject? The question is reasonable, and We will endeavor to answer it as briefly and as clearly as possible. The answer may be comprised in one phrase—*Gallicanism revived*.[5] It would lead us too far to go into the history or to discuss the principles of Gallicanism. . . .

Its principles, so far as they were theological,[6] consisted in a revival of the Decrees of Constance declaring the superiority of the Council over the Pope, in limiting the exercise of the papal prerogative to what is contained in the canons, without apparently granting him the power of exceptions or dispensations, and especially in regard to the received usages, rules, and institutions of the French Church; finally, in the declaration made in the fourth and last article, which we give textually, in a literal translation, as it contains the gist of Gallicanism as lately revived, to the utter astonishment of all Christendom.

"Likewise in questions of faith (we declare) that the Sovereign Pontiff has the principal part, and that his decrees regard the Churches, all and singular; nevertheless that his judgment is not irreformable, unless ratified by the consent of the Church."

Any comparison between the power of the Pontiff and that of a general Council, outside the time of a papal schism, is clearly preposterous, from the Catholic standpoint. For as all Catholic divines admit that there can be no general Council without the Pope, the question as to which is greater would resolve itself into this: is the Council of Bishops, together with the Pope, superior to the Pope alone; or this, is the Pope alone superior to the Pope with the Council of Bishops? Every one sees, at a glance, how very absurd such a comparison would be, and will hence infer that the Council of Constance could not possibly have intended to extend their decrees beyond the time of schism.

The attempt to limit the exercise of the papal jurisdiction by the canons, of which the Pontiff is the divinely accredited interpreter, and in which he may dispense in case of need, was clearly a limitation of the power of the Keys given to him in its plenitude, in the person of Peter by our Lord Himself; while the reservation specially made in behalf of the customs received in the Gallican Church seemed to look towards setting up a national church, whose local laws and customs should be of paramount authority. Happily, the dangerous principle was not carried out to its full extent, thanks to the deeply seated and abiding loyalty of the noble French hierarchy; else schism would have been the necessary result.

But the most dangerous of all the articles, as has been already intimated, was the fourth requiring the consent of the Church as an essential condition for rendering the judgment of the Pontiff on questions of faith—final and irreformable. This principle once admitted, many practical difficulties of a most embarrassing nature would arise, which would render the Papal decision of little or no effect. For how long should we wait for this consent of the Church, before accepting the Papal judgment as final? What consent would be required; that of a minority, or a majority of the Bishops of Christendom, or a moral unanimity? Should this consent be express or implied—a tacit and merely negative acquiescence of a clearly marked acceptance? And in the meantime, the proscribed error or heresy would have full time to spread and to seduce thousands, perhaps millions of the faithful. . . .

The fourth article seems to refer chiefly to the consent of the Church *subsequent* to the Pontiff's judgment; but besides this, there is an *antecedent* and a *concomitant* consent of the Church. The latter suffers no difficulty, when it refers to that given by the Bishops assembled in general Council under the presidency of the Pontiff in person or through his legates. This has never failed to be given, and according to the essential Constitution of the Church, it can never fail; else the Council would and could not be general, but would be plainly schismatical, and its decisions null and void. The antecedent consent of the Church, though by no means essential to irreformable finality of the Papal judgment, which derives its divine solidity from the immediate concession of Christ and His solemn promises to Peter and his successors, has, however, been often secured in advance; as has been already seen in the historical and doctrinal exposition of the Vatican Council given above.

In fact, all students of Church History, and all who are even slightly acquainted with the method of procedure invariably adopted by the Holy See in its doctrinal decisions, cannot fail to have remarked the patient and protracted deliberations which invariably precede the issuing of such judgments. No industry is spared, no means left untried, to ascertain the doctrine of the Church as contained in the deposit of Scripture and tradition. Sometimes, as in the case of defining the Immaculate Conception, all the Bishops of Christendom are previously consulted; sometimes, general Councils are convened; sometimes particular synods; in all cases, the matter in issue is maturely discussed by repeated Congregations of Cardinals aided by the most learned theologians: and no decision is made until the whole ground has been accurately and fully surveyed in all its parts and bearings. Thus, before the condemnation of Jansenism, from forty to fifty Congregations of Cardinals were held, many of them in the presence of the Pontiff, and the deliberations extended over the space of two years. Very generally also, provincial or national Councils are held on the spot where the new error has been first broached, and the judgment pronounced in these inferior Courts of the Church are carried up for final adjudication to the Supreme Court of Christendom, whose decision is final and infallible.

Without this permanent, ever living and present supreme tribunal for finally settling controversies on faith and morals, sufficient provision would not have been made by our Dear Lord for the faith of the Church, which He purchased with His blood, and secured from error by His infallible promises. General Councils cannot be convened except at long intervals, and under the pressure of the greatest emergencies. It is only with the greatest difficulty, that nearly a thousand Bishops, scattered over the whole world, can be brought together in general Council; and often the political condition of the world is so disturbed as to render such meetings impracticable. Accordingly, we find that nearly three hundred years elapsed before the meeting of the first general Council at Nice in 325; and three hundred and six years have elapsed from the close of the last general Council of Trent in 1563 and the opening of the first of the Vatican in 1869; while more than two hundred and fifty years intervened between the eighth and the ninth general Councils.

Under these circumstances, how could heresies be condemned, and the ruin of the Church be averted, unless Christ our Lord had given to the successor of Peter the prerogative to pronounce authoritative judgment with unerring and infallible certainty? To what other tribunal can recourse be had for finally settling controversies and preserving unity? Plainly to none other, as even, apart from the solemn declarations and promises of Christ, all Church History proclaims, with a thousand tongues. Most of the heresies which have in various ages sprung up in the Church have been solemnly condemned by the Roman Pontiffs, without the intervention of general Councils; and, as we have already seen, in no case has it ever occurred that the Church dispersed over the world did not adhere to and concur in the Papal decisions thus rendered. The facts of Church History thus furnish a clear and conclusive comment on the promises of Christ, and exhibit the infallibility of the Church as essentially identical with that of the Roman Pontiff pronouncing *ex Cathedra*, through the Apostolic authority imparted to him by the divine Founder of the Church. It is in this sense that Suarez, the great theologian and champion of Papal Infallibility, writes: "When the Pontiff defines, the Church speaks through her head; nor is the body separated from the head, nor is the head separated from the body."[7] According to the essential Constitution of the Church as divinely settled, such a separation is clearly impossible; the head gives life and movement to the body, the head directs and leads, the body obeys and follows. In the human body, the head may be separated from the members, but death immediately and necessarily ensues from the separation: the Church, which is the body of Christ, is immortal; and therefore no separation can possibly take place.

Thus, from the Catholic standpoint, whichsoever way we turn, we cannot logically believe in the Infallibility of the Church, without, at the same time, admitting the Official Infallibility of its visible head, the Roman Pontiff. And it is not at all to be wondered at that this cardinal point of Catholic doctrine should have been defined in the Council of the Vatican, as it had been so publicly impugned, with so much evil to the Church, since the close of the last general Council of Trent; particularly as the opposition to it has lately been re-awakened in a manner so fierce and so determined. It was surely time to settle finally a question which has produced so much excitement, to the great embarrassment and disedification of the faithful.

The decision presents nothing new in substance; it is only a solemn and authoritative definition of what has always been the general belief of Catholic Christendom, and which, from what we have already shown, has been admitted in practice, even by that small portion of Catholics who denied it in theory. These, in fact, could not have done otherwise; for resistance to the formal definitions of the Pontiff on matters of faith and morals, or yielding to them only external respect and not internal assent, would have placed them at once outside the pale of Catholic communion.

We pass now, Venerable and Beloved Brethren, to the second proposition which We promised briefly to illustrate.

II. *There is no valid reason for asserting that the definition will or should so greatly startle or shock the prejudices of non-Catholics, as to prevent or even retard their Conversion to the true faith.*

Why should it? If non-Catholics and unbelievers choose to believe less than we, or nothing at all, why should they be particularly shocked if we believe more or something? As We have already shown, it is not a question here of the innate or natural infallibility of man, but of the infallibility of *God*, who is true to His promises, omnipotent in His action, and faithful in carrying out effectually His high purposes, in spite of the weakness of the instrument He employs. And, in this view of the case, it is surely as easy for Him to guard from error one man appointed by Himself as the teacher and leader of His people, as it is to guard a thousand dispersed over the world. And if there be any difference of degree it would seem more obvious and reasonable for Him to guard from error in preference the head, that the body might not be led astray, to secure the foundation, that the edifice might not totter or fall, to enlighten and fortify the shepherd, that the whole flock of sheep and lambs might not be scattered, devoured by wolves, or led to poisonous instead of wholesome pastures.

A long acquaintance and a friendly discussion with intelligent and candid non-Catholics running through a period of more than the third of a century, has impressed Us with the conviction, that what they admire most in the Catholic controvertist is candor, directness, and an openness which leaves no suspicion that anything is left in the background or meant to be concealed. They admire a man, who feels strong enough to accept the whole position, and who is bold enough to meet every issue and to decline no responsibility.

The first things which strike a cultivated non-Catholic, when his attention is called to the Catholic Church, are its world-wide grandeur of extension, its superhuman and marvelous unity of faith and its tenacious consistency in so steadily adhering to principle amid weal and woe; and above all, its wonderful antiquity, indicated so strikingly in its long line of Pontiffs reaching back, through the wreck of kingdoms and the vicissitudes of human affairs, to the time when Peter and Paul first came poor strangers and pilgrims to the Eternal City, to set up the standard of the Crucified in the magnificent Metropolis and mistress of the world. The range of human history can present no parallel to this line of Venerable Pontiffs, through whose energetic exertions and untiring zeal apostles were ordained and successively sent out to convert the nations, and to knit them as fast as converted to the great Roman centre of unity, so that in the course of a few centuries the world became Christian, even far beyond the boundaries of the Roman empire. Thus was accomplished the promise of Christ, the great divine Shepherd of the flock, through the agency of His delegated chief shepherd: "And other sheep I have which are not of this fold; them also must I call, and there shall be *One Sheepfold under the one Shepherd.*" (Jn. 10:16)

The chief agents, under Christ, of this marvelous transformation were manifestly the Roman Pontiffs; and to them, whenever it is a question of the Church, all eyes are spontaneously directed. Now, in discussing with Protestants, we take this high standpoint, as our beginning, and from it we easily survey the whole field and point out all its bearings, with the official Infallibility of the Pontiffs established, and along with it the necessary adherence of the body to the head; we explain at once the secret of that wonderful unity and tenacity of faith which so puzzles the unbeliever in supernatural interposition and guidance. The fidelity of Christ in fulfilling His promise, that the gates of hell shall not prevail against His Church built upon Peter as a rock, and that his faith should not fail that he might safely and securely confirm his brethren, makes clear what else would be wellnigh, if not wholly, inexplicable.

True, without expressly maintaining the official Infallibility of the Pope as an article of faith, we have hitherto been able to explain and defend triumphantly the Infallibility of the Church, and to answer the objection as to the subject, or seat of Infallibility. But we have done so more or less haltingly in the view of the more intelligent and shrewder class of non-Catholic inquirers. Our usual answer has been, that, even admitting the separate fallibility of the head and of the body apart from the head, the two conjoined constitute the seat of Infallibility divinely guaranteed. This last proposition always has been and it still is the Catholic doctrine; but its explanation would probably be more satisfactory to the intelligent mind, if our process began with the head and thence proceeded to the body. It is much more simple and far more readily understood; and it obviates many objections which have been already sufficiently alluded to. The promises of Christ were first made to Peter, and then to the apostles along with Peter: he was full sharer in all the promises made to the apostolic college, while he had divinely secured to him prerogatives bestowed on none of the rest, nor on the entire college apart from him; and what is true of Peter and the apostles, is also true of the Pope and the Bishops.

While professing their belief in the divine mission of the apostles and in the inspiration of the New Testament, evangelical Protestants admit the Infallibility of Peter and of the other apostles, at least of such of them as were inspired writers. Why was this gift of Infallibility conferred on them? Plainly, that the whole body of Christians who would be instructed by their writings might not be necessarily led into error. It was for the security and common good of Christendom that this extraordinary gift was divinely bestowed. The Infallibility of the other apostles did not descend to their successors, the individual bishops; because these were to have charge of only particular and local churches, and their error would thus not affect or mislead the whole body, and it might moreover be readily remedied by the ordinary powers left by Christ with His divinely constituted Church. The case was widely different with Peter and his successors, whose jurisdiction was to remain world-wide, and whose error—if official error there could be—would necessarily taint and ruin the entire body of the Church. For, from the very beginning of the Church, from and before the days of Irenaeus, in the second century, it was a generally received axiom and rule of conduct, that "all other churches—that is, the faithful who are everywhere, MUST OF NECESSITY AGREE with the Roman Church."[8]

It may indeed happen, that ignorant and prejudiced men will sneer at and calumniate this doctrine, as making an idol of a man; but with the clear and, we trust, satisfactory explanations of the true meaning of the doctrine, as already furnished, we may well afford to disregard all such misrepresentations, which can mislead only those who wish to be misled. The Catholic Church has been so long accustomed to be assailed by such weapons, that she looks upon them as harmless to herself, and injurious only to those who wield them. The great and essential question is this: is the Church a divine or is it merely a human institution? If the former, no candid man with ordinary intelligence can be shocked or startled at its claiming official Infallibility for its divinely constituted head, foundation rock, and chief shepherd, in virtue of the solemn promises of Christ, who is God, and whose word cannot pass away unfulfilled. If the latter, then there can be plainly no question of infallibility whatsoever; and accordingly we are not at all surprised that the human sects lay no claim to this prerogative in theory, whatever they may do in practice.

But even in all well-regulated human societies, whether religious or civil, there always exists, besides a chief executive, a supreme judge or court, to which all cases in controversy are or may be ultimately referred, and whose decision is final and irreformable—that is, in so far infallible, that no remedy can be found in case of error. This is the case with our own free government; the judgments of the Supreme Court can be reversed by no other tribunal. It is not, indeed, intrinsically infallible, because nothing that is merely human is or can be infallible, and because in human things, which so soon pass away, infallibility is not essential. It is not so in divine things, upon which eternity depends, and in which error may be fatal for eternity; and accordingly we find, that our Blessed Lord, in His infinite goodness and wisdom, was pleased to guarantee from error His appointed supreme judge, that his decisions might be safely looked up to, in all ages, by His people, as not only final but infallible; as, in fact, His own judgments pronounced in His name by His own Vicar and minister plenipotentiary on earth. Thus He redeems His solemn promise made to Peter: "To thee will I give the keys of the kingdom of heaven; and whatsoever thou shalt bind on earth, it shall be bound in heaven, and whatsoever thou shalt lose on earth, it shall be loosed in heaven." (Mt. 16:18) Was ever promise more ample; was ever promise kept more faithfully? Let the solemn verdict of eighteen centuries answer.

To illustrate the Gallican principle, as compared with that of the Catholic Church, let us for a moment apply the former to the judgments of our Supreme Court. Suppose it were a principle of law with us,—that the judgments of the Supreme Court were not final until after the consent and concurrence of all or the most of the inferior Courts would have been previously asked and obtained! The legal mind would shudder at the bare thought; and even common-sense would be revolted, and would regard the new principle as disorganizing and necessarily leading to anarchy. The inferior Courts are all well enough within their own sphere and attributions; but to give them the power to revise and nullify the decisions of the Supreme Court would lead to the ruin of all well regulated jurisprudence, and consequently of all social order and security.

And this shows how groundless is the allegation, that declaring the judgments of the Supreme Court in the Catholic Church, or of the Sovereign Pontiff, final and infallible, carries with it the abrogation of the judicial power of the Bishops, who are also judges of the faith. They are judges, indeed, but inferior and subordinate judges in their own respective Dioceses; and this right is not only not impaired, but it is rather strengthened by proclaiming the judgments of the Supreme Court of the Church final and irreformable. Each Court is thus left in its own appropriate sphere, and there is and can be no clashing whatsoever between their respective powers, the inferior judges freely admitting that their decisions may be revised and reversed by him whom they recognize as the supreme judge by divine appointment. When assembled in Council with the Supreme Judge, they are associate judges, who must pronounce judgment in unison with their Chief; as always has been the case, and as from the very nature and divine Constitution of the Church, must always and necessarily be the case. The head and the members have always been united; and so long as the promises of Christ will endure, they always will and must be united. The history of all general Councils clearly establishes this; and of none is it more conspicuously true than of the present glorious Council of the Vatican. Fidelity to the Pope by the Bishops secures to the latter the fidelity and obedience of both priests and people under their jurisdiction; while the rejection of the papal authority has invariably ended in the Bishops becoming the slaves of the civil power, or the subservient instruments of the flocks over whom they are placed; all history proclaims this truth.

We pass now, Venerable and Beloved Brethren, to the illustration of the third proposition which We undertook to establish; and We must necessarily be brief, not to overstep the legitimate limits of a Pastoral Letter.

III. *The definition should afford no reasonable cause of complaint to civil governments, even to those which are free, or professed to be based upon what is called* LIBERALISM.

We have already, We trust, sufficiently shown that the definition will make no *practical* change whatever either in the *modus operandi*, or in the extent of the field to which the papal prerogative will still be confined, namely, to that of faith and morals. We cannot see how civil governments can take any reasonable umbrage at the solemn declaration of what has thus always been so generally believed, and so universally acted on in the Church, without any detriment to their real interests.

No intention whatsoever is entertained, or even so much as thought of, to interfere with existing civil governments. On the contrary, the Church and the Popes will always inculcate on her children, as in times past, the sacred duty of obedience to the existing powers, whether monarchical, liberal, or republican, in all things connected with the well-being of society, and the legitimate objects of civil government; and the Church and the Popes, as heretofore, will always continue to protest, in the name of God and of the right, against all encroachments of the civil power on the spiritual domain, and on the legitimate and time-honored rights of the Church. In all this, no change whatever need be apprehended; and all attempts to get up undue excitement as to imaginary projects of the Church and the Papacy against the rights or stability of existing civil governments, should be discarded at once, as not only signally mischievous, but as wholly groundless and purely malicious. . . .

The time has long passed—for three centuries—when Pontiffs, acting in accordance with the generally received and clearly established jurisprudence of the ages of faith, hurled the thunderbolts of excommunication, with annexed sentence of deposition, at the heads of tyrannical sovereigns, who crushed their people, and sacrilegiously invaded the rights of the Church. We have changed all that, and we have discovered an easier, though perhaps not a safer or wiser way, for getting rid of tyrants, and even of good though unpopular sovereigns. Bloody revolutions and blind mobs have but too often been substituted for what even the enemies of the Church must regard as the comparatively mild and wise adjudication of the Supreme Pontiffs, to whose sentence all once looked for a redress of grievances else unbearable. Bloodshed, rapine, confiscation have but too often taken the place of the sublime Pontifical arbitratorship between kings and peoples adopted by our fathers in the Middle Ages, when all were of one faith, and the tower of Babel with its confusion of tongues had not yet cursed the world with its dinning discord of creeds, and before infidelity became rife in the midst of Christian nations hitherto governed in accordance with the sound principles of Christianity.

Whether the change has been for the real good of mankind, or for the true and sound progress of humanity, we leave to others to pronounce. . . .

Governments, like garments, must fit, or suit the people for whom they are formed. Some may need a monarchy; some may prefer a republic. The Church leaves all this to regulate itself, according to the choice of the people, or the circumstances of time and place, confining herself to teaching both sovereigns and peoples their respective duties, as laid down by the law of Christ. She teaches boldly and fearlessly, though she may sometimes be able only to cry out in the wilderness to those who will not heed her voice. . . .

Beloved Brethren, there is *liberty* and *liberty;* there is perhaps likewise *liberalism* and *liberalism.* There is the true, and there is the counterfeit coin. There are three kinds of liberty, on each of which allow Us briefly to unfold Our thought.

1. There is the highest grade of liberty established by Christ Himself, "the liberty of the glory of the children of God." (Rom. 8:21) This is the liberty which Christ promised as the result of divine truth; "and you shall know the truth and the truth shall make you free;"(Jn. 8:32) and again, "if therefore the Son shall make you free, you shall be free indeed."(Jn. 8:36) It is the blessed state to which only Christianity can bring us; in which, ceasing to be the slaves of sin, we breathe the pure and free air of God's children, and our hearts swell with the feeling of exultation at having our bonds broken, the snares of the devil destroyed, and ourselves free with the freedom with which God has freed us; for "where the spirit of God is, there is liberty,"(Jn. 8:34) and "whosoever committeth sin is the servant of sin;"(2 Cor. 3:17) nor can such a slave chant the peans of victory, without, at the same time, shaking his heavy chains.

This is the liberty which the Catholic Church has always inculcated, and it is this teaching precisely which has rendered possible any other kind of liberty. We thus owe all modern civil liberty to the humanizing influence in the Christian masses of this precious leaven of Gospel liberty diffused among them by the Popes and the Church. Without this, true, real, solid civil liberty were an utter impossibility.

2. The second kind of liberty, and the highest possible type of it in civil governments, is that in which, whatever be the form of government, the rights of all citizens are respected and protected alike; in which, if it be a republic, the majority rules while respecting the rights of the minority; in which the taxes are equitably levied upon all citizens in proportion to their ability or means, and do not exceed what is necessary for carrying on the government; above all, in which the property and the just rights and laws of the Church are respected, and left inviolate, and in which all citizens, ecclesiastics included, are equally protected by the law, not only as written, but as executed: in which, in a word, without discrimination, especially as between the rich and the poor, all are equally protected in their legitimate rights, all are equal before the law, and all are equally governed and are equally benefited by the law. This theory of liberty was, in substance, laid down by the Catholic schoolmen of the Middle Ages, but it has seldom, if ever, been fully realized in this imperfect world.

3. Has this species of liberty, or has any kind of liberty worthy the name, been guaranteed to the people by these European governments which profess to be governed by free institutions under the name of *Liberalism!* Alas! Beloved Brethren, that we cannot answer in the affirmative in regard to all or even the most of them. Inaugurated by revolution, the first step of these liberal governments has usually been, to seize upon and confiscate the property of the Church, to trample upon her dearest rights and liberties, to expel her ministers, such of them at least as they might choose to regard as obnoxious, to suppress her monasteries and convents, to turn her poor, helpless, religious women into the streets, and to desecrate her holiest sanctuaries.[9] Even when the storm had passed, and they had settled down into something of a normal state, it usually happened that the exchequer was empty, and that the population was ground down with excessive taxes. In most of them, what is called *liberty* thus becomes not only an expensive luxury, but an instrument for the still greater oppression of the masses of the people. As vast standing armies are necessary to sustain the new order of things, a most oppressive conscription, pervading all classes of the people, takes the place of the hitherto comparatively mild method adopted for recruiting the ranks of the army; and their taxes are fearfully increased, and the

people are deprived of their substance and of their personal liberty. Among those who are the loudest champions of liberty, practice is not always in accordance with professions; and it is but fair to judge the latter by the former. Look at Italy, look at Spain, for the most recent and striking examples of what We here state.

It was necessary to state these things, Beloved Brethren, that you might be enabled to understand how it is, that the Pontiffs have so often protested against the excesses committed by these so-called European Liberals, in the hallowed name of liberty, which they, in too many cases, employ as a cloak for malice. The Popes have never uttered one word of censure against true liberty such as We have endeavored to depict it; on the contrary, they have done everything in their power to foster its growth. It is against the false principles which have been engrafted on the tree of liberty, not against the tree itself, that they have raised their voice of warning. It is but fair to judge their words and their acts by this standard of sadly existing facts based as they were upon false and dangerous principles subversive of all religion and of all justice.

And now, Venerable and Beloved Brethren, we have completed our task, imperfectly indeed but earnestly, and We must come to a conclusion, wishing you all blessings, both temporal and spiritual, and asking your fervent prayers in Our behalf, We remain in life and unto death your devoted Father in Christ,

Martin John Spalding,
Archbishop of Baltimore.

Given at Rome, outside the Flaminian Gate, on the Feast of it. Vincent de Paul, 19th July, 1870.

NOTES

1. One of the most earnest debates and interesting votes of the assembled Fathers regarded the retention or omission of a comma. The text often passed through seven or eight revisions, before it was regarded as satisfactory.

2. The final vote took place in the fourth public Session, held on the 18th July: it stood Placet 533, non Placet 2. The last preliminary vote in the public Congregation a few days previously stood Placet 451, non Placet 88, Placet with modification 62. Most of the last class voted Placet at the Session, while most of the non Placet voters chose to absent themselves, though they were perfectly free to vote, as the example of two of their number proved. Comparing the total number of voters on this occasion with that of the Fathers who originally belonged to the Council, We notice a falling off of two hundred and twenty-nine, of whom about twelve had departed this life, and the remainder, with the exception above indicated, had been permitted for legitimate causes to return to their Dioceses, except a few of them

were detained by illness. The great majority of them were in favor of the Infallibility. See Giornale di Roma, July 18, 1870.

The total number of speeches delivered since the opening of the Council was about 420, of which about one hundred were on the question of Papal Infallibility, either in the general or in the special discussion.

3. St. Thomas, Summa, 2. 2. Quaestio 1. Art. X.

4. The case of Honorius forms no exception; for 1, Honorius expressly says in his Letters to Sergius that he meant to define nothing, and he was condemned precisely because he temporized and would not define; 2, because in his Letters he clearly taught the sound Catholic doctrine, only enjoining silence as to the use of certain terms, then new in the Church; and 3d, because his Letters were not addressed to a general council of the whole Church, and were rather private than public and official—at least they were not published, even in the East, until several years later. The first Letter was written to Sergius in 633, and eight years afterwards—in 641—the Emperor Heraclius, in exculpating himself to Pope John II, Honorius' successor, for having published his edict—the Ecthesis—which enjoined silence on the disputants, similar to that imposed by Honorius, lays the whole responsibility thereof on Sergius, who, he declares, composed the Edict. Evidently, Sergius had not communicated the Letter to the Emperor, probably because its contents if published would not have suited his wily purpose of secretly introducing, under another form, the Entychian heresy. Thus falls to the ground the only case upon which the opponents of Infallibility have continued to insist. This entire subject has been exhausted by many recent learned writers.

5. We do not wish to be understood as here intending to cast any reflection whatsoever on the course adopted by those Bishops of Christendom, who, using their clear right of discussion in the Council, questioned the opportuneness or propriety of the definition. We refer to various publications outside the Council, which appeared in Germany and France during the last eight months: such as that entitled Janus, which filled all good Catholics with horror. Many of those were conceived in the worst *spirit*, far worse even than that of the older Gallicans, and they were openly scandalous, going in some instances to the very verge of heresy. They greatly contributed to render necessary and to hasten the very definition they were intended to oppose. The Presidents, with the concurrence of the great body of the Fathers of the Council, entered a Solemn Protest against two of these pestilent pamphlets, written in French, as replete with false statements, affecting the good name of the Council and that of the Holy Father himself.

6. Of the first article in the Declaration, which denies any temporal power of the Pope over sovereigns or governments, We will have occasion to speak further on.

7. Cum Pontifex definit, Ecclesia per caput suum loquitur; neque corpus separatur a Capite, neque caput a corpore.—Definit Fidel, O. 23, N. 27.

8. Ad quam (R. Ecclesiam) necesse est omnem convenire ecclesiam, id est omnes qui sunt undique fideles. Contra Haer. L. iii. c. 3. Bossuet and De Marca, unsuspected witnesses, both translate *convenire* by *s'accorder*—agree with—which is its undoubted meaning. So if the Roman Church could teach error, all the other churches would necessarily be led astray from the faith.

9. We ourselves have seen beautiful churches in Italy, with marble altars and noble paintings and statuary of the first masters, turned into military magazines and barracks; and all this in the name of liberty!

A SELECTED BIBLIOGRAPHY

PRIMARY SOURCES:

D' Aubigne's "History of the Great Reformation in Germany and Switzerland" Reviewed (Baltimore: J. Murphy, 1844).

Sketches of the Early Catholic Missions of Kentucky (Louisville, 1844).

General Evidences of Catholicity (Louisville: Webb, 1847).

Sketches of the Life, Times and Character of the Rt. Rev. Benedict Joseph Flaget (Louisville: Webb and Levering, 1852).

An Address to the Impartial Public on the Intolerant Spirit of the Times (1854).

Miscellanea: comprising reviews, lectures, and essays, on history, theology, and miscellaneous subjects (Louisville: Webb and Levering, 1855).

The History of the Protestant Reformation (2 vols.; Louisville: Webb and Levering, 1860).

SECONDARY SOURCES:

Adam A. Micek, *The Apologetics of Martin John Spalding* (Washington, D.C.: Catholic University of America Press, 1951).

Barbara Schlaud, S.S.J., "Peter Richard Kenrick and Martin John Spalding: A Study of Their Positions on Papal Infallibility" (unpublished University of St. Michael's College, Master's Thesis, Toronto, 1979).

David Spalding, "Martin John Spalding, Legislator," *Records of the American Catholic Historical Society of Philadelphia* LXXV (Sept. 1964), 131-160.

John Lancaster Spalding, *The Life of the Most Rev. M. J. Spalding, D.D. Archbishop of Baltimore* (New York: Catholic Publication Society, 1873).

Thomas W. Spalding, *Martin John Spalding: American Churchman* (Washington, D.C.: Catholic University of America Press, 1973).

Part IV

AMERICANISM AND MODERNISM, 1880-1910

5

John Ireland

*John Ireland (1838-1918), first Archbishop of St. Paul, became
known in the American hierarchy as the "consecrated blizzard of the
Northwest." His zealous advocacy of American values and his attempts
to bring the Catholic Church into conformity with those values made
him the chief American Catholic spokesman for the optimism of the
"Gilded Age."*

*Like other Americans caught in the sweep of manifest destiny, Ire-
land believed that America had a special mission in the world. He also
believed that the American Catholic Church had come of age and
should be a significant influence upon the development of international
Catholicism. In Europe as well as in the United States, Ireland tried to
establish harmony between the values of Catholicism and those of the
late nineteenth century. His enemies saw him as the potential head of a
schismatic church, one that was democratic in structure and reductionist
in theology. Because of his attempts to accommodate the church to
American values, he was accused of "Americanism" on both sides of
the Atlantic. In 1899, Pope Leo XIII, in an encyclical, Testem Benevolentiae, condemned the so-called heresy of "Americanism"—a heresy
that many of Ireland's opponents believed he held. Ireland himself,
however, denied that any of the positions he had ever articulated were
condemned by the encyclical.*

*Ireland was born in Burnchurch, Ireland to Richard and Judith
Naughton Ireland during the years of the Irish famine. At the age of
twelve, he emigrated to the United States with his family and joined the
westward migration to Chicago and then to St. Paul in 1852. In 1853,
he went to the College of Meximieux in the Diocese of Belley, France,
for a classical education. In 1857, he entered the seminary at Montbel
in France, graduating in 1861. That same year he returned to St. Paul*

to join the Union Army as a Catholic chaplain. From 1862 to 1875, he ministered in St. Paul as curate and then rector of the Cathedral of St. Paul. In 1875, he was consecrated coadjutor bishop of the diocese, becoming Archbishop of St. Paul in 1888.

The following selection manifests a number of Ireland's Americanist concerns. The address was given on October 18, 1893 in Baltimore on the occasion of the twenty-fifth anniversary of the episcopal consecration of James Cardinal Gibbons of Baltimore. Ireland took this opportunity to raise the banner of harmony between the values of the age and those of Catholicism. He encouraged the hierarchy and clergy to be independent leaders in reforming the church and making a Catholic contribution to American society. He tried to demonstrate that such leadership was already present in Gibbons and Pope Leo XIII. He also seems to be responding to the American nativists' charges that Catholicism is foreign to Americanism. Here he sees the world as a place of opportunity and progress and positively evaluates the aspirations of the age. The church, too slow to understand the new age, needs to conciliate in order to Christianize the ages' aspirations. God works both in the age and in the church; both need, therefore, to be harmonized and to correct and change each other's "accidental" accumulations.

TEXT

"THE CHURCH AND THE AGE"
(OCTOBER 18, 1893)
Source: John Ireland, *The Church and Modern Society*
(New York: D. H. McBride & Co., 1903), 105-131.

. . . This evening, it is my privilege to honor a man among men. The record of the Cardinal Archbishop of Baltimore! I speak it with pride and exultation. It is the record I should have traced for the ideal bishop and leader of men in these solemn times through which the Church is passing.

CHURCH AND ERA

The times are solemn. In no other epoch of history, since the beginning of the Christian era, did changes so profound and so far-reaching take place. Discoveries and inventions have opened to us a new material world. Social and political conditions have been transformed. Intellectual curiosity peers with keenest eye into the recesses of sky and earth. Intellectual ambition, maddened by wondrous successes in many fields, puts on daring pinions and challenges all limitations of knowledge. The human heart is emboldened to the strangest dreams, and frets itself into desperate efforts before all barriers to the fulfillment of its desires. Let all things be new, is the watchword of humanity to-day, and to make all things new is humanity's strong resolve. To this end are pledged its most fierce activities, which, wherever in the realm of man they are put forth, are exemplified in the stream and electricity of the new material creation.

In the midst of times so solemn the Catholic Church moves and works, purposing, under the terms of her charter, to conquer to Christ minds and hearts, individuals and society. Her mission to the world is the same as it has been during nineteen hundred years; but the world has changed and is changing. With the new order have come new needs, new hopes, new aspirations. To conquer the new world to Christ, the Church must herself be new, adapting herself in manner of life and in method of action to the conditions of the new order, thus proving herself, while ever ancient, to be ever new, as truth from heaven is and ever must be.

Now is the opportunity for great and singular men among the sons of God's Church. To-day, routine is fatal; to-day the common is exhausted senility. The crisis demands the new, the extraordinary, and with it the Catholic Church will score the grandest of her victories in the grandest of history's ages.

The Church and the age are at war. I voice the fact with sorrow. Both Church and age are at fault. I explain my words. When I speak of Church and age in conflict one with the other, I take the age as portrayed by many representatives of the age, and I take the Church as portrayed by many representatives of the Church. Church and age, rightly understood, are not at war.

I blame the age. Elated with its material and intellectual successes, it is proud and it exaggerates its powers. It imagines that the natural, which has served it so well, is all sufficient; it tends to the exclusion of the supernatural; it puts on the cloak of secularism. In its worship of the new, it regards whatever is old with suspicion. It asks why its church may not be new, as well as its chemistry, or its biology. A church bearing on her front the marks of nineteen centuries is, in its eyes, out of date and out of place. Pride and thoughtlessness are the evil and misleading characteristics of the age.

I blame the Church. I speak as a Catholic. I know the divine elements in the Church. I have full faith that those elements are at all times guarded by the abiding presence of the Holy Spirit. But I know, also, the human elements in the Church, and I know that upon those human elements much of the Church's weal depends. The Church has had her more brilliant epochs of light and glory, according as pastors and people scanned the world with clearer vision and unsheathed the spiritual sword with greater alacrity. The dependency of the Church upon her human elements is too easily forgotten, although the Church herself authoritatively teaches that undue reliance upon divine grace is a sin of presumption.

I am not afraid to say that, during the century whose sun is now setting, many leaders of thought in the Church have made the mistake of being too slow to understand the new age and too slow to extend to it the conciliatory hand of friendship. They were not without their reasons. The Church, in her divine elements, is unchangeable, supremely conservative; her dread of change, so righteous in a degree, is easily carried beyond its legitimate frontier, and made to cover ground where change is proper. The movements of the age were frequently ushered into existence under most repellent and inauspicious forms. The revolution of 1789, whose waters, rushing and destructive as the maddest mountain torrent, were crested with the crimson of blood, was the loud signal of the new era. The standard-bearers of the age often raised aloft the insignia of impiety and of social anarchy. Certain Catholics, indeed, as Lamennais, sought to establish an alliance between the church and the age; but they were imprudent in speech, and, in their impatience, they invoked failure upon themselves and discouragement upon their allies.[1] But with all these excuses, churchmen thought and acted too slowly. They failed to grasp the age, to Christianize its aspirations, and to guide its forward march. The age passed beyond them. There were a few Lacordaires, who recognized and proclaimed the duties of the hour: but timid companions abandoned them: reactionaries accused them of dangerous liberalism, of semi-heresy; and they were forced to be silent.[2] The many saw but the vices of the age, which they readily anathamatized; its good and noble tendencies they either ignored or denied. For them the age was the dark world against which Christ had warned His followers. The task of winning it to the gospel was a forlorn hope. It was a task to be accomplished only through some stupendous miracle from heaven, and, until the miracle would come, the ministers of Christ must withdraw into winter quarters, sacristies, and sanctuaries, where, surrounded by a small band of chosen souls, they might guard themselves and their friends from the all-pervading contagion. The age, abandoned to itself and to false and mischievous guides, irritated by the isolation and the unfriendliness of the Church, became hardened in its secularism, and taught itself to despise and hate religion. This deplorable condition was prevalent in some countries more than in others; but from none was it wholly absent. The Church had seemingly furled her flag of battle, her flag of victory.[3]

MISSION OF CHURCH TO AGE

It was a mistake and a misfortune. "Go, teach all nations," Christ had said once for all time. In obedience to this command the first apostles hastened through the Roman Empire, preaching to the sages of Athens on the Hill of Mars, to the patricians and senators of Rome in the courts of emperors, to the slaves in their huts, and the Roman Empire was Christianized. Even if our age had been radically evil and erring, the methods and the zeal of the early apostles would have won it to the Saviour. But, in veriest fact, the present age, pagan as it may be in its language and in its extravagances, is, in its depths, instinct with Christian emotions; it worships unwittingly at Christian shrines, and only awaits the warm contact of Christ's Church to avow itself Christian.

I indicate the opportunity for the great and singular churchman. His work is to bridge the chasm separating the Church from the age, to dispel the mists of prejudice which prevent the one from seeing the other as it is, to bring the Church to the age, and the age to the Church.

Men must be taught that the Church and the age are not hopelessly separated.

The age has, assuredly, its sins and its errors, and these the Church never will condone. But sins and errors are the accidentals, not the essentials, of the age. For my part, I see in the present age one of the mighty upheavals which, from time to time, occur in humanity, producing and signalizing the ascending stages in its continuous progress. Humanity, strengthened by centuries of toil and of reflection, nourished and permeated by principles of Christian truth, is now lifting its whole mass upward to higher regions of light and liberty, and demanding full and universal enjoyment of its God-given rights. All this is praiseworthy; all this is noble and beautiful. This is what we are asked to accept when we are asked to accept the age. When we accept the age, we reserve to ourselves the right to rebuke it for its defects; in accepting it we put ourselves in a position to correct it.

The Church, too, has her accidentals and her essentials. We should distinguish accidentals from essentials; we should be ready, while jealously guarding the essentials, to abandon the accidentals, as circumstances of time and place demand. What the Church at any time was, certain people hold she must ever remain. They do her much harm, making her rigid and unbending, incapable of adapting herself to new and changing surroundings. The Church, created by Christ for all time, lives in every age and is of every age. We find, consequently, in her outward features the variable and the contingent. The Church, at one time imperialistic in her political alliances, was, at another, feudalistic; but she never committed herself in principle to imperalism or to feudalism. She spoke Greek in Athens and Latin in Rome, and her sons wore the chlamys or the toga; but she was never confined to Greece or to Italy. In later days she lisped the nascent languages of Goth and Frank, and, in her steppings through their lands, showed not a little of their uncultured bearing and of their unformed civilization; but she was never limited in life and conditions to the life and conditions of Goth or Frank. Her scientific knowledge was scant as that of the epoch; her social legislation and customs, as rude and tentative. She was merely partaking, in her human elements, of the life of her epoch, her divine elements always remaining the self-same. Two or three centuries ago she was courtly and aristocratic under the temporal sway of the Fifth Charles of Spain, or of the Fourteenth Louis of France; but this again was a passing phase in her existence, and at other times she may be as democratic in her demeanor as the most earnest democracy would desire. Her canon law, which is the expression of her adaptability to environment, received the impress, now of Charlemagne, now of Hapsburgh or Bourbon edicts; but never was she herself mummified in Justinian or Bourbon molds, and her canon law may be as American as it was Roman, as much the reflection of the twentieth century as it was of the middle ages. Were not all this true, the Church would not be Catholic, as her founder was Catholic, the teacher and Saviour of all ages and of all nations. Let us be as broad and as Catholic in our conception of the Church as Christ was, and we shall have no difficulty in recognizing her fitness to all lands and to all ages—past as well as present, and present and future as well as past.

What! the Church of the living God, the Church of ten thousand victories over pagans and barbarians, over heresies and false philosophies, over defiant kings and unruly peoples—the great, freedom-loving, truth-giving, civilizing Catholic Church—this Church of the nineteenth century afraid of any century! not seeing in the ambitions of the nineteenth century the fervent ebullitions of her own noble sentiments, and in its achievements for the elevation of mankind the germinations of her own Christlike plantings! this Church not eager for the fray, not precipitating herself with love irresistible upon this modern world to claim it, to bless it, to own it for Christ, to foster and encourage its hopes or to rectify and remedy its defects, and with her impetuous arm to lift it to the very summit of its highest aspirations—to which by the Church's aid alone this doubting, quivering, hoping, despairing world can ever attain! Far, far, from Catholics be the chilling, un-Catholic thought!

I preach the new, the most glorious crusade. Church and age! Unite them in the name of humanity, in the name of God.

Church and age! They pulsate alike: the God of nature works in one, the God of supernatural revelation works in the other—in both the self-same God.

CHARACTERISTICS OF THE AGE

Let us note the chief characteristics of the age. The age is ambitious of knowledge. Its searchings know no rest and submit to no limitations. Be it so. The Catholic Church proclaims that all truth, natural as well as supernatural, is from God, and that the mind grows more God-like as it absorbs truth in more generous proportions. Two sources of knowledge there are, according to Catholic teaching, both from God— the reason of man and the voice of God in revelation. Between reason and revelation there never can be a contradiction; the so-called war between faith and science is a war between the misrepresentations of science and the misrepresentations of faith, or, rather, between the ignorance of some scientists and the ignorance of some theologians. The Church has no fear of natural truth; yea, from it strongest proofs come to her of the truth of supernatural revelation. The discoveries of the age, whether in minute animalcules or in vast fiery orbs, demonstrate God. Through all the laws of the universe they show forth an absolute cause, all-wise, all-powerful, eternal. The fruits of all historical research, of all social and moral inquiry, give us Christ rising from the dead and raising the world from the dead. They gave us Christ's Church as the enduring embodiment of Christ's mission. The knowledge of the age! The age has not a sufficiency of knowledge; and the need of the hour, the duty of the Church, is to stimulate the age to deeper researches, to more extensive surveyings, until it has left untouched no particle of matter that may conceal a secret, no incident of history, no act in the life of humanity, that may solve a problem. The knowledge of the age! The Church blesses it; the Church promotes its onward growth with all her might, with all her light.

It is an age of liberty, civil and political; it is the age of democracy—the people, tired of the unrestricted sway of sovereigns, have themselves become sovereigns, and exercise with more or less directness the power which was primarily theirs by divine ordinance. The age of democracy! The Catholic Church, I am sure, has no fear of democracy, this flowering of her own most sacred principles of the equality, fraternity, and liberty of all men, in Christ and through Christ. These principles are found upon every page of the gospel. From the moment they were first confided to the Church they have been ceaselessly leavening minds and hearts towards the full recognition of the rights and the dignity of man, towards the elevation of the multitude, and the enjoyment of freedom from unnecessary restrictions, and of social happiness mingled with as few sorrows as earth's planet permits. The whole history of the Catholic Church is the record of the enfranchisement of the slave, the curbing of the tyranny of kings, the defense of the poor, of woman, of the people, of all the social entities that pride and passion choose to trample upon. The great theologians of the Church lay the foundations of political democracy which to-day attains its perfect form. They prove that all political power comes from God through the people, that kings and princes are the people's delegates, and that when rulers become tyrants the inalienable right of revolution belongs to the people. The Church is at home under all forms of government. The one condition of the legitimacy of a form of government, in the eyes of the Church, is that it be accepted by the people. The Church has never said that she prefers one form of government above another. But, so far as I may from my own thoughts interpret the principles of the Church, I say that the government of the people, by the people, and for the people, is, more than any other, the polity under which the Catholic Church, the church of the people, breathes air most congenial to her mind and heart.[4]

It is an age of battlings for social justice to all men, for the right of all men to live in the frugal comfort becoming rational creatures. Very well! Is it not Catholic doctrine that birth into the world is man's title to a sufficiency of the things of the world? Is not the plea for social justice and social well-being the loud outburst of the cry which has ever been going up from the bosom of the Church since the words were spoken by her founder: "Seek first the kingdom of God and His justice and all these things shall be added unto you"? (Mt. 6:33) It is not sufficiently understood that the principles which underlie the social movement of the times in its legitimate demands are constantly taught in schools of Catholic theology; as, for instance, the principle which, to the surprise of his fellow-countrymen, Cardinal Manning proclaimed: that in case of extreme necessity, one may use, as far as it is needed to save life, the property of others. We have, of late, been so accustomed to lock up our teachings in seminary and sanctuary that when they appear in active evolution in the broad arena of life they are not recognized by Catholics; nay, are even feared and disowned by them.

It is an age of material progress, of inventions, of the subjugation of nature's forces to the service of man, of the building up of man's empire over all irrational creation. Will the Church condemn the age for this? It is her teaching that the earth was given to man that he dominate over it. Progress along lines of all human activity is the divine ordering. That the stagnation of human energies provokes God's anger, is the lesson of the parable of the talents.

CATHOLIC RELATIONS TO THE AGE

I have described the intellectual attitude which it befits us to assume towards the age. What should our practical relations with it be? Let them be all that the warmest apostolic zeal and the best human prudence counsel. We desire to win the age. Let us not, then, stand isolated from it. Our place is in the world as well as in the sanctuary; in the world, wherever we can prove our love for it or render it a service. We cannot influence men at long range; close contact is needed. Let us be with them in the things that are theirs—material interests, social welfare, civil weal—so that they may be with us in the things that are ours—the interests of religion. Let us be with them because their interests are ours, and ours are theirs, because nature and grace must not be separated.

The age loves knowledge: let us be patrons of knowledge. Let us be the most erudite historians, the most experienced scientists, the most acute philosophers; and history, science, and philosophy will not be divorced from religion. The age demands liberty with good government: let us be models of patriotism, of civil virtue, of loyalty to the country's institutions; and no suspicion will ever rest on us that we are the advocates of buried regimes, the enemies of liberty, civil or political. The age pleads for social justice and the amelioration of the masses: in social movements let us be most active, most useful; and men will recognize the truth that religion, having the promises of the life to come, has those, too, of the life that is, and seeing in the Church the friend and the protectress of their terrestrial interests, they will put faith in her pledges of supernatural rewards. The age exults in its material progress, its inventions, and discoveries; let us exult with it and recognize its claims to stupendous achievements; let us, books of history in hand, show to the age that the earliest leaders in modern material progress were sons of the Church; let us embrace every opportunity to work for further victories of mind over matter; and no man will dare speak to the Church a word of reproach in the name of progress.

And in all that we undertake or do, let us labor earnestly and energetically. The world succeeds in its enterprises through tireless perseverance and Titanic labors. It is in such wise that we shall succeed in our task. The half-hearted manner in which we evangelize the age deserves and entails failure. Steam and electricity in religion cooperating with divine grace will triumph; old-fashioned, easy-going methods mean defeat. We have not heretofore won the age; let us not put all the blame upon the age.

But I am afraid, one will say, of the opposition that I shall encounter if I speak as you speak this evening, if I act as you advise me to act. Do not, I pray, lose time in thinking of opposition that may come to you. If you dread opposition, you are not "of the seed of those men by whom salvation is brought to Israel."(1 Isacc. 5:12) Opposition is sure to come. In every historic transition there are reactionaries, who would feign push back into Erie the waters of Niagara—men, to whom all change is perilous, all innovation damnable liberalism, or, even, rank heresy. Heed them not; pass onward with Christ and His Church.

But the age, another says, is wedded to its idols; it is turned away from the Church and will not listen. The age will listen, if minds and hearts properly attuned speak to it. Men are always convertible to God (Wis. 1:14); the age is convertible to Him. I know as well as you the errors and the evils of the age, and you and I condemn them, even as God and His Church condemn them. I know that movements, holy and legitimate in themselves, are directed towards things false and pernicious, and that by many advocates of the age natural truth is made a protest against revealed religion; liberty becomes license and anarchy, and social justice means the violation of private right to property. Against this misdirection of the movements of the age, Catholics should labor with all their might. But to do so effectively, Catholics must first prove that they are heart and soul in sympathy with the movements themselves, and actively devoted to the advancement of all that is good and true in them. No one will say that during the nineteenth century Catholics have not, in loud speech and brave acts, made opposition to all the bad tendencies visible in the movements of the age. If, however, their opposition failed to arrest those tendencies, may not the cause be that they did not make clear their love for what is good in the age, while expressing their hatred of what is bad in it? The age believed that it was attacked in all its aims and activities; it regarded as its enemies those

who spoke, and it refused to hearken to them. To hold the age to truth
and justice, Catholics must be in it and of it; they must be fair to it,
recognizing what is good no less than what is bad in it; they must love
what is good in it, and work in aid of all its legitimate aspirations.

PROVIDENTIAL MEN OF THE AGE

The Church and the age! Their union is assured. The nineteenth
century has seen in its latter days men "by whom salvation is brought to
Israel." I name a few: Von Ketteler, of Mayence; Lavigerie, of Carthage; Manning, of Westminster; Gibbons, of Baltimore; Leo, of
Rome.[5] Two we especially revere.

Leo, I hail thee, pontiff of thy age, providential chieftain of the
Church in a great crisis of her history! How true it is that God has care
of His Church! It seemed to be a supreme moment in her life among
men. The abyss between her and the age was widening; governments
warred against her; peoples distrusted her; the intellectual and social
movements of humanity ignored her. Catholics, priests and laymen, ter-
rified and disheartened, isolated themselves from the active world and
made of their isolation a rule, almost a dogma. Humanly speaking, the
horizon was dark with fateful forebodings. Leo comes to the helm;
quickly he discerns the dangers from angry elements, from shoals and
breakers, and, under his hand, the ship moves in new courses; she sur-
mounts the highest billows, fearless of their fury; she reaches calm seas,
where triumphantly she ploughs the waters—the peerless queen.

Leo speaks to the age in its own language, and the age understands
him. He tells the age what the mind of the Church is in regard to its
hopes and aspirations, and the age wonders and admires. He acts, and
demands that others act, for the furtherance of those hopes and aspirations under all their legitimate forms, and the age praises and loves the
name of Leo.

Leo charges the age to go forward in its discoveries and inventions.
He writes: "Because all that is true must of necessity have come from
God, whatever of truth human investigation brings out, is recognized by
the Church as a reflection of the divine mind. The Church is not
opposed to the discovery of new things; she is not opposed to the searching for things that will add to the elegance and the comfort of life: nay
rather, the Church, as the enemy of apathy and idleness, ardently
desires that the minds of men be exercised and cultivated and made to
produce rich fruits."[6]

He opens to the scholarship of the world the archives of the Vatican, establishes universities in Europe and America, raises the standard of studies in the schools of the Church, and thus strives to place the Church in the van of the world's race for knowledge.

By his encyclical on "The Condition of Labor," he makes himself the pontiff of the working man; he gives to labor its charter, teaching labor not only its duties, of which it had heard so much, but, also its rights, of which it had heard so little. The poor, the oppressed, the masses of the people now know that the Church is with them, not merely as their counselor, but as their defender and their champion.

Leo's encyclical to the Catholics of France tenders to democracy the long-coveted approval of the Church.[7] Empires and monarchies had claimed as exclusively their own the smiles of the Church: these smiles are now bestowed upon the republic, the highest embodiment of popular rights. God be praised that we have lived to know and to love Leo!

In letters, in private conversation, Leo urges bishops, priests, and laymen to be ambassadors of the Church, to bear in her name to peoples and governments, not the sword of war, but the olive branch of amity and concord. His letters to Decurtins and De Mun are examples of his enlightened zeal. "I try to do everything, everywhere, for the Church," said Leo to me, "and so would I have bishops do, wherever circumstances permit." Nor does Leo restrict for Catholics the lines of action to confraternities and religious associations. In his letter to the Bishop of Grenoble, he counsels Catholics to work for truth and virtue wherever they are allowed to work and with men who, though not themselves Catholics, are led by their good sense and their natural instincts of righteousness to do what is right and to oppose what is evil.[8]

Leo has the courage of his high mission. Pope as he is, he has opponents within the Church; men whose sickly nerves suffer from the vibrations of the ship moving under his hand with accelerated velocity; reactionaries, who think that all the wisdom and all the providential guidance of the Church are with the past; obstinate advocates of self-interest, who place their own views and their own likings above the welfare of the Church of Christ. But in spite of all opposition Leo works, and Leo reigns. The Roman Pontificate is to-day invested before governments and peoples with prestige and moral power unknown to it for years; the Church is out upon the broad world, esteemed and listened to as she has not hitherto been in this century. Whole nations are saved! Leo is doing for France what France is unable to do; he is uniting her people, giving to her a durable government, and staying the hand of religious persecution. Say what some may, such are in France the results of the Papal encyclicals in favor of the Republic.

Leo shows forth in especial splendor the Church's catholicity—her divinely-begotten fitness for all ages and all nations. He withdraws the Church from political and social entanglements, makes her independent of the transient traditions of the past, and sets her before the world radiant in her native beauty and freedom, prepared to embrace and bless the new humanity of the twentieth century, as she embraced and blessed the humanity of preceding centuries, the Church of to-day as of yesterday, the Church of tomorrow as of to-day.

True, much is yet to be done before the union of Church and age is complete; but the work has been begun and is progressing. May Leo live yet many years! May Leo's spirit long dominate in the Vatican! All will then be well. Meanwhile, in America, let us be loyal to Leo, and work as earnestly as he does for the welfare of Church and of humanity, and in full accord with his teachings. We are especially favored by Leo. He lives among us in the person of his chosen friend and representative, one who makes the pontiff known to us as none other could, and who, in the acts and discourses by which he interprets Leo's mind, proves daily to us that Leo is, indeed, the pontiff of the age. The Church and the age! Rome and America! Their intimate union is heralded in the command of Monsignor Satolli to the Catholics of America: "Go forward on the road of progress, bearing in one hand the book of Christian truth—Christ's gospel—and in the other the Constitution of the United States."

Gibbons, of Baltimore: I cannot give to my words the warmth of my heart; I will give to them its sincerity. I have spoken of the providential Pope of Rome. I speak now of the providential Archbishop of Baltimore. Often have I thanked God that in this latter quarter of the nineteenth century Cardinal Gibbons has been given to us as primate, as leader. Catholic of Catholics, American of Americans, a bishop of his age and of his country, he is to America what Leo is to Christendom. Aye, far beyond America does his influence extend. Men's influence is not confined by the frontiers of nations, and Gibbons is European as Manning is American. A special mission is reserved to the American Cardinal. In America, the Church and the age have fairest field to display their activities, and in America more speedily than elsewhere is the problem of their reconciliation to be solved. The world has a supreme interest in this reconciliation, and watches intently the prelate who in America leads the forces of the Church. The name of Cardinal Gibbons lights up the pages of nearly every European book which treats of modern social and political questions. The ripplings of his influence cross the threshold of the Vatican. Leo, the mighty inspirer of men, is himself not seldom inspired and encouraged by his faithful lieutenants, from whom he asks: "Watchman, what of the night?" And the historic incident of

the Knights of Labor, whose condemnation by the Roman Congregations Cardinal Gibbons was able to avert, exercised, I am sure, no small
influence upon the preparation of the encyclical "The Condition of
Labor."

But Cardinal Gibbons belongs to America; let him be judged by
his work in America.

The work of Cardinal Gibbons forms an epoch in the history of the
Church in America. He has made the Church known to the people of
America; he has demonstrated the fitness of the Church for America,
the natural alliance existing between the Church and the freedom-giving
democratic institutions of America. Thanks to him the scales have fallen
from the eyes of non-Catholics; prejudices have vanished. He, the great
churchman, is also the great citizen. In him Church and country are
united, and the magnetism of the union pervades the whole land, teaching laggard Catholics to love America, teaching well-disposed non-Catholics to trust the Church. Church and country, Church and age, modern
aspirations and ancient truths, republican liberty and spiritual prince-
dom—harmonized, drawn into bonds of warm amity, laboring together
for the progress and happiness of humanity! How great the mission
assigned to Cardinal Gibbons! How precious the work done by him in
fulfillment of it!

I need not tell what qualities of mind and heart have brought the
reward of success to the labors of Cardinal Gibbons. The nation knows
them. He is large-minded; his vision cannot be narrowed to a one-sided
consideration of men or things. He is large-hearted; his sympathies are
limited only by the frontiers of humanity. He is ready for every noble
work, patriotic, intellectual, social, philanthropic, as well as religious,
and, in the prosecution of it, joins hands with laborer and capitalist,
with white man and black man, with Catholic, Protestant, and Jew. He
is brave; he has the courage to speak and to act according to his convictions; he rejoices when men work with him; he works when men fall
away from him. Cardinal Gibbons, the most outspoken of Catholics,
the most loyal co-laborer of the Pope of Rome, is the American of
Americans. I desire to accentuate his patriotism, for it has been a wondrous factor in his success. We have heard it said that frequent declarations of patriotism are unseeming in loyal citizens, whose silent lives
ought to give sufficient evidence of their civic virtue. Then let it be said,
too, that frequent declarations of religious faith are not in place among
devoted Christians; then, let the *Credo* be seldom repeated.

I have spoken my tribute to the Cardinal Archbishop of Baltimore.
A wide field remains ungleaned from which others may gather other
tributes.

My whole observation of the times, and in particular of this memorable Columbian year, convinces me that the Church has now her season of grace in America, and I often put to myself the anxious question: Will she profit by it? At times my soul sinks downward to the borderland of pessimism. I hate pessimism; I believe it to be one of the worst crimes against God and humanity; it puts an end to progress. Yet it tempts me, when I read in so many souls indifference and inertia, when I hear of the trifles with which soldiers of truth busy themselves, when I perceive the vast crowd looking backward lest they see the eastern horizon purpled by the rays of the new sun, and moving at slowest pace lest perchance they leave the ruts of the past and overtake the world, whose salvation is their God-given mission. But this evening, far from me is pessimism driven. I feel that religion will surely conquer. My soul throbs with hope. For I remember the God above me; I remember the leaders He has given to the Church—in Rome, Leo XIII; in America, Cardinal Gibbons. What one man can do is wondrous; what could not ten men—a hundred men do? O Catholic Church, fruitful mother of heroes, give us in unstinted measure men, sons of thy own greatness and of thy own power!

The jubilee of Cardinal Gibbons is not a celebration of song and tinsel; it is a lesson to bishops, priests, and laymen of God's Church in America.

NOTES

1. In 1830 Lamennais and his associates, chief among whom were Montalembert and Lacordaire, established the famous journal *L'Avenir*. It had for its device: "Dieu et Liberté," and for its mission, the alliance of the Church with democracy. Of *L'Avenir*, Le Père Chocarne writes in his "Life of Lacordaire": "The smallest care of ardent and absolute spirits is to reckon with opportuneness, patience, and time; their mistake is to forget that the logic of facts is not so hurried as the logic of ideas; that if the grain of wheat entrusted to the earth does not attain to maturity until long months have passed, the growth of an idea in the cold and slow soil of the public mind demands yet longer time; that it is much, in the lifetime of men, to have thrown into the world a fecund thought, leaving to a subsequent generation to see it germinate and blossom. This was the mistake of the men of *L'Avenir*."

Those remarks do not, of course, apply to Lamennais' writings after his secession.

Lamennais seceded from the Church. For Lamennais' secession from the Church, and the writings which he published after his secession, no excuse can be offered. But this much may, perhaps, be said, that if he had been left to deal with Rome alone, even after the Encyclical *Mirari Vos* had appeared, the strong probabilities are that he would have remained a dutiful son of the Church. Vide Spuller: "Vie de Lamennais," Brownson: Works, vol. xx, page 265; Mrs. Oliphant: "Memoir of Count de Montalembert," chap. vi.

[Ed. Félicité Robert de Lamennais (1782-1845), a French priest, was a well-known religious and political author who tried to reconcile the Catholic Church in France with the democratic age. Some of his ideas were condemned in two papal encyclicals, *Mirari Vos* (1832) and *Singulari Nos* (1834). After these condemnations, he left the Catholic Church and continued to write on political topics.

Charles René Forbes Montalembert (1810-1870), a lay French Catholic historian and politician, was, like Lamennais an ardent liberal Catholic who desired to see the Church freed from the control of the state. Unlike Lamennais, he remained in the Catholic Church after *Mirari Vos* and continued to advocate liberal views on the relationship of the church and the state in France.

Henri Dominique Lacordaire (1802-1861) was a famous French Dominican preacher who was a follower of Lamennais until the papal condemnations. Even after disassociating himself from Lamennais, however, he continued to foster the liberal movement in politics.]

2. Lacordaire lived to see the dawn of his triumph. In his latter days he was able to write to one of his friends: "In the time of *L' Avenir* we were rash men, blasphemers, heretics. Forty bishops reported to the Holy See seventy-two propositions taken from our writings. To-day, what a change!" Had he lived thirty years longer, and been able to read Leo's Encyclical to the French Catholics, and the Encyclical "On the Condition of Labor," what a reward was his for devotion to liberty and to democracy! "I die," he said in his last moments, "a penitent Catholic and an impenitent liberal." Feared and frowned upon by the authorities of the State, ignored and suspected by those of the Church in France, abandoned by his own brethren, he never changed, never despaired. Lacordaire lived for the future, and the future in which he put his trust has justified him.

3. Vide "La Papauté, le Socialisme et la Démocratie," par Anatole Leroy-Beaulieu, chaps i. and xvi.

4. Some foreign writers reject for *a priori* reasons political democracy and discredit the possibility of harmonious relations between the Church and republican institutions. Catholic theologians of high standing in the schools of the Church have amply vindicated what the writers referred to style "the pretended dogma of popular sovereignty." The hostility to the Church which the same writers seem to expect from a republic is perhaps founded upon politico-religious complications which unfortunately exist in certain republics, but which are in no way to be ascribed to the nature of a republican form of government. America is the most democratic of democracies, and in no country in the world is the Church more unhampered in her action. The letter [*Au milieu des sollicitudes*, 17 February 1892] of His Holiness, Leo XIII, on the duty of the Catholics of France towards the French Republic should reassure all who apprehend danger to religion from republican institutions.

5. [Ed. Wilhelm Emmanuel von Ketteler (1811-1877), Bishop of Mainz from 1850 to 1877, spent most of his episcopal life trying to free the German Catholic Church from state controls. He had a keen interest in social questions and was con-

sidered by many historians one of the primary influences upon the developments that led to Pope Leo XIII's encyclical *Rerum Novarum* (1891).

Charles Martel Allemand Lavigiere (1825-1892), French Bishop of Nancy from 1863 to 1867, Archbishop of Algiers from 1867 to 1884 and Cardinal Primate of Carthage from 1884 to 1892, is best known for his attempts to reconcile French Catholics to the republican form of government, his advocacy of Pope Leo XIII's policies in this regard, and his promotion of the anti-slavery movement in North Africa.

Henry Edward Manning (1808-1892), Archbishop of Westminster from 1865 to 1892, was a convert to Catholicism from Anglicanism. He was an ardent supporter of papal infallibility at the First Vatican Council and after the council became a vocal advocate of social justice in England.]

6. [Ed. Encyclical: "Immortale Dei," 1885.]

7. [Ed. The reference here is to Leo XIII's encyclical *Au milieu des sollicitudes.*]

8. Litterae ad Episcopum Gratianipolitanum, 1892.

[Ed. Albert de Mun (1841-1914) was an orator and journalist who dedicated his life to the re-Christianization of France, helped to launch Catholic social reform movements, and pioneered as a parliamentarian to enact social legislation.

Gaspar Decurtins (1855-1916) was a Swiss politician who like de Nun was interested and involved in the social and economic reform movements of his day. He tried to relate Christian doctrines to these problems, becoming a major exponent of the Swiss Catholic social movement.]

A SELECTED BIBLIOGRAPHY

PRIMARY SOURCES:

The Apostolic Church (St. Paul, Minn.: North-Western Chronicle, 1882).

The Church and Modern Society (New York: D.H. McBride & Co., 1896).

The Church and Modern Society. (St. Paul, Minn.: The Pioneer Press, 1904).

Archives of the Minnesota Historical Society, St. Paul.

SECONDARY SOURCES:

Dennis Joseph Dease, "The Theological Influence of Orestes Brownson and Isaac Hecker on John Ireland's Americanist Ecclesiology" (Ph.D. dissertation, Catholic University of America, 1978).

John T. Farrell, "Archbishop Ireland and Manifest Destiny," *Catholic Historical Review* XXXIII (1948), 269-301.

James H. Moynihan, *The Life of Archbishop John Ireland* (New York: Harper & Brothers, 1953).

Margaret Mary Reher, I.H.M., "The Church and the Kingdom of God in America: The Ecclesiology of the Americanists" (Ph.D. dissertation, Fordham University, 1972).

Thomas Wangler, "The Ecclesiology of Archbishop John Ireland, Its Nature, Development and Influence" (Ph.D. dissertation, Marquette University, 1968).

_____, "John Ireland's Emergence as a Liberal Catholic and Americanist, 1875-1887," *Records of the American Catholic Historical Society* LXXXI (June, 1970), 67-81.

_____, "John Ireland and the Origins of Liberal Catholicism in the United States," *Catholic Historical Review* 56 (1971) 617-629.

_____, "The Birth of Americanism: Westward the Apocalyptic Candlestick," *Harvard Theological Review* 65 (1972), 415-36.

Part V

SOCIAL JUSTICE, 1840-1940

6

John Hughes

JOHN HUGHES: A CHRISTIAN ECONOMY

John Hughes (1797-1864), fourth Bishop of New York, was a combative apostle for American Catholicism in his struggles against the lay trustees, the Common School Society of New York, and the "Protestant Crusade." He was also a representative of romantic Catholicism in the United States. Although he was never a consistent nor a systematic romantic thinker, he did idealize pre-Reformation Christendom (as had some of the Catholic romantics) and tried to integrate religion and social values. He rejected in particular the divorce of religious from economic values and called for the incorporation of a Christian anthropology into economic theory and practice. He rejected, in other words, the total autonomy of a capitalistic economic theory and practice and advocated a return to the more integral practices of medieval Christendom. In his judgment, the medieval Catholic Church had been the buffer against an exaggerated individualism and an excessively capitalistic spirit. The Protestant Reformation broke this buffer and thus released these twin evils in contemporary society.

Hughes was born in Annaloghan, Ireland, in the Province of Ulster, to Patrick and Margaret Hughes. In 1817, he emigrated to the United States and shortly thereafter enrolled in Mount St. Mary's College and Seminary in Emmitsburg, Maryland (1819-1826). After ordination to the priesthood in 1826, he assumed various pastoral duties in Philadelphia where he earned his reputation as an articulate and bellicose Catholic warrior. In 1838, he was consecrated Coadjutor Bishop of New York, becoming bishop in 1840. For the remaining twenty-three years of his life, he served the immigrant Catholic community in New York.

The following selection reflects his criticism of incipient capitalism and his advocacy of Christianity as the necessary basis for determining

197

the common good in society. Hughes delivered this address before the Calvert Institute of Baltimore and the Carroll Institute of Philadelphia on the 17th and 18th of January 1844. The speech was one of a number of popular addresses given before the immigrant and native American Catholic communities of those cities. Orestes A. Brownson, when reviewing this work, called Hughes "one of the ablest and most enlightened men of the times," an opinion he may have revised later in his life. Like Hughes, Brownson saw the laboring man's current distressful economic circumstances as a result of the Protestant Reformation's rejection of the Catholic Church's authority. "The rejection of that authority left men without the necessary moral restraints on their natural selfishness, free to regulate all individual and social matters according to the dictates of the self-interests of individuals and governments, instead of the dictates of Christian duty and love."[1] The only solution to current problems was to return to the authority of the "Church of Christ." The Church represented the only rival to the "Mammon" that "reigns in modern society," "and we cannot remedy this evil without some power stronger even than the money-god."[2]

In this article Hughes seems to be drawing upon William Cobbett's thesis, articulated in his History of The Reformation in England and Ireland (1824-1827), that individualistic or selfish capitalism arose simultaneously with the Protestant "revolt" against Catholicism. Such views were common among American Catholic apologists in middle nineteenth-century America.[3]

NOTES

1. *Brownson Quarterly Review* (April, 1844), 278-280.
2. *Ibid.*, p. 280.
3. Cf., e.g., Martin John Spalding, *Miscellanea* (Baltimore, 1894), pp. 455-505.

TEXT

A LECTURE ON THE IMPORTANCE OF A CHRISTIAN BASIS
FOR THE SCIENCE OF POLITICAL ECONOMY,
AND ITS APPLICATION TO THE AFFAIRS OF LIFE

Source: Lawrence Kehoe (ed.), Complete Works of the Most Rev. John Hughes, D.D.,
Archbishop of New York; comprising his sermons, letters, lectures,
speeches, etc. (2 vols., New York, 1865), I, 513-534.

Political Economy professes to treat of the material wealth of nations, and to trace out the laws which govern and regulate its tendencies to increase or diminution. By material wealth, it would have us to understand not only the precious metals, as gold and silver, but all descriptions of property, having an exchangeable value. Whatever substance, whether in the heavens above, or in the earth beneath, or in the waters under the earth, is consecrated to the use of mankind, by the expenditure of human capital, or human labor, passes, *ipso facto*, under the scientific dominion of Political Economy. . . .

Of its two great primary departments, the one comprises the inhabitants of the earth; the other embraces the material things which are required, and can be supplied, for the physical sustenance or enjoyment of these inhabitants. Now, it is found that these material things, before they can be fully prepared for the purposes of sustenance and pleasure, require the expenditure of capital, either in money, or labor, or both. Such things are divided into two stages of time; the one commencing with the first expenditure of capital on the raw material, and ending at the term of expenditure, when the thing is entirely prepared, and passes over to its use. This comprehends all the industrial pursuits and occupations of mankind; and the whole is designated by the term *production*. The other stage begins when the object is applied to its use; and this stage is called by the general term *consumption*. The latter of these terms represents the wants, whether real or artificial, of society; the former designates the supply of these wants. Population is also classed under two corresponding divisions; namely, *producers* and *consumers*.

But in general, the science has, so far been conducted rather in conformity to the special interests of particular nations, than according to any principles of universal origin or application. The countries which have paid most attention to this subject, in a scientific point of view, are France and England; and the works emanating from these countries, represent very distinctly, the national type, according to which the study has been prosecuted. Hence, although there are found in their treatises, principles supposed to be of universal application, still the actual condition of society, the nature of industrial pursuits, the bearing of commercial laws, peculiar to those countries, have come in so powerfully in modifying the views of their political economists, that their best principles cannot be appreciated, except by a just discrimination of all the circumstances, in which one nation differs from another.

Thus, for instance, confining our remarks to England, with which we are better acquainted, we are met with a distribution of the population into classes, which are not formed in our own country. These are, landlords, capitalists, and laborers. Generally in this country, the same individual represents all three. He is the owner of the soil, which he cultivates; and his means of carrying on agriculture, constitutes his capital. The three classes are indeed, found; but that which constitutes the rule in England, is only the exception here. It is not, perhaps, the fault of Political Economy, as a science, that it seems to regard wealth as the *end*, and human *beings* as only the *means*, in order for its attainment. We would not venture to make this a reproach; and yet we cannot help making it a subject of regret. Its writers did not create the science; they only embodied a copy of its workings in practical life, as they found it in the relations of men. The prominence which is given to wealth, in tracing out the most certain rules for the acquisition of it, cannot but have had an injurious moral effect, in so far as it enhanced the ideal value of riches in the estimation of the human mind. There perhaps never was a period, when men entered on the pursuit of wealth, with so much of what might be called almost desperate determination to succeed, as the period in which we live. And we may entertain a reasonable doubt, whether it be not owing to this, that individuals in high and honorable stations, have so frequently (and of late as never before,) jeoparded and sacrificed an unblemished character, rather than miss the opportunity of rapidly acquiring wealth; the means of which, circumstances and confidence had placed within their reach. Cupidity is a natural propensity of man; and it is to be feared that the theoretic, and practical, political economy of our age, has encouraged and whetted the passion instead of moderating and regulating its violence. It is certain, that self-interest is the great motive principle of human exertion; but it is equally certain, that Political Economy, as a science, omits what would be essential in a true definition of a man's interest. Of this we shall be convinced, if we examine the moral principle on which, whether in the practice of modern nations, or in the theory of writers, Political Economy is founded. If we follow it up to the mysterious link which connects it with the spiritual or moral world, in the breast of man, we shall find that it acts exclusively on that of personal interest. So much so indeed, that if England and France, and the nations of modern times, in general instead of being Christians, or at least professing Christianity, were Heathens, it would still be almost unnecessary to change a single word in the actual Philosophy or ethics of Political Economy. Here then, it is, that the importance of a Christian basis demands our attention. The advantages and disadvantage of position between Landlord and Tenant—between the Capitalist and the Laborer, are such, that if mere material self-interest alone be left to regulate their relations, it is easy to foresee that the weaker are liable to fall victims to the interests and power of the stronger. The truth of this proposition is manifest now, in the condition of England, where these relations are, and have been in existence for a long time. Now, if Christianity were admitted as an element in Political Economy, man—human nature—in consideration of the value which it has acquired by the Redemption, would be the first and principal object of solicitude, and all things else would be estimated by reference to this. Man's interest would be graduated on a scale proportioned to the whole of his nature, combining the spiritual with the corporeal; and the whole of his destiny, extending to eternity, as well as time. Then, indeed, self-interest thus understood, would constitute a principle sufficiently high and sufficiently ample to combine the acquisition of wealth, with sacred regard for the rights and privileges of human beings. But this is not the case. The landlords, capitalists, and laborers of England, are supposed to represent three great departments of capital; the one in territory—the other in money—and the third in muscular strength, or mechanical skill. Each is supposed to be free, and the only motive which is furnished in the present system, is that of individual advantage. But it happens necessarily, that what would be the advantage of one class, is directly opposed to the interests of another; and then each adhering to the common principle, it is clear that he or they who have most power to hold out, will be able to damage or destroy the antagonist interest of the other. The influences to be derived from a high and enlightened appreciation of human worth, according to the standard of revelation, seem to have been shut out from the practical and theoretic economy of modern nations. The interest of the body, in its relation with material wealth, limited, of course, to this present life, is the narrow and ignoble sphere within which political economy affects to move.

ENGLAND'S ECONOMY

I must not proceed, however, with views of this kind, until I shall have anticipated an objection which has already, perhaps, arisen in your minds, in seeming refutation of what is here advanced. And this is, that the immense wealth, the wonderful power, and unequalled prosperity of England, as a nation, is a practical proof of the soundness of her Political Economy. Or, it may be, that an assumption, which has often been proclaimed, has presented itself to your mind as a yet stronger refutation, namely: that the wealth of England, her power and prosperity are owing to her profession of the Protestant reiigion, and the play of those energies which that religion is supposed to foster and develope. Now, with the qualifications which will occur during the course of these remarks, I admit the truth of both these observations. That England is the wealthiest nation on the globe, is indisputable. But it is to be remarked, that this wealth is in the hands of a small portion of her inhabitants; and we can form some idea of its amount from the fact, that we read of private individuals, whose annual income is not less than half a million of pounds sterling. That must, indeed, be a wealthy country, in which the income of a private gentleman, for a period of twelve months, would be sufficient to pay the salary of our President for nearly a hundred years! But perhaps no stronger instance could be adduced, to show how unequally the wealth of England is distributed among its inhabitants, than such a case as this, contrasted with the hundreds of thousands and millions of the people, who are sunk and sinking under the combined evils of moral and physical destitution. Taking the population of the three kingdoms together, as constituting one political family, it will be found that there is no nation of the world, and above all no Christian nation, in which there is such an amount of poverty and wretchedness as in England.

She has, indeed, fought the great battle for wealth with other countries, and has, by universal consent, gained the victory. But how comes it that, while a few of her sons are rioting in the spoils of the vanquished, the cries of the wounded and dying of her own battalions, are heard on every side? How comes it that, in Ireland, out of a population of between eight and nine millions, there are over two millions absolutely dependent on the charity of others, scarcely a degree above their own condition? How comes it that, in Scotland, misery and destitution are hardly less general, and, from other causes, perhaps even more excruciating still? How comes it that, in England itself, distress among the laboring classes presses, at intervals, to such an extreme point, as to threaten, from time to time, insurrection and revolution? How comes it, in fine, to happen that, while the dogs of landlords and capitalists are well fed and well housed—while their horses are daintily provided for, the sons and daughters of Britons around them go forth with gaunt looks and sunken features, through want of food? These are results which *puzzle* political economists, but which never could have happened, if Political Economy had not been transferred from the Christian basis on which it was originally reared in that country, to the inadequate foundations of mere individual interest. I am willing, then, to ascribe to the Protestant religion, the credit of England's wealth; but her poverty, and the destitution of her millions, must, I insist upon it, be charged to the same account. This, however, only in so far as these results have been brought about by the Political Economy of that country. Other causes may have contributed to both—such as the system of colonization and military conquest, in which England has been no less distinguished. Neither would I have it to be understood, that I regard the national character of the people of that country as differing essentially from that of other nations. If it be true, as some say it is, that, as a nation or as individuals, they are proverbially selfish, I do not ascribe it so much to any inherent deficiency of moral excellence or feeling, as I do to their system of Public Economy, which has so long prevailed, that it has gradually become, as it were ingrained into the habits, principles, sentiments and associations of the people. Unfortunately, the same feelings with the prevalence of the same system, are extending to other nations; and if they should continue, as appears quite likely, it may be difficult, at no distant day, to determine which will be entitled to pre-eminence on this score. There is, it is but just to add, perhaps no other nation in which there is a greater readiness to come to the relief of public distress, when it can be remedied, than in England. But the root of the disease is deep in the social condition of the country: and the highest effort of modern statesmen, political economists, and philanthropists, is to apply palliatives to the evils which it must produce, without daring to eradicate or disturb the principle from which they flow.

Let us, then, go back to the origin of this system, and trace its workings in connection with Political Economy, and we shall, perhaps be able to discover the sources from which both the wealth and the poverty of England have been derived. At the beginning of the sixteenth century, England, as a manufacturing country, had no pre-eminence, and was scarcely equal to France, Italy, Spain and the Netherlands. Up till that period, the profession of the same religion had established, throughout all these nations, a certain type of uniformity, in reference to moral as well as religious questions, constituting a standard common to them all. This, however, did not interfere with the peculiar genius and national characteristics of each people. But, in reference more especially to certain social questions, such as the exercise of charity, making provision for the poor, seasons of religious observances, days of rest, and the like, the usages of the different nations approached sufficiently near to uniformity. England, as is known, broke away from this religious connection. The Christianity which she embraced in its stead was based upon an entirely different principle, as regards the social relations. The merit of good works was rejected as an erroneous doctrine, and it was ascertained that salvation is by faith *alone*. This is not the time nor the place to inquire which of these two systems is true, in a theological point of view. But they are mentioned in contrast, as having been calculated to affect most seriously the social relations, especially in reference to the condition of the poor. Up to that period, the influence of the Christian religion on the hearts of the people was sufficient to provide, by voluntary contribution, for the necessities of the destitute; and it was a great safeguard for that unfortunate class, that the wealthy were under the conviction, right or wrong, of the importance and advantage to themselves, of doing good to their neighbor. When the universal belief was, that even "a cup of cold water given in the name of a disciple, should not be without its reward," the efforts and sacrifices made spontaneously, to remedy or provide against distress, could not have been regarded either as vain or unproductive expenditure of capital.

But another and more obvious result of the change was, in the increased production which England was enabled to bring forth, in consequence of having abolished the religious holidays of the ancient church. These, at that time, were little short in number of one day in each week. The original motive for their institution was not exclusively religious. Those days furnished seasons of rest for the serfs or slaves of the middle ages; and thus, by diminishing the profits of their lords, and furnishing themselves with such opportunities of education and moral elevation as the times afforded, prepared them gradually for the free condition. By abolishing them, England was enabled to present a production of nearly two months' labor, in each year, more than the other States that still adhered to the ancient system. The consequence of this was, that, by increasing the amount, she diminished the value of her productions. Through this diminution in their value, she was enabled to undersell her rivals, first in all neutral foreign markets; and then, following up, with energy and perseverance, the advantages thus gained, she was enabled to undersell them in their own countries, and take possession of their own markets. Thus she began to drain other countries of their circulating medium, which became again a new instrument in developing still further the advantages of her position. . . .

Thus, precisely, has it happened in the history of manufactures in England, as compared with the other nations of Europe. The results of the entire national industry, during some forty or forty-five days in each year, gave her the first advantage over her rivals. This brought her capital, and drained from them their resources. It made her strong, and left them weak and exhausted. By means of capital she was enabled not only to increase the quantity, but also to improve the quality, of her productions, to a degree which they could not rival; and if, at different subsequent periods, they attempted to revive their manufactures, even by artificial means British skill and British capital were prompt, even at a little sacrifice, if necessary, to effect their extinguishment. Thus, England became a monopolist in the market of nations—thus, their wealth flowed to her workshops—thus, competition was destroyed abroad; and the foundation laid at home for that super-abundance of riches by which she has been enabled to borrow from her own subjects almost the whole of her national debt, amounting to some eight hundred millions of pounds sterling. It is not pretended that this is the only cause of the great aggregate wealth of England; but so far as it comes under the head of Political Economy, it was one great cause, of which the comparative poverty of other European nations is as manifestly another consequence. Here, then, we see the principle of interest operating in its national form; and, thus concentrated, powerful enough to sustain England, in competition, against the world. But having been successful in putting down all foreign competition, how did this principle operate on the condition of its own inhabitants? The contest now is among those three classes into which Political Economy is pleased to distribute her people. The interest of the manufacturer, as a capitalist, is in the profits of his production. When the markets are brisk and the demand great, he will make large returns by his investments. But still, if he can cheapen the cost of production, he will be increasing his profits on both sides. Hence the laborer must maintain his interest, against that of the capitalist. Both are free; and labor is a commodity liable to rise and fall, like every other thing, with the fluctuations of trade. But the position of the laborer is unfortunate, inasmuch as the interests of the capitalist must be provided for before his can be reached. He may, indeed, refuse to work for less than fair wages; but no matter how just his pretensions on that score, the hunger that stands at the portals of his dwelling, threatening both himself and his family, if he do not work, renders him perfectly unequal to the contest. He must give in; for the same policy which annihilated competition in other nations, employs that same competition at home, for the increase of profits by the reduction of wages, or even the occasional suspension of labor altogether. Add to this the introduction of machinery, within the last fifty years. It is estimated that the machinery of England, in the various departments of industrial production, is equal to the labor of a hundred millions of workmen. Besides at the present time, almost every nation has, at length, been aroused to the subject of manufactures, and has come to the conclusion that it is wiser to encourage and employ its own laborers, than to spend the amount of money which such employment may cost in the purchase of British goods. If, then, we take the actual condition of the poorer classes of Great Britain, depending in a great measure on this class of employment for the means of life, in connection with the rising manufactures of other States, and take in the future which statesmen ought to anticipate, it will appear doubtful whether, even in an economical point of view, the policy of England has not been a shortsighted policy after all.

Let us now turn to the condition of the agricultural laborers of Great Britain. One would suppose that *their* condition should be improved by the transition of so many from their ranks to those of manufacturing industry. But this is not the case; for, as a class, they are not so well off as they were several centuries ago. They cannot, at present, obtain for a day's wages more than one-fourth of the amount of food which could be purchased for a day's labor, up to the reign of Henry VIII. In an act, or rather the preamble of an act, passed in his reign, 1533, "beef, pork, mutton, and veal" are mentioned as the ordinary "food of the poorer sort;" so that the agricultural laborers of the present day require to have three hundred per cent, *added* to their actual wages, in order to live as well as their predecessors did, three centuries ago! Here is an awful deterioration in their condition. A precarious, and, at best, a scanty supply of the cheapest, and, consequently, poorest kind of food, is all they can now obtain in exchange or recompense for their incessant toil. And hence they are described and represented, in public and official documents, as on the verge of absolute pauperism. Why and how has all this come to happen? The question is the more startling, because, during this period, the aggregate wealth of the nation has increased many hundred fold. To my mind, however, the answer is simple. It has happened, because, during this period, the whole practical economy of the country has been transferred from the ancient basis, and left to be regulated on the exclusive principle of universal, material self-interest. It is all very fine, to talk, as *we* Americans do, of the "immense wealth of England;" and, as the English themselves do, of the "sturdy reliance and manly bearing of a British operative"—as contrasted with the humble deportment of corresponding classes in other European States. But Political Economy has not seen, or, seeing, has not dared to denounce the social blunder—the mockery of freedom—which are presented in the spectacle of the starving laborer maintaining a contest of competition with the bloated capitalist. Each, in that contest, is referred back to his own interest; and while the interest of the one is to increase, or at least not diminish, his capital, the interest of the other is simply to escape a death of starvation which is pressing on him.

If these remarks be deemed sufficient to explain *why* the condition of the laboring classes is so much deteriorated from former times, we may now proceed to explain *how* the thing has been brought about.

In order to do this, it will be necessary to recur briefly to the social condition of England antecedent to the change of religion in that country. Nothing is more true, than that a large portion of the wealth and of the real estate of the country were in the hands of the clergy. The origin of their title was as just and as authentic as that of any other property in Europe. The wealth which they possessed was the growth of time— the result of their own industry, economy, and the gradual increase in the value of their estates. The church, and its principles—or rather, the principle of Christianity, working out through the living agencies of the church—had become interwoven, to a certain extent, with all the relations of social life. It operated as an invisible bond, binding together the various ranks, classes, and conditions of the whole people; and correcting or reconciling the antagonism of mere material interests, by the influence of other interests relating to another world. It was as the cement in the social edifice. After the serfs of the middle ages had passed into the condition of tenants and free laborers, those who occupied or cultivated the lands of the monasteries and of the church had kind and indulgent landlords to deal with. In fact, all this property, as to its advantages, belonged rather to the poor at large, than to those who were its nominal proprietors. The law of the church regulated its uses. Its revenues, by this law, were divided into three portions. The first was sacred to the maintenance of the poor; the second was appropriated to the repairs of the churches, and the improvement of ecclesiastical property. Out of the third, the clergy were entitled to their support; and if still there remained a surplus, this also was a charge on their conscience, as belonging to the poor. It is not pretended in these remarks, that this law was, in all cases, strictly observed. But yet, the absence of all destitution and suffering among the poor, except in seasons of famine, is a sufficient proof that it was substantially attended to; since we find that there was no other poor law needed in the country, except that of Him who said, "The poor you have always with you, and when you *will*, you can do good unto them."

When the change of religion took place in England, the possession of those ecclesiastical estates, and this wealth, constituted perhaps the greatest *error* of the church. They excited the cupidity of the monarch and his parasites. And if monasteries were denounced as citadels of luxury, indolence, and crime—if celibacy was held up as a variation from the law of God, and an injury to the welfare of the State, the motives of the declaimers against both are fairly liable to suspicion, when it is remembered that the wealth of the assailed was to become the prey and patrimony of the assailant. The secular clergy were, with few exceptions, brought into the measures of the monarch. The inmates of the cloisters, male and female, were turned adrift on the world, and added to the ranks of the destitute whom they had hitherto been accustomed to relieve. The estates of the church were seized by the ancestors of many of the landlords and noble families of the present day. The fathers and mothers of the poor in the religious communities of both sexes, that were scattered from point to point over the surface of England, were driven from their peaceful abodes, and their estates seized in the private right of private individuals. The consequence of all this was, that in less than half a century there was not concern enough for the poor left remaining in the hearts of the people to provide for their support, without the aid, or rather the coercion of an *act of Parliament*. This is the first instance in the annals of Christian nations, in which the principles of religion were found insufficient to furnish a spontaneous provision for the destitute. The burthens of their support necessarily fell upon the occupants and cultivators of the soil. The lands of the church were rented out on the principle of the proprietor's interest, modified only by two considerations—one was the extent of competition among the applicants; and the other was, the amount of rent which might be exacted without depriving the tenants and their families of the means, at least necessary, for subsistence. Hence, weighty rents; and as the landlords were for the most part, the law-makers also, hence too, in process of time, those statutes in favor of landlord interests, which in our days are familiarly known under the designation of corn-laws. Does not every one see that all such legislation, whatever may be its other effects, must tend to diminish the wages of all the productive and laboring classes, by either diminishing the quantity, or raising the price, of bread? So that if you look to the relations thus created between the laborers of England and the other two classes into which political economists have divided the population, namely, landlords and capitalists, it would seem as if the whole practical purpose of public economy has been to reduce the working people down to that condition in which Malthus[1] has discovered what he calls the "natural standard of wages"—which means, perhaps, a little more than is barely sufficient to keep the workman's soul and body together.

It is impossible not to perceive, in all this, the injurious effect of the principle to which we have already, more than once, alluded, as the actual *regulator* of Political Economy in Great Britain, namely, *self-interest*.

Viewed according to the light of this principle, it was perfectly natural for those who were at once landlords and lawmakers, to secure to themselves the largest amount of rents; and to throw off, on others, the weight of every public burthen. In former times, the system presented the resources of the poor, from the very land which produced the crop. But now, the whole crop is claimed for the benefit of the landlord; and the tax, for the support of the poor, is to be gathered, not from those who grow the wheat, but from those who eat the bread; that is to say, in every nine cases out of ten, from the laboring classes themselves. Thus the laboring classes of England are placed as in a cleft stick, between capitalists and landlords and feel the effects of pressure from both sides: from the one side, in the reduction of wages; and from the other, in the increased prices of food.

The consequence now is, that in that country, including the three kingdoms, there is poverty and distress, such as cannot be found in the civilized world besides. In other countries there is less of aggregate wealth; but in no nation is there to be found so much, or such intense, misery, as among the poor of England. Nothing can show this more fully than the official reports made, from time to time, by order of Parliament, on their condition. Leaving the condition of the agricultural laborers aside, the reports on the condition of laborers in mines and manufactories present a picture of physical and moral destitution such as it is appalling to contemplate. We read, for instance, of children's being employed from the age of seven years and upward. And why is this? Because a child is as good as an adult person in waiting on the evolutions of machinery. Now the wages of a child is less than that of a man, and interest whispers to the employer to give the child the preference. It matters not that the delicate limbs of such beings are unable to support their bodies during the long hours of labor. It matters not that they become deformed, and contract physical maladies, which will accompany them through the remainder of their wretched lives. These things go on—for interest so determines it—until Parliament is at length obliged to pass enactments to interdict such outrages off the rights of childhood.

It is quite honorable to the feelings of the English people that they should sympathize in the sufferings of those who are in the condition of slaves throughout the world. But while her gaze can extend across the Atlantic; and while her honest and genuine sympathy is often disgraced by the *cant* and fanaticism of those who would be its organs, surely it cannot be wrong for us to sympathize with those of her own population, whom avarice, or the interests of capital have buried in the bowels of the earth in her mining districts. Delicate women and tender children, as reported to Parliament, were found in the mines, *with harness fitted to them*, and obliged to drag loads on their hands and knees, after the manner of beasts. Passing from these again, to the pauper class, we see that the Public Economy directs their classification in a manner such as, in some countries, would be regarded as a violation of the rights of human nature. The dearest ties—even those which constitute the last sweet drop, in the cup of poverty, are rudely disregarded and ruptured. Husbands and wives, parents and children, brothers and sisters, are separated from each other, and distributed in the establishments of public relief, as if they were malefactors, guilty of some social crime. Now, the worst feature in this system of Political Economy is, not precisely that the facts are so; but that the prejudices of the nation, like the principles of the science itself, as looking to individual interest as the life-spring of society, do not allow them even to conceive that things ought to be otherwise. And so true is this, that, according to the recognized principle, you may pass all the various members of society in review, and you will be unable to discover to whom the fault belongs; and in fact, according to the principle of self-interest, the fault belongs nowhere! Every man for himself.

SOCIALIST THEORIES AND PROGRAMS

It is the contemplation of all this that has impelled many benevolent, but, as I conceive, mistaken persons, to conclude that society in general is organized on a vicious principle. Individuals of this description have stood forth, in France, England, and this country also, flattering themselves with the hope of being able to withdraw some portion of their fellow-beings from the miseries which they regard as essentially connected with the actual state of things. For this purpose, various schemes, and schools of Political Economy have made their appearance, encouraging separate systems of private socialism, founded each on some favorite theory. These either have failed, or will fail; and principally for the reason that, while they have discovered the *self-interest* which operates so injuriously in the present systems, they have not discovered in those which they would substitute any other principle of sufficient power to correct it. This can be done only through a renovated faith, and a practical exercise of the virtues prescribed by religion. The tendency of society in general, at least in all that appertains to Political Economy, is in the opposite direction; and there is but little hope that its course will be arrested until nations, as well as individuals, shall have been punished for their great social error.

RELIGIOUS SOLUTIONS

How much ink has been shed in describing the evils which now press on the people, at least the laboring classes, of Great Britain! How much of profound meditation has been employed, in vain efforts to find a solution for the social problem of that country! And though many of her statesmen have begun to trace these evils back to their true cause, yet few have proclaimed the discovery, and fewer still have ventured to suggest the true remedy. Sometimes the evils are charged to one cause, sometimes to another. Now, it is the "restrictions on commerce;" and now, is an "excess of population over and above the wants of consumption." But no one has, as yet, contended for the true cause; that is, the absence of a religious power which should be able to extend the obligation of *duties*, in exact proportion with the extension of *rights*. The social machine, in its relations to Political Economy, has been left to regulate itself, by the spring of mere individual interest; and it is manifest that the weights and balances necessary to restore its equilibrium and to regulate its motion, cannot be adjusted except by the invocation of some *extrinsic* power, such as can be found in practical Christianity alone. The earth is not expected to furnish itself with light and heat: these come from the sun. So also, with regard to the practical Political Economy of modern nations—unless its lips be touched and purified with living coals from the altars of Divine Religion, it can never accomplish the entire purpose, according to which society is an institution of God. Any religion which can accomplish this, whatever may be the truth or the error of its other dogmas, will have rendered essential service to humanity. It is on this account that Political Economy, as a science, appears to me inadequate and defective. It would be more complete, and certainly more exalted, if, instead of regarding man as the mere "producer" and "consumer" of material wealth, it took cognizance of his intellectual, moral, and religious nature. It may, however, be objected, that these faculties, being spiritual and not material, have nothing to do with the subject. This seems to me an unfounded conclusion. The ancient Persians, for instance, held, as a religious opinion, that anything which could defile the waters of the ocean was sinful. Here, then, is an important branch of Political Economy—maritime commerce—affected by a religious conviction. . . .

In assuming the "importance of a Christian basis" for Political Economy, I did not indeed imagine, as you may easily conceive, that the system now so deeply and almost universally established, could be transferred to any other foundation than that on which it rests. But when I consider the *nature* of the evils which press upon so large a portion of modern society, it seems to me that a preventive, if not a remedy, is discoverable in the Political Economy (so to call it) of the old Catholic Church. She had, preeminently, the faculty of guiding the affections and energies of mankind, in the direction most required by the actual wants of society in given times and circumstances. She differed from the modern religions, essentially on *one* great point; namely, that, while they teach that salvation is "by faith alone," and that good works have no merit, though they are provided for, as consequences of faith, *she* taught that they are to be concomitants of belief; that faith without works, is dead in itself! and that whatever good we do to one of the least of Christ's disciples, He will reward as if done to himself. This is the *turning point* of difference between the Political Economy of the Catholic Church and that of the religions which have been substituted in its stead. Thus, she created an interest not to be estimated by the acquisition or exchange of material wealth, but by the consideration of advantages in the spiritual order and in the life to come. This doctrine, like the principle of life in the human body, vivified the spirit, and influenced the actions of all her members. Besides, she conceived human nature as having been *exalted* and *ennobled* through the Incarnation and Redemption, by the Son of God. Hence she valued human beings according to the high dignity of their ransom, irrespective of wealth or poverty. She has, indeed, been reproached with the tendency to abridge the rights of men. But the explanation of this is to be found in the fact, that the inherent selfishness of fallen humanity prompts them to claim injurious immunities; while, as she conceived, her office was to apportion *duties* according to the means which providence furnished for the discharge of them. Men are prompt to assert their rights; but prone to forget that every right is accompanied with a corresponding duty. To every class and condition she assigned its own peculiar range of Christian obligation. To sovereigns and legislators, those of justice and mercy in the enactment and execution of laws. To the rich, moderation in enjoyment, and liberality toward the poor. To the poor, patience under their trials, and affection toward their wealthier brethren. Toward all, the common obligation of loving one another, not in word, but in *deed*. Neither was this by a uniform development of the principles of the Christian doctrine from the pulpit alone, but by a rigid process of self-examination and self-accusation, which was incumbent on every individual, when preparing for the Sacraments of Penance and of the Holy Eucharist. Here, the lawgiver, the landlord, the capitalist, and the laborer—all men of all classes—were required to stand at least once a year in *judgment upon themselves*, in the presence of God and of his minister.

Far be it from me to insinuate or assert, that these great leading duties are not set forth to the people by the religions which have taken the place of the Catholic faith in Great Britain. But I think it will be evident that, in them all, there are wanting the means for their practical inculcation. First, because the paramount motive has been utterly destroyed by rejecting the "merit of good works," and proclaiming "salvation by faith alone." It is, indeed, alleged that, by a higher motive still, works, as the consequence, or fruits, or evidence, of faith, are provided for. But still, those who enjoin works of this kind, since they declare them to be of "no merit" in the sight of God, seem to pull down with one hand what they have built up with the other. Besides this, in the new system of religion, every man claims to be the judge of his moral duties, as well as of his religious faith. Thus you perceive that the only motives left, as inducements for the performance of good works, in this system, are essentially of the *human* and *temporal* order. Now the manifestations of these fundamental principles are obvious, in the social developments under the influence of the two religions. Of its consequences, in the one case, the preceding remarks of this lecture are a sufficient exhibition. Rights are claimed—interests are prosecuted—every one that can, throws the burthen from himself. Each is the judge of his own moral and social duties—and self-love blinds him against what would require the sacrifice of his material interests, even if religion presented any adequate motive for making that sacrifice. Wealth is accumulating enormously on one side—poverty, deep and distressing, spreads on the other: England is the richest and the poorest country on the globe; and where, or to whom, belongs the guilt of this social anomaly, no man can determine!

The type of the other doctrine has developed itself in those principles and institutions which incur the censure, and sometimes the hatred, even of those who are the victims of their overthrow. If they were errors in religion, it is the more to be regretted, as they would have been blessings in Social, if not in Political Economy. They would have been, first of all, a merciful resource for the condition of the poor, which now constitutes the great *puzzle* of Political Economists, throughout the three kingdoms. The interests of man—taking in his spiritual nature and his eternal destiny—would be surveyed from a high and holy eminence. And when the rich man gave of his abundance to the needy, he would be acting, not *against*, but according to this principle of *Christian* interest. When the prince or the noble, moved by the *"Amor Jesu nobilis,"* descended from his elevated position, to put on the sandals, the garment, and the girdle of religious poverty, in some monastic order, he understood, perfectly well, what he was about—comprehended the advantage of the step; and, whether he was mistaken or not, his determination was of infinite importance to the condition of the destitute. He became poor from a religious motive, having first, perhaps, given his property to the relief of the class to whose condition he attached himself. He became their mediator with the rich—his own example had a powerful influence on them—he represented the necessity of alms-deeds—he spoke of their common Saviour, as having, in his own person, selected the condition of poverty; and reminded them that whatever they did for their suffering brethren, was done for Christ.

It was by the spirit of this doctrine of good works, that hospitals and asylums for the afflicted, sprang, as if spontaneously, into existence, in all parts of Great Britain, as well as of other European countries. It was by this that every kind of social evil, whether in physical suffering or in moral destitution, found whole armies of *volunteers*, ready to go in the face of pestilence and death, and this without human recompense, to counteract its ravages. It was by this, that individuals were constantly found ready to devote themselves to every species of good works.

The question in connection with this subject, is not whether these individuals were acting under a genuine principle of Christianity or not—but it is, whether their devotion had any bearing upon the Political Economy of the country. That it had, is in my mind, beyond dispute. Firstly: In such a state of things, no poor law would be necessary. Secondly: The burthen of their support would not be regarded as a burthen, but as a privilege, and would fall on individuals in the rank of landlords and capitalists, instead of laborers as at present. Thirdly: The expense of supporting the poor would not be increased by the enormous sums which are paid to state officers, in that department. Fourthly: The ecclesiastical revenues, which have now quite a different direction, would be applied to that purpose. Fifthly: But besides all this, the influence of the doctrine I have alluded to, would infuse a spirit of gentle kindness into the treatment of the poor, which would leave no room for those dark and bitter passions against society, with which their breasts are now, too often, agitated; for it is a shocking feature of our times, that distinguished writers on Political Economy, have gone so far, as to maintain that poverty when it reaches the point of destitution ought to be treated as "infamy," in order to make the struggle for self support of the sinking laborer "honorable."

If this reasoning, and these reflections be correct we see what has been the cause of the prevailing distress; and what would have been the preventive or the remedy. And in either case, the great social calamity which is every day becoming more and more formidable, in the estimation of British statesmen and political economists, instead of being, as it now is, apparently irremediable, would never have existed at all.

Some may imagine that in following out this subject, my judgment has been warped by a natural partiality for the religion to which I belong. This is, indeed, possible; but I can only say, that if it be true, I am entirely unconscious of it. Neither, at the present day, are these views peculiar to Catholics: a declaration briefly uttered, among others, by a distinguished Protestant statesman, Lord John Manners, expresses a similar conclusion, when he says, "that the re-establishment of the monasteries which have been destroyed, can alone provide a suitable remedy for the condition of the poor."

What, we may now ask, would be the influence of the Political Economy of the ancient Church on the class of society immediately next above pauperism: Of this we may judge by the fact already noticed, that during its prevalence, the English laborer could exchange a day's work for four or five times the quantity of food which a day's labor will now bring. But what it may be asked, had the doctrines of the Church to do with a result like this? They had simply this: that from principles already referred to, her policy, if I can use the expression, was directed to, or at least resulted in, two consequences;—one was, to keep up the value of labor; the other, to keep down the price of bread. Both of these objects were included in the economy of religious festivals, which gave increased value to labor, by diminishing the amount of production. Rich and poor, assembled on an equality around the altars. Those days furnished leisure for the poor to be instructed, at least, in their Christian hopes and duties; as well as to repose from toil. The ceremonies of the Church—the grandeur and beauty of its architecture—the works of painting, and art, and music which could be enjoyed within its walls—exercised a refining influence on their feelings and manners, in the absence of that popular education which the multiplication of books and the improvements in knowledge have since so much facilitated. It is to be observed, however, to those who understand no more of the subject, than the silly charge that, "the Church in all this encouraged idleness," a more unfounded imputation could scarcely be conceived. The principle of the Church, on that subject, may be seen in the rules of her religious orders. In these, you will find time so distributed, as to allow periods for labor—for reading—prayer—repose—but not one moment for idleness. It is to be remembered, also, that these holidays in no way interfered with the crops or productions of the earth. For, not only was labor allowed, but in many cases, absolutely enjoined, even on Sundays, when the inclemencies of the season endangered the productions of the earth.

What then was the result in the light of Political Economy? Simply that which was most important for the consideration of the laboring classes. The evils of over-production were provided against; and thus, the value and adequate price of labor were maintained. Had this system been continued, seasons of rest would have been provided for, and regularly distributed, at intervals, throughout the year. But these days were abolished; and after capitalists had realized the advantages of the change, its rebound fell, with terrible effect, upon the laborers. Even at reduced wages, they have to encounter seasons when employment is denied for weeks and months. And why is this? It is from over-production;—the very evil which the economy of the Church in the observance of holidays was calculated to prevent. In the actual condition of the laborers the want of employment is synonymous with the want of food; and when the cry of distress rings in the ears of their rulers, it is too often ascribed to other, than the real causes. The author of the "Essay on Population," Malthus, startled Europe with the theory, that mankind increases in a ratio disproportioned to the means of their support. He maintained that, inasmuch as population increases in a geometrical ratio, and the agricultural productions of the earth, only in an arithmetical degree; therefore a time must come, when the excess of the former over the amount of the latter, would require that a large portion of the human race should perish! In this, there is some ground to believe, that he was misled by confounding the excess of "production" with excess of "population." If the island of Great Britain were the only agricultural soil on the globe, then, indeed, with its present population, his theory might be correct. But the earth is teeming with fertility, which the industry of man has not yet turned to account. If the interested policy of England allowed other nations to send their surplus agricultural produce, in fair exchange, for her industrial fabrics, there would be no need for the invention of this theory. It is estimated that the valley of the Mississippi, alone, could furnish the staple of life for a population of one hundred and twenty-five millions. And yet the genius of Political Economy, in England, was such as to conceal this fact from the mind of Malthus. And instead of allowing the bread of that valley to reach the hungry operatives of Manchester;—in other words, instead of diminishing the material interests of the British landholder, he allowed himself, to be thrown on the horrible alternative of recommending, as a prospective remedy, that the increase of population should, as much as possible, be prevented by restraints on the marriage of the poor. But what is more surprising still, is that his theory should have been received with approbation by distinguished writers on Political Economy. Indeed, so far is this true, that the doctrine is now boldly asserted, that in reality the pauper has no more right to quarter himself on the public for support than the rich man; that if he be so supported, it is owing to the humanity of the public, but not due, as a right, to his condition. The universal doctrine prevalent is, that every man has "a right to do what he pleases with his own;" consequently, that, unless compelled by law, he has a right to refuse relief from his property, and leave the sufferer to die! When Sir Robert Peel, on a late occasion, declared, in Parliament, that property had "duties as well as rights," the sentiment was re-echoed by the press, with one chorus of astonishment; as if an axiom of morals, as old as the Christian religion, were a recent discovery made by the minister.

But, supposing we admit the correctness of the conclusion at which Malthus arrived, how awful and retributive is the vindication which it furnishes of the social economy of the Church in the sanctioning of voluntary celibacy! The nation that denounced celibacy when it was a voluntary choice, in the clergy and in the monastic institutions, are reduced to the necessity of recommending the *enforcement of it* by compulsion, in regard to the poor. If that institution had continued, how great would have been the public economy in the support of the clergy! One-twentieth part of the revenues of the Church, at the present time, would be sufficient to support a single, that is, unmarried clergyman, in the proportion of one to every one thousand souls of the population. If it be said, that the ecclesiastical revenues return to the people, through some other channel, a better condition would be that nineteen-twentieths of it should not have been taken from them at all. But even the economy would not be the only advantage. The influence of such a ministry of religion, acting in a moral direction, could not but produce the happiest effects among that portion of mankind who are compelled to toil daily for the means of subsistence. Their pleasures would be of a more rational, more elevating, and, at the same time, more economical description. Their feelings and manners would be softened and improved, by the influence of religion and frequent intercourse with its ministers. Their moral faculties would be cultivated; and, if the trials of life bore heavily upon them, religion would still be near, to console them with the promised hopes and joys of another world.

Such are the results of Political Economy, as based on the principle of individual material interest. It might possibly suffice, if the means of protecting—each his own interest—were *equal* in the hands of all. But what chance have the poor against the rich? the weak against the strong, under such a system? When all the social elements of material industry, of consumption, production, capital and labor, wealth of nations in general, *all* resolve themselves, by common consent and established usage, into mere personal selfishness? Could any other result have been reason-

ably expected, by men who understand the feelings and passions of poor
fallen nature? And what remedy can be applied now? Alas! whatever
remedy either wisdom or philanthropy might suggest, will come too late
for many of the victims that are sinking under this state of things. And
it is feared, even by wise men, that they will lead, at no remote period,
if they continue on, to some social catastrophe, such as one shudders to
think of. Unquestionably, in the system itself, there are elements for
mitigating these miseries. But the measures for that purpose can only be
presented in the aggregate of *abstract* interest, and are still violently
opposed by the selfishness of coteries, and of individuals who have
power to resist them. The only way to apply a corrective to the *root* of
the evil, would be, not indeed to destroy the principle of interest, but to
enlarge it, to an extent corresponding with the whole nature and destiny
of man, as made known through the lessons of our Divine Redeemer.
Bring *temporal* interests into harmony with *spiritual*—infuse some portion
of the attributes of God, justice and mercy, into the minds and hearts of
princes, of legislators, of nobles, of landlords; yea, if possible, of capitalists and money-changers themselves, as the *Christian* rules, for their
thoughts and actions toward the weaker classes of their countrymen.
Persuade them, not only that there *is* a God in heaven, but also that He
is the common Father of all, rich and poor; that they ought to love each
other. Bring their hearts nearer to each other—unite and bind them
together, not only as citizens of the same country, but also as aspirants
to the same immortal life and eternal glory. Any effort toward this will
be a step in the great cause of society and human nature. All this the
Church would have done, without seeming to spend a thought upon it,
if you had allowed her to continue the peaceful mission with which her
Founder sent her forth to the nations of the earth. In times of barbarism
she was the means of erecting for your forefathers a noble and majestic
social edifice, sufficiently ample to shield and protect them all. She
would have enlarged, improved, and adorned it, in proportion to your
increasing numbers, and the varying wants of your condition. But you
overthrew this, and built for yourselves an incongruous and misshapen
structure. You are fain to call it a social edifice! But no; its true name is
a temple of interest. Princes, and lords, and capitalists are indeed well
provided for, beneath its glittering arches—a few others still may find
protection within its vestibule; but as for you, oh ye millions of the poor
and laboring classes, who are called and compelled to worship at its
shrine, ye are strewn around its outer porches; and, instead of its sheltering you from the storm and the rains of adversity, you are even
drenched with the waters that descend from its roof. Go back among the
ruins of former things, you may still find and trace out the deep founda-

tions of the better edifice you destroyed. And, if there be no other hope for you, cooperate with Divine Religion in rearing up its stately walls, and its capacious dome, beneath which, even as regards your temporal condition, you, or at least, the heirs of your condition, your children, may yet find shelter and protection.

NOTE

1. [Ed. Thomas Malthus, 1766-1834, was a Church of England clergyman whose "Essay on the Principle of Population" (London, 1798; rev. ed., 1803) argued for moral restraint in marriage in order to check the growth of population. Population, he held, when unchecked either by governmental means or by natural vices and disasters, tends to increase in geometrical ratio while food and sustenance increase in an arithmetrical ratio. A geometrically-increasing population would eventually not have enough food. He also advocated the abolition of the poor laws in England in order to protect the limited means of the country for those who truly deserved them.]

A SELECTED BIBLIOGRAPHY

PRIMARY SOURCES:

John Hughes and John Breckenridge, *Controversy Between Rev. Messrs. Hughes and Breckenridge, on the Subject "Is the Protestant Religion the Religion of Christ?"* (Philadelphia: E. Cummiskey, 1833).

————, *A Discussion of the Question, Is the Roman Catholic Religion, in any or in all its Principles or Doctrines, Inimical to the Civil or Religious Liberty and of the Question, Is the Presbyterian Religion in any or in all its Principles or Doctrines Inimical to Civil or Religious Liberty* (Philadelphia: Carey and Lea, 1836).

Lawrence Kehoe, (ed.), *Complete Works of the Most Rev. John Hughes, D.D., Archbishop of New York; comprising his sermons, letters, lectures, speeches, etc.* (2 vols.; New York: Lawrence Kehoe, 1865).

SECONDARY SOURCES:

Jay P. Dolan, "A Critical Period in American Catholicism," *The Review of Politics* 35 (October, 1973), 523-536.

John R.G. Hassard, *Life of The Most Reverend John Hughes, D.D., First Archbishop of New York, with Extracts from his Private Correspondence* (New York: D. Appleton & Co., 1866).

Richard Shaw, *Dagger John: The Unquiet Life and Times of Archbishop John Hughes of New York* (New York: Paulist Press, 1977).

7

Edward McGlynn

Edward McGlynn (1837-1900) was a controversial priest of New York City who identified himself with the poor and unemployed and became an articulate spokesman for social justice. For McGlynn, charity was not sufficient to respond to the needs of the poor. One had to understand the root causes of the conditions of poverty and do something to eradicate those causes, establishing a just foundation for the economic life of the American people. McGlynn eventually became convinced by Henry George that the fundamental remedy to economic and social injustice was in a single tax that would fairly distribute fiscal responsibility and provide economic opportunities for the workingmen of the country.[1] McGlynn was eventually charged with socialism because of his position on social justice and his political advocacy of Henry George for mayor of New York City. Like other social reformers in New York City, e.g., the Protestant social gospeler Walter Rauschenbusch, McGlynn had pastoral experience with poverty; his calls for social justice, therefore, were not grounded solely in social theories, but in social theories that were responsive to practical experiences of poverty and human degradation.

Edward McGlynn, the seventh of eleven children, was born on September 27, 1837 to Peter and Sarah McGlynn, middle class Irish Catholics who had immigrated to New York City in 1824. He was educated in the New York public schools until the age of thirteen (1850) when he was sent to the Urban College of Propaganda in Rome where he received his education for the priesthood. In 1859, he became Vice President of the newly established American College in Rome and a year later received his doctorate in theology. He returned to the United States in 1860, after ten years in Rome, and accepted a number of pastoral positions in the Diocese of New York (i.e., assistant pastor of St.

220

Joseph's, New York City, 1860-66; pastor of St. Stephen's, New York City, 1866-86; pastor of St. Mary's, Newburgh, New York, 1895-1900). In 1886, he was suspended from the priesthood for supporting Henry George and was excommunicated from the Catholic Church in 1887 for, among other things, disobedience. During the period of his excommunication, 1887 to 1892, he served as President of the Anti-Poverty Society in New York City. In 1892, he was reinstated in the Church and died on January 7, 1900, as pastor of St. Mary's in Newburgh, New York.

The following selection is a speech Dr. McGlynn gave repeatedly from 1887 to the end of his life. In it he calls for a new crusade on behalf of the poor, proclaiming that the Fatherhood of God and the brotherhood of man, essential Christian doctrines, are the primary motivating forces behind the movement. The new crusade was undertaken, like most of the older Christian crusades, for the liberation of mankind from the prisons of poverty, ignorance, disease, and selfish materialism. This new crusade was not just another social movement; it was "necessarily a religious movement."

NOTE

1. On the single tax theory, see James Jeremiah Green, "The Impact of Henry George's Theories on American Catholics" (unpublished, University of Notre Dame, Ph.D. dissertation, 1956).

TEXT

"THE CROSS OF A NEW CRUSADE"

Source: The Standard, April 2, 1887, pp. 2-3

ADDRESS BY DR. McGLYNN IN THE ACADEMY OF MUSIC
NEW YORK CITY
TUESDAY EVENING, MARCH 29, 1887

Ladies and Gentlemen: . . .

The cross of the new crusade is not raised in hostility to the cross of Christ. The very thought of a crusade and of the honored badge of a crusade—the holy ensign of the cross—is entirely borrowed from Him.

The crusades of old, that brought a good thing, and with it a new name into the world, were inspired by tenderest reverence for the cross of Christ and affection for the places, even on the sea sands, on the mountain side, and at the city gates, where He had walked and slept and suffered and taught and died. It was the enthusiastic love of the cross, and of the magnificent teachings of the cross, that fired the hearts of men and made them undertake and carry on for centuries the old crusades.

It was a man of God—a hermit—consecrated by peculiar sanctity of life, profession and practice to the service of Christ, who became the preacher of the holy war that took for itself the name of a crusade. The crusade was to ransom from captivity the tomb of Christ; to redeem thousands and tens of thousands of Christian men and women who were enslaved under the hated ensign of the Saracen Invaders; to emancipate individual men and women in countless multitudes from horrible chattel slavery. It was to restore to Christendom the possession of the places that had been made sacred by the life, the tears, the music of His voice, and the expiring cry upon the cross of Him who gave name to Christendom. . . .

When the first crusade was proclaimed at the Council of Clermont the happy thought—no doubt inspired—seized upon the multitude of making the Cross of Christ, no matter of how rich or cheap material it might be, the badge of the holy war.

And so women rent their garments, and men took off their raiment, and making strips of them formed crosses with which to deck the breasts of the soldiers of the cross. And it was this badge of the cross of Christ, the ensign of the holy war, that gave to all our modern languages the word crusade.

And so the cross of a new crusade need not be any material emblem, but it stands for the acceptance by men and women, by whomsoever will hear, of the call, the trumpet blast, that invites them to forget themselves, to set aside their wretched strifes, to utterly renounce the injustice in which they may have been engaged, and to take on a new enthusiasm of humanity in believing, in working, in battling, in suffering, and, if need be, in dying, for the right, for a great truth that I shall not be guilty of the indiscretion of calling a new truth, for a truth that, like all great truths, must in its germ and in its essence be as old as God himself in eternity, and as old as the world, or the race of men in time. And so it is a new crusade, to which you are invited, for the proclaiming, the propagating, and the enforcing of an ancient truth—a truth that is eminently consonant with the great truth of Christianity itself—and, properly understood, resolves itself into the very essence, the very core of all religion as taught us by Him, who spake as never

man spake before or since, and in homely accents, and in simple parables, taught the poor, the lowly and the oppressed the comforting doctrine, so full of truth and light, of the fatherhood of one God and the
universal brotherhood of man.

This new crusade then, while, to use a modern phrase, there is
nothing sectarian about it, is necessarily a religious movement. And
permit me to say, and I am not at all singular in the saying of it, if it
were not a religious movement you might at the very outset count me
out of it; for I think that any cause, any movement, any object that
enlists the thought of men and the affections of the hearts of men must
have a religious inspiration, a religious justification and a religious consummation, or the cause is not worth wasting our breath, our time and
our strength upon. It were useless to prate about truth and beauty and
goodness and justice and humanity, and the brotherhood of man, if this
truth and justice and goodness and beauty, and this universal brotherhood, found not their source and their centre, their type, their ideal,
their justification, in God himself.

That all great causes must necessarily be religious was not hidden
from the sages of pagan antiquity any more than it is hidden from us.
For whatever fires the heart of man—in the sense in which the heart of
man means affection, love, forgetfulness of self, enthusiasm for something outside of self—in this sense whatever fires the heart of man must
come from a source that is not only outside of man, but above man.

When we talk of justice we must mean something more than a
mere abstraction, or else we are talking most unphilosophically. There
must be a standard of justice. There must be a standard of truth. There
must be somewhere an ideal beauty, an ideal holiness, an ideal justice,
an ideal truth, and that ideal must be above all men and angels. It must
be a source from which all men and angels shall in their measure partake of truth, of holiness, of beauty, of justice. And that for me is God.
God is the perfect justice, the eternal, the infinite, the absolute purity,
goodness and truth. . . .

And now, therefore, this is—if I need one at all—my excuse for
having stepped forth from the pulpit to stand upon other platforms, and
to talk of justice, of truth, of charity, of love (applause); to talk to men
who, perhaps, sad to say, have learned to hate with a peculiar intensity
the church of which I was but an humble servant, to talk to men who
thought, or thought they thought, that there was no God. I felt that it
was not amiss to take reverently, as if from the very ark of God, the precious truth and bring it out and scatter it broadcast among men, fearing
not that it should ever be soiled or contaminated by coming into closer
contact with the minds and the hearts of any of God's children. And I

felt, if I needed justification, more than justified in this, by the thought of the example of Him who taught wherever men would hear Him, whether in the courts of the temple or by the wayside, or from the boat of the fisherman or on the summit of the mount; who taught the multitude, and never ceased to teach in homely parables the truths of God; taught to Scribes and Pharisees, Sadducees and Essenes; taught to priests of the temple, and to disciples of John, as well as to those whom he called his disciples, the great truths that are most precious, most simple, and most universal, of the essential relations of the minds and the hearts of God's children to their Creator, to their Father, to their God.

The reason why I have felt it almost a sin to refuse any invitation that came to me to speak for any great public cause of truth or justice or morality was just that. I feel that it is amiss for us to hide whatever light may be given to us under a bushel, but that rather should we let our light shine before men, that men seeing may be attracted by the beauty of truth, and may perchance desire to know more of it, and may come in from the highways and the byways, and from halls where meetings are held that are political or social, or whatsoever you will, to learn more of that better way, to inquire if there be not other truths, if not so essential yet most important in guarding, in building up, in strengthening and making perfect the great essential truths of the fatherhood of God and the brotherhood of man.

And now if you will permit I will let you into a little secret, and I am somewhat comforted in this indiscretion of telling you the secret, because I observe with some gratification that there are quite enough of you here to-night to keep the secret. The secret is this: It is my opinion—of course that does not add any great weight to it—but the secret is that it is my opinion that the Christian church would speedily gather in the whole world into the flock of Christ if she would preach more generously and more self-sacrificingly to men and women and children wherever they will listen to her, and would carry out with all her wondrously potent influences the blessed lesson of the fatherhood of God and the brotherhood of man. I may quote the authority of a gentle spirit, who, in a discussion in which I took part before the Nineteenth Century Club not very long ago, while he spoke on the agnostic side of the question under discussion—which was the alleged failure of agnosticism—yet said most tenderly beautiful things about the character of Christ, and professed the most tender reverence for that character, and told this great truth to the nominally Christian men and women who filled that hall: "If you and all Christians would but carry out the precepts of your Master, very speedily there would be but few agnostics in the world." And what emphasized the lesson coming from such a source was the fact that he was neither by race nor training a Christian; he was a scion of the great old Hebrew race who spoke thus reverently and beautifully and truly of Him whom we call Lord and Master.

And I may say that during a certain political campaign that may, perhaps, be considered to have passed into ancient history—I believe it is actually nearly three or four months ago—not a few men said to me that they were attracted to the movement in which I took a humble part by the religion that they found in it; by the fact that it was opening to them a new vista; that it was bringing them back to God; that it was making them feel ashamed, as it were, of the bitterness that they had cherished in their hearts against the very name of God, because God had been presented to them as a monster, as an ogre, as a being who made laws that necessarily resulted in the poverty, the degradation and the crime of a very large portion of His children; of an alleged father who did not know how to provide for his children, and who gave certain privileges to a chosen few of the children to impoverish, to degrade, to enslave, and to rob the greater part of their brethren.

When they began to hear of a man telling that God was the father who by beautiful laws of justice, by simple universal economic laws, had provided admirably for His children, had provided a table so long and so wide and so well supplied with all manner of good things that there never could be too many at that table—never the slightest fear that the poorest and weakest need be crowded away from it—a man who came to preach, not so much a new political economy as to teach the old and the best political economy, that the more mouths that come into the world the more hands come with them to feed the mouths; and that the larger and the denser the population, all the better for the country, because all the better the facilities of production and exchange; a man who taught them that Malthusianism, taking name from an alleged Christian minister, was a blasphemy against the Most High; and that while God's children come into the world with diversity of gifts, of physical strength, of intellect, of heart and fancy, yet they all come stamped ineffaceably with the same image of the Father and the King, His and His alone the image, and His the superscription, and that, therefore, in spite of these inequalities of stature, or of wit, or of weight, or of brain, or of fancy, there is an essential equality that far transcends all these inequalities, the essential image of God in the capacity to know the truth, and to love the good and to do the right, and therefore an essential equality of all men as against all other men under the common, beneficent, just, wise and merciful rule of an all-loving Father.

And I confess that from very early years, as a boy and a very young man, and a very young clergyman, I was tormented by these problems.

I have been blessed, or cursed, as you will, from my earliest childhood with a decided enlargement of the heart. From a very early day I wondered and pondered and I tormented myself with the question, Why is there so much misery in the world? Why are there so many barefooted and ragged children? Why are there so many seeking bread and seeking it in vain? Why are there so many who look upon what we are told in the Scriptures is in some measure a curse—the curse of labor—look upon it as a priceless boon, and crave with intensest earnestness the mere chance to work even for a wretched pittance, as if in the very work itself they found something wonderfully good and beautiful and comforting? I wondered and tormented myself with the question why it was that so many who toil not, neither do they spin, are dressed in all the colors of the rainbow, and are actually sated with the good things of this world, and find life itself a bore. And while they are thus sated with the good things of the world they begin to ask themselves: Is this pleasure? Is life worth living? Is the game worth the candle? And not a few of them say in the bitterness of their souls as they grow old, "It is a pretty tiresome thing, after all, for a man for seventy years every day to be pulling on and off his stockings." That disease of mine of enlargement of the heart had a great deal to do with drawing or driving me into the priesthood of the Catholic church; because there I saw a ministry consecrated to the preaching of the highest truths, to a life of renunciation for the sake of the brethren, to the doing of gentle deeds of Christlike charity; and I repeat, and I shall never tire of repeating, that I find justification for loving every social cause, every economic cause, every political cause, whose object is the diminution—rather let us say the abolition—of poverty, for the diffusion of knowledge, for the refinement and the civilization of these images of God all around us—a cause in which I must sympathize, and for which, as far as I can, I must speak and labor; and I never for a moment fancied on that, to me, most sacred day, when, full of reverence, I bowed before a Christian altar, to receive the consecration of Christ's priesthood, that I was to rise from that prostrate attitude any the less a man, any the less the citizen. I felt that the priesthood of Christ gave to manhood and citizenship a new grace and dignity, that in a spiritual sense it gave new loftiness to the man's stature and made him capable of being more unselfish, if he would not be recreant to the best interests of humanity—of aiding the poor, of comforting the afflicted—that it enabled the man, not entirely unaided by supernatural lights and graces, to do something in his time to make the world appear more beautiful and more comfortable for the children of men. If we read history aright we shall see that all the great triumphs of the cause of Christ came where the Church sent out her missionaries to be the friends and fathers of the people, to teach them art and literature and science while teaching the priceless truths of religion.

The missionaries of Christ went out with the self-same spirit, lowliness, poverty and self-renunciation as the Master himself had gone out to teach man by example as well as by word how good a thing it is to deny ourselves, to labor, to do, to suffer and even to die for our brethren. The Church did a great work when she began to teach to the downtrodden; when she taught the abject slave that was crushed beneath the chariot of a Roman conqueror that he was all of a man, and not only taught him that he was the child of God, but also taught the proud Roman emperor upon his throne that he was only a man who one day must stand wretched and miserable and naked before the throne of Him whose majesty he had outraged by oppressing even the least of the brethren who bore in their natures the image and impress of the King. The Christian church gained a magnificent patrimony, upon which it has been banking for centuries, and the allegiance of all the nations of Europe, by sending out her priests with the great lesson for men's hearts that it was to the poor and lowly and oppressed that they were sent, "For of such is the Kingdom of Heaven."

It was then they went out from this Christian church with the divine injunction to gather up the waifs and strays and fragments of humanity, the blind, the poor, and foundlings and insane, to gather up from the wayside all that suffer from tyranny and heedlessness, to gather them up with tenderness and reverence, even as they gathered up the sacred particles of the sacrament of Christ upon the altar, lest they should suffer profanation—it was when they went forth with such lessons in their hearts that they conquered the world.

They never went to apologize to the Roman emperor. (Thunders of applause.) They never went to seek an interview. (Applause.) They went on with supreme cool indifference to preach the Gospel, to gather up the fragments of Christian humanity in the persons of the poor. (Applause.) The Roman emperor gave orders that their heads should be cut off. And these Christian ministers, strangely enough, seemed to enjoy having their heads cut off. They actually at times foolishly went out of their way to have their heads cut off, and sometimes bounded unnecessarily into the arena to proclaim themselves Christians, when they could just as well have kept out of the way and kept their heads upon their shoulders. Why did they enjoy having their heads cut off? Why? They did not fear men as long as they followed the teaching of the Master. That man who has a great truth in him, in his head or in his heart, can preach the truth a hundred times better with his head cut off than with his head on his shoulders.

I think I can gather from your applause and from your cheering that you think you discover in that last remark of mine something of a parable not entirely inapplicable to myself.

I assure you that when I started out with the sentence I had not the slightest intention of making any personal application. At the same time if this very respectable jury finds in it any applicableness to my case I shall not be guilty of the indiscretion of questioning the verdict.

Now, dear friends, what I have said thus far is something of an explanation and a justification of the part of a Christian minister, of a Catholic priest, feeling it not amiss, thinking it even a duty to leave his sanctuary, to put off his gown, and even in secular attire, and before what may be called secular audiences, to discourse of justice and of truth; and it will be a sad day for the world when the strange and unnatural divorce shall have full sway between the church and society, between the altars of the church and the family altars, between the teachings in the church and the teachings in the school, in the market place, in the highways, and in the byways—and by this I do not mean for one moment to insinuate, but the very reverse—I do not for a moment mean to insinuate that ecclesiastical authorities shall control politics and commerce and the development of nationalities, but that there shall be so truly religious a spirit permeating the minds and hearts of men that wherever they go they shall feel the unspeakable comfort of knowing that in the great causes they are promoting they have the sanctions and benedictions of sweet religion.

The crusade that we have chosen to call a "new crusade" is for the enforcing of one of those great truths of which I have already spoken to you—the truth that, with diversity of natural gifts, God has given an equality of essential rights to all His children just because they are His children; that for every mouth He sends into the world to be fed, He sends, with rare exceptions, a pair of hands to feed it; that He had made us land animals, and not fishes or birds, and therefore He has made us to live upon the land and not to fly in the air or swim in the water, and that because He has made us land animals, and because He has made us at all, He has given us the right with these two hands somehow or other to root, to scratch and to dig for a living in order to feed these mouths; and that any man or set of men, who shall by law or in any other way deny, impair, diminish or restrain the equal right of every human being to the possession of the general bounties of nature, the sunlight, the air, the water and the land, is guilty of blasphemy against the goodness of the universal Father. They are perverting under the name of law the right of men; they are desecrating the holy name of law to sanction a monstrous injustice. Under the name of right they are doing a horrid wrong; under the pretense of guarding the best interests of society they are opposing the very germinal principle of rightly ordained society. They are guilty of the monstrous crime of making hundreds of thousands, yea, millions, of God's creatures feel that this life is a wretched mistake, or worse than that—the joke of some most hateful fiend rather than the gift of an all-wise and all-loving Father.

It was not for nothing that He who came to save the souls of men did so much to minister to the relief of their bodily wants. He healed their diseases; He raised their dead; He cured their distempers; He bore their sorrows; He felt compassion for the multitude; lest they should faint by the wayside, He miraculously supplemented the laws of nature and fed them with miraculous loaves and fishes in the wilderness. He did all this, because doing it He knew full well that the bodies of men as well as their souls are the creatures of God, and that their bodies and the capacities of those bodies are but signs and symbols of the spiritual things within, even as all the vast universe of God is but His garment, is but the sign and symbol and the thin veil that surrounds Him, through the rifts in which we catch on every hand glimpses of God and of heaven.

The heavens are telling the glory of God. There is a greater heaven here, vaster and more wondrous than the physical universe, in the intelligent mind and the affectionate heart of the least of God's creatures. All the multitudinous and multifarious beauties and glories of the physical world are not equal to the dignity and the sanctity of the mind and the heart of the least of God's children; and therefore it is that Christ tells us that at the very peril of our souls we must look after the bodies of these little ones; we must feed the hungry; we must comfort and, as far as we can, heal the sick; we must provide shelter for the homeless; we must look after the weak, the blind, the halt, and the insane. Is all this a mistake? No; it is a part of true religion, because it is the sign and the symbol of spiritual things. It is because of the proper care of the bodies of men, of the proper feeding of those bodies, of the proper sheltering of them, that we make it possible for human nature to expand as a beautiful flower under the influence of genial warmth and refreshing breezes and showers, and so the lilies and flowers of every virtue may the more readily expand if the mind and the heart of the child are able to look up and to feel that God the Father has not been entirely unmindful of the wants of the child.

This is the word of an apostle of Christ: "This is true religion—to visit the widow and the fatherless in their affliction, and to keep one's self unspotted from the world." So it is necessarily a part of true religion to insist on what is essentially the equality of man, regardless of the comparatively trifling differences in their gifts and acquirements. This is the political economy, the teaching and reducing of which to practice are the core and essence of this new crusade. All men, inalienably, always, everywhere, have a common right to all the general bounties of nature; and this is in perfect and beautiful keeping with the other law of labor that every mouth has two hands with which to feed itself, a necessary corollary of which is that these hands must have equal direct or indirect access to the general bounties of nature out of which to make a living. That is the whole of the doctrine of this new crusade in a nutshell, that the land as well the sunlight, and the air, and the waters, and the fishes, and the mines in the bowels of the earth, all these things that were made by the Creator through the beautiful processes of nature, belong equally to the human family, to the community, to the people, to all the children of God. The law of labor requires that these natural materials shall be brought into such relations with men that they shall afford to them food, raiment, shelter; for the erection of works not merely of utility, but of ornament; that out of these materials the children of men shall have equal, indefeasible rights to pluck, to catch, to delve, in order not merely to satisfy the necessities of the animal body or to keep it from the inclemency of the blast, but to do more than this—to make the very shelter itself a thing of beauty, to make the home a kind of temple in which there may be a family altar; to erect great public works that shall serve not merely purposes of utility, but shall educate the eye and the fancy, and shall gladden the habitations of men during their brief temporal abode; to add something to the mere garments that shall clothe and preserve the body from the inclemency of the atmosphere; to make even the raiment of man a work of art; to give a charm and a grace and a dignity even to the mere feeding of the animal. All men then have this right; and it is a part of the gospel of this new crusade that while we may make much allowance for the ignorance in which these great cardinal truths are too often forgotten, the barbarism and the slavery in which, because of might, right went under and stayed under for centuries; while we may be very indulgent to the errors and even be willing to forgive in some measure the crimes of the past, we hold aloft the banner upon which is inscribed this truth, that ever and always in the past, the present and the future the earth and the fulness thereof were given by God, and therefore should belong to all the children of God.

The crimes and the horrors of history are chiefly due to the forgetting of that great truth, because of the sordid passions of the few, who, being stronger of mind and swifter of foot and more cunning of brain, used their gifts to enslave and to rob their brethren. But might never has made, and in the Book of God never can make, right. You may find it prudent to surrender your purse to the highwayman, but you shall never find it in your hearts to think that that surrender gives him any right to hold it. And you may, perhaps, think it a discreet thing, if a man with a big sword in his hand stands ready to cut your head off if you want to speak a certain word, to keep your mouth shut and not speak that word until some other day. But at the same time, if that word happens to be the truth, the man with the sword ready to cut off your head does not make it a falsehood.

Now, what are we going to do about it? . . .

The first thing is to keep talking just the way I am talking to-night, at all times, in season and out of season, to any crowd that will listen to us who are supposed to belong to the labor party.

There are laboring men and laboring men. There is a broad distinction between the kinds of laboring men. There are those who labor with their hands and those who work with their jaws. And one may work very successfully and accomplish many good things with the jaws. This class of men have been called by the handworkers—facetiously and somewhat contemptuously—jawsmiths. I have never done much with my hands, so I suppose I may consider myself as belonging to the jawsmiths; and, after all, I think the truth is imparted more by talking than by writing. Writing is all very well in its way, but there is a touch of magnetism about the human voice, about the expression of a man's countenance, that makes the spoken word much more effectual than the written. The best example of this is in the teaching of our Lord and Master. He taught by word of mouth. The command was to go and preach—to go and teach. So I want you to have respect for talking.

Then the next thing is to write; to circulate the truth by books, newspapers—any way that we can manage to dovetail it in; to wedge it in, to smuggle it in, to get it in in any way. Now, if you can convince the majority of the people, especially of the ungentle sex, of this doctrine, of what they have got to do, than we are going to teach the majority of the ungentle sex by the exercise of the right of suffrage to change their institutions so as to undo the wrong and to bring man closer to God.

Cardinal McCloskey, the Lord rest his soul, by means of a message from Rome, about four years ago, got word that there were some heretical doctrines being preached, and he sent to me to inquire what all this was about. He had got a copy of a report of a speech of mine, and, although it was two months old, it was news to the good cardinal. "Why," he said to me, "here, you want to divide up Manhattan Island into little bits, and give each of us one of the bits." I said: "Oh, no; there is no such meaning there." And then I proceeded to explain to him just what we want to do, as I shall now try to explain it to you. Take this whole island of Manhattan—what is it worth? Without the houses and buildings—just merely for agricultural purposes—not much; but for the sake of its capacity for building houses on it—say a thousand million dollars. Why is it worth that? Simply for its capacity to keep men and women and children from falling through into the centre. All these people of New York must sit, lie down, work, eat and suffer upon Manhattan Island.

What is it that gives this peculiar value? It is the aggregation of population; it is the density of population; it is the necessities of the million and a half of people here; it is because of the peculiar, subtle something—this ethereal, immaterial something—that this aggregation of population gives it. It is because of the touch of shoulder to shoulder, because of the nearness of man to man, because of the wondrous multiplication of the productive powers of men and of the miraculous multiplication of the powers of exchange between man and man that are created by this density of population that this ground of Manhattan Island takes on this peculiar and this enormous value. Now, who has the benefit of this? It is individuals who have inherited from grandfathers a few acres of land. It is our dense population which gives it its value. To whom does this belong? To those that made it. It belongs to society, it is the outcome of society; it is the very shadow of society that follows society just as the shadow follows the man who walks hither and thither. Take away the aggregation of the people and Manhattan Island will be worth less than the $24 for which I believe at one time it was purchased.

How are we going to give back to the poor man what belongs to him? How shall we have that beautiful state of things in which naught shall be ill and all shall be well? Simply by confiscating rent and allowing people nominally to own if you choose the whole of Manhattan Island, if it will do them any good to nominally own it; but while they have the distinguished satisfaction of seeming to own it we are going to scoop the meat out of the shell and allow them to have the shell. And how are we going to do that? By simply taxing all this land and all kindred bounties of nature to the full amount of their rental value. If there isn't any rental value then there won't be any tax. If there is any rental value then it will be precisely what that value is. If the rental value goes up, up goes the tax. If the rental value comes down, down comes the tax. If the rental value ceases, then the tax ceases. Don't you see? It is as clear as the nose on your face. . . .

That is what we mean by taxing and appropriating rental value. We would simply tax all these bounties of nature, where there is a scramble for them, to the full rental value. In a new community, where the people are few, land is comparatively limitless; there is no such thing as rent; the land is pretty equally distributed; there is no choice; it would be a senseless thing for men to quarrel about it; there is land enough for all. What is the law of rent? Where there is competition for a larger or choicer portion of the common bounties, for a portion of land that is nearer a river, that is next to the junction of two great rivers, that is near to a great city, for a corner lot, say at the corner of Broadway and Wall street, or at Broadway and Twenty-third street, there rent exists. And how is the competition for the use of such land to be decided? Simply by allowing it to go to the highest bidder. Thus would be provided, through the exercise of the taxing power, a fund for the common treasury, a munificent fund growing with the growth of population and civilization, supplied by a beautiful providential law, a simple, economic law that works with the same simplicity and the same regularity as the law of gravitation itself—a magnificent ever-increasing fund to supply the wants of increasing civilization and increasing population.

This magnificent fund would go to support all public burdens; it would do a great deal more than is done at present by the tax levy; you would have larger, more beautiful and more numerous parks; you would be able to sweep away the greater part of the wretched rookeries that, under the name of tenement houses, are a sin and a shame, and a blot upon the fair name and fame of this beautiful city, and instead of those the best class of houses will be built, and we will have parks, with trees and flowers and the singing of birds, to make glad and beautify this island and God's children, and will thereby add enormously to the value of the surrounding land; and then it would no longer sound Quixotic to talk of building free rapid transit railroads on solid foundations, on which trains could travel at the rate of thirty miles an hour for twenty, thirty or forty miles into the suburbs, to give homes to all the people, from which they could come and go every day, and in which they could enjoy some of nature's life, by which they could get the sun and the air, green fields and flowers. This is no fancy sketch; it is entirely feasible, and in every view it could be brought about if a majority of citizens, convinced of the truth of this doctrine, would carry it into practice and deposit their ballots in the ballot box in favor of this thing.

One of the greatest beneficial consequences of this just and necessary reform, of this restoration to all of what belongs to all, would be this: The artificial value that is now given to land, even beyond this enormous value which we have just discussed, would cease; the giving to individual men what God never intended they should have—the absolute ownership of land—would cease. If there was no individual ownership in land then there would be no such thing as speculative value in land. Then no man would be such a fool as to pay rent to keep land fenced in from year to year, preventing everybody else from doing anything with it. That man, if he nominally owned it, must pay the full rental value of it. Even if he were a fool, he would soon see there was no fun in that kind of thing, and he would give it up and let somebody else take it. You see what would be the result. There would be a consequent increase in the building trades; houses would spring up all over the city of New York, and the tenement houses would be depopulated, and the owners would be glad to sell them cheap to the city, so they could be destroyed to make breathing places for the people.

Capital will then find nothing to invest in except human labor and its products. Don't you see the general demand for human labor that will result? In every society there is capital, and it is the instinct of men not to keep capital lying idle if they can use it, and the only manner in which they can use it is by producing something, so that there will be a steady demand for labor. But a more steady demand for labor comes from something else. It comes from the law of hunger, of cold, of the need to have some soft spot to lie down and sleep, and so whether capital employs labor or not, you may be sure, if labor gets a chance, it will employ itself. The average man is not going to lie down and die of hunger if he can get any kind of a fair chance to dig in the soil for food; the average man is not going to perish by the winter's cold if he can get a chance to provide himself shelter; nor to freeze if he can get access to raw materials to make clothes for himself. And so, in this beautiful condition of things there will always be a demand for labor, and then it will be strictly true and proper to say to any able-bodied man or woman that comes begging: "Why, you are not sick—why should you beg?" "I can't find work." "Oh, that is not true; in this community there is always enough work for all; there is always a demand for labor exceeding the supply."

And that leads us to another beautiful consequence—high wages. Oh, that is a grand thing for us labor people. How does that come about? Why, by a reversal of the terrible law that at present makes wages always keep tending down. Why? Because with the increase of population comes this increased value of land. Don't you notice how great fortunes are accumulating here, as they have accumulated in England and elsewhere? They are becoming amassed more and more in the hands of a few.

Now, all this will be changed; it will necessarily have to be changed by this beautiful and simple law that we have just spoken of. These enormous fortunes will be distributed, and wages will become higher.

Why? Because then it will be the capitalist that will have to be running around after the laborer and begging him to be kind enough to work for him, and not the laborer that shall be running after the capitalist and begging him as if he were a divinity to give him a chance to live.

So, then, we laboring men shall enjoy this unutterably comforting spectacle of reversing the present order of things by seeing not seven poor devils of workmen running after one lord of a capitalist and begging him to employ them, but the seven poor devils of capitalists running after one workman and begging him to work for them. And he will put on lordly ways and feel that he is the lord of creation, the joint owner of the soil, and that he has something in his muscular and sinewy arms, in his well-preserved health, preserved by chastity, sobriety and healthy muscular exercise, that the poor capitalists have not; that he has got something more precious that these capitalists can't do without, and so he dictates his terms, and he says, "Now, how much will you seven people bid for my labor?" And one poor capitalist says, "Well, for a starter I will say $3 a day." "No, no," "$3.25," "$3.50," "$4," "$4.50," "$5," and finally, when the capitalists begin to thin out in that competition, he knocks himself down to the man who will give him five, or six, or seven dollars.

What will be the proper wages resulting from that competition of the seven capitalists for the labor of that one man? Do you know what the wages will be? Just precisely what they ought to be, exactly; neither one cent more nor one cent less. How does that come about? By that law that works just like the law of gravitation. What are economic wages? In the very essence and nature of things what are wages anyhow? They are what the workman produces by his labor out of the materials to which he has legitimate access. What he has put into that raw material is his, and he sells it to somebody else, and for what should he sell? For a perfect equivalent. And so the wages of the man will be an absolute and perfect equivalent for what he has done, for this transmutation of his nerves, of his brain, of his sinews, of his time, into something new and strange, rich and rare, that he has developed out of that raw material, and so economic wages will be a perfect equivalent for the time and muscle and so on that he has put into that thing and that will determine itself as a matter of course, just as water finds its level. Directly or indirectly in a true system of economic government every man shall have absolutely his own, a free field and no favor, but absolutely justice to all, favoritism to none.

But in addition to these natural wages that this man shall get for what he has produced will come his magnificent share as a joint stockholder or owner in the common estate. He will be getting through the common treasury the use and the benefit of a rental in things that the mere man in the barbarous, rustic state has little or no conception of.

This leads us to that other consequence of this law of God that, instead of being afraid of having too many children in a family or too many people in a city or too many people in a country, we shall be asking God to send us more of these good things, and we shall be saying we shall never have enough. Some of you gray-bearded gentlemen in this audience here are old enough to remember that there used once to be a common notion in this country of ours that we couldn't have too many people, and we used to think that every man that came into this country—every able-bodied man—was worth $1,000 to $1,500 to the country. In the southern portion of this country, not very many years ago, a man used to be supposed to have a well defined value. A man was worth his $1,000, his $1,200 or his $1,500, wasn't he? And every able-bodied man, every able-bodied woman, every healthy child that comes into this country, whether from Heaven or from Europe, is money in the pocket of the country. Why? For the reason that we have just explained, that density of population, thick population, creates this subtle something, this immaterial something, that adds so enormously to the value of all natural bounties. Do you not observe that it is only where there are dense populations that you can have anything like civilization? Have you reflected upon the fact that the very word civilization comes from the same root as city—*civitas*. The very words *civitas* and *civis* are supposed to come from a word which means "coming together," and it is logically, historically and philosophically true, as well as etymologically.

Coming together—you are coming together, shoulder to shoulder, elbow to elbow, helping one another. That is civilization—facility of exchange. . . . Here civilization will increase by density of population, and it is a crime against this economic law to be talking about the danger of overpopulation.

And that is keeping with that other—forgive the remark—rot about overproduction. Overproduction of good things! Overproduction of houses! Overproduction of clothes! Overproduction of food! "What fools these mortals be!" Overproduction! It is underconsumption, not overproduction.

I am going to prove to you now that there is not any overproduction. You just pass the word around that all these things that have been overproduced, the houses that have impaired the real estate market—have broken the market—and the glut of dry goods and silks and sealskins and groceries and things, are going to be distributed free; that anybody that needs these things can come and have them for the mere trouble of taking them away. I want to know how long would that overproduction continue to distress our souls. Not very long, which proves to a demonstration that there is plenty of demand for these things. But the trouble is that the poor devils who are suffering cold for the want of sealskins and hunger for the want of groceries can't get at these things because they haven't the means with which to buy them.

So the trouble is not overproduction, but it is the unjust arrangements of society by which so large a portion of the people either cannot get work at all or have to work at starvation wages. And because when there is a so-called overproduction and underconsumption there comes commercial depression—stagnation in trade—a large portion of the people are thrown out of work and in their misery are willing then to work for lower wages—for anything that will keep them from starving and from perishing. Then there is a revival in trade. Then people say: "Now is a good time to get in the goods, because they can be got so cheap—because labor is cheap. Now is a good time to build, because labor is cheap." And so gradually there is a cessation of this commercial depression, and times begin to get a little better, and then they begin to get what is called good, and the moment the times begin to be good and business begins to prosper, then the man that is sitting there, neither working nor spinning, but eating and drinking, begins to say: "Ha, ha, times are good. Business is prospering. Real estate will go up." And so it does. Land will go up. There is a need for building more houses. There is a need for more factories, and land goes up, and so a large and constantly increasing portion of the profits of both capital and labor go to pay the unjust rent to the landlord. But when we shall have appropriated to the common treasury the economic rent, all that condition must necessarily cease, and as men will be able to get steady employment or steadily to employ themselves, and will get the highest wages that the very law of wages itself will permit, they will not be so foolish when the wants of their bodies are admirably supplied as to work themselves to death, to continue to degrade themselves into mere working machines. And so, with the increase of general wealth, the raising of wages and the general wellbeing, will commence, voluntarily and naturally, a shortening of the hours of work. It doesn't require any law of the legislature, or any strike, or any rule of a trades union or any similar society to determine these things. Men will then be more free than they ever have been before to work or not to work as they please; to work long hours or short hours, as it suits best their tastes, their desires and their convenience. If a man wants to work, very good. If a man does not want to work there will be nobody to coerce him, and so we shall restore in a great measure individual liberty. We shall restore what hitherto has been singularly characteristic of our country, but is fast ceasing to be so characteristic of it—the magnificent individualism of Americans.

Let us be humble and acknowledge what is the truth, that the boasted superiority of the American people in their inventive genius is the liberality that has presided over the forming of all their institutions. Things that have been hitherto characteristic of American men and women, and of American civilization, were not due, are not due, so much to any superiority of ourselves bodily or mentally as to the magnificent opportunities that, under the providence of God, came to this new people from what used to be considered the boundless and illimitable resources of this wide continent. The peculiar inventiveness of the American people came from the need on the part of a few men to subdue a continent, to make locomotion from one end of it to the other possible within a reasonable space of time. But these characteristics, and the homely virtues that were also characteristic of the American people, were due not so much to difference of race as to difference of condition, and now with changing conditions many of these characteristics and characteristic influences and virtues have disappeared, and we are fast becoming assimilated to those older societies both in their criminal luxuries and in the horrible chasm that separates the rich from the poor.

And now, last of all, I would appeal to all you men and women to take up the cross of this new crusade. And, though you will not impress upon your forehead and wear upon your breast any material emblem thereof, let at least the mighty controlling thought take possession of your minds, the divine enthusiasm seize upon your hearts. Take, then, the cross of this new crusade of justice and truth for humanity. Do what you can to help us in what we are trying to do, in the words of the great Christian poet of England, "To justify the ways of God to men;" to give leisure to God's children from the "carking cares," as the same poet says, from imbruting and ceaseless toil, from degradation and want, and the worse degradation of the fear of want; to give them plenty, so that they shall say with glad and loving hearts their grace—not a mere form of words, but grace before meat and after meat—and feel that it is not a mockery to say, "Bless, O Lord, these Thy gifts which we are to receive from Thy bountiful hands"—a mockery too often over the cup of tea and dry bread which is the too common food and drink of the working women of this city to-day. Make room at the Father's table for all of His children.

Go, then, into the highways and byways. Not merely invite them, but compel them to come in and sit at the Father's table and feast and make merry and be glad in His presence. And give them leisure from this degrading, ceaseless toil to beautify their minds and hearts and worship their Maker, to glorify the Christ in humanity; to read books and to enjoy works of art, not depending for these upon individual charities, but with twenty or fifty art schools and Cooper Unions provided for out of the common treasury.

And when men's bodily necessities have been satisfied, when their minds shall begin to be cultivated, and they shall have begun to take on as a common thing the graces and refinements of culture and science and art, then you will have by the doing of natural justice, by the following of God's economic laws, a way prepared for the coming of the kingdom of heaven. Then will blasphemy cease upon the lips of the children of men, and man will recognize the handiwork of his Creator. Shall we not make some attempt to prepare the way for the coming of that better day foretold by the Master of old, who, as he gathered around him the faithful few, foretold that the little flock should grow and spread until it shall take in all the kingdoms of the earth? Shall we not do our share toward hastening the time that was foretold by the Master when He taught us to look up and say, "Our Father who art in heaven," and then to say, "Thy kingdom come; Thy will be done *on earth* as it is in heaven"?

While, therefore, it is eminently proper for a Christian to teach the blessedness of suffering after Christ's example, and for His dear sake, to teach that there is a higher and better something beyond all this, yet at the same time it is a blasphemy against the Maker thus continually to make light of the sufferings of the poor, and to be guilty of the folly of saying that it is a good thing to continue to foster, preserve and perpetuate poverty in the world. As if, forsooth, if we should abolish poverty our occupation would be gone! that there would be nothing for us charitable people to do—as if it would be right to carefully abstain from purifying the whole system and to persist in plastering a sore leg instead. It is by the doing of justice, by the inculcation of the law of equality, liberty and fraternity on earth that we shall prepare the way for the glorious millennial day when it shall be something more than a prayer, and in great measure a reality—"Thy kingdom come; Thy will be done on earth as it is in heaven."

Take up, then, the cross of this new crusade, and I, for one, dare to say here, before this vast audience, that I have taken it into my head and heart, and never shall I see the day as long as I live that I shall pluck it out from the one or the other. It were a sad thing indeed to think that any man or set of men should forbid you and me to believe these truths of God, to teach them, to preach them, to love them with a religious enthusiasm or to sacrifice even our very lives in the noble work of making them cheap and common among men; and I stand here and say, without fear of reasonable denial, that all that I have said to-night is eminently consonant with the highest Christian truth and the best Christian justice, and that no condemnation of this truth has ever been heard from the blessed lips of Christ nor from the highest tribunal in His church. Nor is there any more danger or possibility of such condemnation of so clear and salutary an economic truth than there is of the condemnation of the proposition that two and two make four. . . .

A SELECTED BIBLIOGRAPHY

PRIMARY SOURCES:

"The Bugbear of Vaticanism," *American Catholic Quarterly Review*, 1 (January, 1876), 73-100.

"Dr. McGlynn's Pessimistic Philosophy," *The Nation* 43 (December 2, 1886), 450-451.

"Lessons of the New York City Election. The Labor Party View," *The North American Review* 143 (December, 1886), 571-576.

"The New Know-Nothingisms and the Old," *The North American Review* 145 (August, 1887), 192-205.

"Justice Wanted More Than Charity," *The Independent* (December 11, 1890), 3-4.

"The Vatican and the United States," *The Forum* 16 (1893), 11-21.

"Large Fortunes and Low Wages," *Donahoe's Magazine* 34 (July, 1895), 749-753.

"The Results of Cardinal Satolli's Mission," *The Forum* 52 (February, 1897), 695-705.

SECONDARY SOURCES:

Stephen Bell, *Rebel, Priest and Prophet. A Biography of Dr. Edward McGlynn* (New York: The Devin-Adair Co., 1937).

Robert Emmett Curran, *Michael Augstine Corrigan, and the Shaping of Conservative Catholicism in America, 1878-1902* (New York: Arno Press, 1978).

————, "The McGlynn Affair and the Shaping of the New Conservativism in American Catholicism, 1886-1894," *The Catholic Historical Review* 66 (April, 1980), 184-204.

————, "Prelude to 'Americanism': The New York Accademia and Clerical Radicalism in the Late Nineteenth Century," *Church History* 47 (March, 1978), 48-65.

Gerald P. Fogarty, *The Vatican and the American Hierarchy from 1870 to 1965* (Stuttgart: Anton Hiersemann, 1982).

Sylvester L. Malone, *Dr. Edward McGlynn* (New York, 1917; reprint, New York: Arno Press, 1978).

8

John Augustine Ryan

JOHN A. RYAN: ADVOCATE OF SOCIAL JUSTICE

*John A. Ryan (1869-1945), the "Right Reverend New Dealer,"
was the chief Catholic spokesman for economic justice in the United
States throughout the early twentieth century. Influenced by Pope Leo
XIII's encyclical Rerum Novarum (1891), Ryan began to discover the
plight of laborers in the United States. A fundamental concern for a just
wage, therefore, stood at the core of all Ryan's activities. He argued
that a just wage was the worker's right derived from his dignity as an
individual. According to Ryan, the Catholic ethicist should not simply
articulate a priori ethical principles; he had to discern the conditions of
the times and adapt principles of natural law to those conditions. The
ethicist involved in the labor-management problems of the industrial
order had to use the sciences of economics and social psychology within
his own ethics in order to determine the nature of justice in the real
order. Ryan became the first American Catholic ethicist to apply himself
to a scientific study of economics in order to create an ethics of the economic order. Although he opposed classical socialism because he insisted
upon the natural right to private property, nevertheless he sought to
secure and insure the workers' rights to fair wages through the intervention of government. The church also had a role to play in the social
order. Ryan repeatedly prodded American Catholics to concern themselves with the issues of social justice more than they had in the past.
Catholic leaders, whether clerical or lay, had to become better informed
about the problems of the new industrial order and to become involved
in reforming that order in accord with the natural principles of social
justice. Ryan tried to steer Catholics and government between the paths
of socialism and individualistic capitalism. His position resembled that
of a limited socialism, or a restricted capitalism; it appeared to be lim-*

ited socialism when he stressed the good of the whole economic body and when he called upon government to protect this good; it seemed like a restricted capitalism when he appealed to the rights of private property and the need to protect the rights of capitalists in the ownership and management of their own industries.

John Ryan was born in Vermillion, Minnesota to William and Maria Luby Ryan. He matured in a rural Minnesota Irish family that had fled famine Ireland. In those early years he read the *Irish World*, edited by Patrick Ford who had supported Henry George, and was influenced by the thinking of Ignatius Donnelly, founder of the Anti-Monopoly Party and an advocate of populist causes, and by Archbishop John Ireland who was himself an advocate for social reforms. Educated in the local schools in Vermillion, the classical curriculum of St. Thomas Minor Seminary in St. Paul, and the clerical curriculum of St. Paul Seminary, he was ordained in 1898. After ordination, Archbishop Ireland sent Ryan to obtain a doctorate in theology at the Catholic University in Washington, D. C. In 1902, he returned to St. Paul to teach in the seminary, and taught there until 1915. From 1915 to 1939, he taught social ethics at the Catholic University in Washington, became involved in social legislation through the National Conference of Catholic Bishops' Social Action Department, and wrote numerous articles on the social issues of the day. He retired from the Catholic University in 1939, but continued writing and working for social causes in Washington until his death in 1945.

The following selection, written in the midst of the Progressive Era after Ryan's first major work *A Living Wage*, emphasizes the Church's function of preparing the individual for his/her ultimate spiritual destiny and shows how far social teaching and activity are included in the Church's regenerative function. Although he appears to be attacking the Protestant Social Gospel advocates in the first paragraphs and has not himself worked out an inherent connection between individual salvation and issues of social justice, nevertheless he argues that the Church must "inculcate the principles of charity and justice by precept and by action." Pope Leo XIII's encyclical *Rerum Novarum* laid down some general social principles, Ryan points out, but these principles must be applied by each local church to the specific needs and conditions in which it finds itself. This means that the clergy in particular must learn the precise nature of the social problems in the United States, apply the Church's social teachings and become actively engaged in social works that will effectively respond to these distinct problems.

TEXT

"THE CHURCH AND THE WORKINGMAN"

Source: Catholic World 89 (April-September, 1909), 776-82.

"Even though it be only a dream, I like to indulge the thought that some day the Church of the poor will lead them out of bondage, and prove to the unbelieving world its divine mission" (From a private letter of a well-known Catholic social reformer).

The viewpoint indicated in this sentence is sufficiently frequent among Catholics to justify a brief reconsideration of a somewhat hackneyed topic. Among the Protestant churches that display any considerable amount of vitality, the tendency is rapidly growing toward a conception that identifies religion with humanitarianism, while the majority of non-church-goers who admit that religion has any useful function probably share the same conception. In such an environment it is not a matter of surprise that many Catholics should exaggerate the social mission of the Church.

The Church is not merely nor mainly a social reform organization, nor is it her primary mission to reorganize society, or to realize the Kingdom of God upon earth. Her primary sphere is the individual soul, her primary object to save souls, that is, to fit them for the Kingdom of God in heaven. Man's true life, the life of the soul, consists in supernatural union with God, which has its beginning during the brief period of his earthly life, but which is to be completed in the eternal existence to come afterward. Compared with this immortal life, such temporary goods as wealth, liberty, education, or fame, are utterly insignificant. To make these or any other earthly considerations the supreme aim would be as foolish as to continue the activities and amusements of childhood after one had reached maturity. It would be to cling to the accidental and disregard the essential. Scoffers and sceptics may contemn this view as "other-worldly," but they cannot deny that it is the only logical and sane position for men who accept the Christian teaching on life, death, and immortality. Were the Church to treat this present life as anything more than a means to the end, which is immortal life, it would be false to its mission. It might deserve great praise as a philanthropic association, but it would have forfeited all right to the name of Christian Church.

Having thus reasserted the obvious truth that the Church's function is the regeneration and improvement of the individual soul with a view to the life beyond, let us inquire how far this includes social teaching or social activity. Since the soul cannot live righteously except through right conduct, the Church must teach and enforce the principles of right conduct. Now a very large and very important part of conduct falls under the heads of charity and justice. Hence we find that from the beginning the Church propagated these virtues both by word and by action. As regards charity, she taught the brotherhood of man, and strove to make it real through organizations and institutions. In the early centuries of the Christian era, the bishops and priests maintained a parochial system of poor relief to which they gave as much active direction and care as to any of their purely religious functions. In the Middle Ages the Church promoted and supported the monastic system with its innumerable institutions for the relief of all forms of distress. Under her direction and active support to-day, religious communities maintain hospitals for the sick, and homes for all kinds of dependents. To take but one instance, the Church in America collects money for orphan asylums as regularly as for many of her purely religious objects. As regards justice, the Church has always taught the doctrine of individual dignity, rights, and sacredness, and proclaimed that all men are essentially equal. Through this teaching the lot of the slave was humanized, and the institution itself gradually disappeared; serfdom was made bearable, and became in time transformed into a status in which the tiller of the soil enjoyed security of tenure, protection against the exactions of the lord, and a recognized place in the social organism. Owing to her doctrine that labor was honorable and was the universal condition and law of life, the working classes gradually acquired that measure of self-respect and of power which enabled them to set up and maintain for centuries the industrial democracy that prevailed in the mediaeval towns. Her uniform teaching that the earth was given by God to all the children of men, and that the individual proprietor was only a steward of his possessions, was preached and emphasized by the Fathers in language that has brought upon them the charge of communism. The theological principle that the starving man who has no other resource may seize what is necessary from the goods of his neighbor, is merely one particular conclusion from this general doctrine. She also taught that every commodity, including labor, had a certain just or fair price from which men ought not to depart, and that the laborer, like the member of every other social class, had a right to a decent living in accordance with the standards of the group to which he belonged. During the centuries preceding the rise of modern capitalism, when the money-lender was the greatest oppressor of the poor, she forbade the taking of interest. Among her *works* in the interest of social justice and social welfare, two only will be mentioned here: the achievements of her monks in promoting agriculture and settled life in the midst of the anarchic conditions that followed the downfall of the Roman Empire, and her encouragement of the Guilds, those splendid organizations which secured for their members a greater measure of welfare relatively to the possibilities of the time than any other industrial system that has ever existed.

To the general proposition that the Church is obliged to inculcate the principles of charity and justice both by precept and by action, all intelligent persons, whether Catholic or not, will subscribe. Opinions will differ only as to the extent to which she ought to go in this direction. Let us consider first the problem of her function as teacher.

The Church cannot be expected to adopt or advocate any particular programme, either partial or comprehensive, of social reconstruction or social reform. This is as far out of her province as is the advocacy of definite methods of political organization, agriculture, manufactures, or finance. Direct participation in matters of this nature would absorb energies that ought to be devoted to her religious and moral work, and would greatly lessen her influence over the minds and hearts of men. Her attitude toward specific measures of social reform can only be that of judge and guide. When necessity warrants it, she pronounces upon their moral character, condemning them if they are bad, encouraging them if they are good. They come within her province only in so far as they involve the principles of morality.

With regard to the moral aspect of existing social and industrial conditions, the Church does lay down sufficiently definite principles. They are almost all contained in the Encyclical, "On the Condition of Labor," issued by Pope Leo XIII. Passing over his declarations on society, the family, Socialism, the State, woman labor, child labor, organization, and arbitration, let us emphasize his pronouncement that the laborer has a moral claim to a wage that will support himself and his family in reasonable and frugal comfort. Beside this principle let us put the traditional Catholic teaching concerning monopolies, the just price of goods, and fair profits. If these doctrines were enforced throughout the industrial world the social problem would soon be within measurable distance of a satisfactory solution. If all workingmen received living-wages in humane conditions of employment, and if all capital obtained only moderate and reasonable profits, the serious elements of the problem remaining would soon solve themselves.

But the social principles here referred to are all very general in character. They are of very little practical use unless they are made specific and applied in detail to concrete industrial relations. Does the Church satisfactorily perform this task? Well, it is a task that falls upon the bishops and the priests rather than upon the central authority at Rome. For example, the teaching of Pope Leo about a living-wage, child labor, woman labor, oppressive hours of work, etc., can be properly applied to any region only by the local clergy, who are acquainted with the precise circumstances, and whose duty it is to convert general principles into specific regulations. In this connection another extract from the private letter cited above may be found interesting and suggestive: "If the same fate is not to overcome us that has overtaken—and justly—the Church in Europe, the Catholic Church here will have to see that it cannot commend itself to the masses of the people by begging Dives to be more lavish of his crumbs to Lazarus, or by moral inculcations to employers to deal with their employees in a more Christian manner." There is some exaggeration in both clauses of this sentence. The defection of large numbers of the people from the Church in certain countries of Europe cannot be ascribed to any single cause. Some of its causes antedate the beginnings of the modern social question; others are not social or industrial at all; and still others would have produced a large measure of damaging results despite the most intelligent and most active efforts of the clergy. When due allowance has been made for all these factors it must still be admitted that the losses in question would have been very much smaller, possibly would have been comparatively easy to restore, had the clergy, bishops and priests, realized the significance, extent, and vitality of modern democracy, economic and political, and if they had done their best to permeate it with the Christian principles of social justice. On the other hand, where, as in Germany and Belgium, the clergy have made serious efforts to apply these principles both by teaching and action the movement of anti-clericalism has made comparatively little headway. At any rate, the better position of the Church and the superior vitality of religion among the people in these two countries, can be traced quite clearly to the more enlightened attitude of their clergy toward the social problem.

The second clause of the quotation given above underestimates, by implication at least, the value of charity as a remedy for industrial abuses. It cannot, indeed, be too strongly nor too frequently insisted that charity is not a substitute for justice; on the other hand, any solution of the social problem based solely upon conceptions of justice, and not wrought out and continued in the spirit of charity, would be cold, lifeless, and in all probability of short duration. If men endeavor to treat each other merely as equals, ignoring their relation as brothers, they cannot long maintain pure and adequate notions of justice, nor apply the principles of justice fully and fairly to all individuals. The personal and the human element will be wanting. Were employers and employees deliberately and sincerely to attempt to base all their economic relations upon Christian charity, upon the Golden Rule, they would necessarily and automatically place these relations upon a basis of justice. For true and adequate charity includes justice, but justice does not include charity. However, the charity that the writer of the letter condemns is neither true nor adequate; it neither includes justice, nor is of any value in the present situation.

Let it be at once admitted that the clergy of America have done comparatively little to apply the social teachings of the Church, or in particular of the Encyclical "On the Condition of Labor," to our industrial relations. The bishops who have made any pronouncements in the matter could probably be counted on the fingers of one hand, while the priests who have done so are not more numerous proportionally. But there are good reasons for this condition of things. The moral aspects of modern industry are extremely difficult to evaluate correctly; its physical aspects and relations are very complicated and not at all easy of comprehension; and the social problem has only in recent times begun to become acute. Add to these circumstances the fact that the American clergy have for the most part been very busy organizing parishes, building churches and schools, and providing the material equipment of religion generally, and you have a tolerably sufficient explanation of their failure to study the social problem, and expound the social teaching of the Church.

The same conditions account for the comparative inactivity of the American clergy in the matter of social *works*. Up to the present their efforts have been confined to the maintenance of homes for defectives and dependents, and the encouragement of charitable societies. In some of the countries of Europe, particularly Germany and Belgium, and more recently France and Italy, bishops and priests have engaged more or less directly in a great variety of projects for the betterment of social conditions, such as, co-operative societies, rural banks, workingmen's gardens, etc. Obviously activities of this kind are not the primary duty of the clergy, but are undertaken merely as means to the religious and moral improvement of the people. The extent to which any priest or bishop ought to engage in them is a matter of local expediency. So far as general principles are concerned, a priest could with as much propriety assist and direct building societies, co-operative associations of all sorts, settlement houses, consumer's leagues, child labor associations, and a great variety of other social reform activities, as he now assists and directs orphan asylums, parochial schools, St. Vincent de Paul societies, or temperance societies. None of these is a purely religious institution; all of them may be made effective aids to Christian life and Christian faith.

The necessity for both social teaching and social works by our American clergy is very great and very urgent. To this extent the sentence quoted in the body of this paper is not an exaggeration. There is a very real danger that large masses of our workingmen will, before many years have gone by, have accepted unchristian views concerning social and industrial institutions, and will have come to look upon the Church as indifferent to human rights and careful only about the rights of property. Let any one who doubts this statement take the trouble to get the confidence and the opinions of a considerable number of intelligent Catholic trade unionists, and to become regular readers of one or two representative labor journals. We are now discussing things as they are, not things as we should like to see them, nor yet things as they were fifteen or twenty-five years ago. Persons who are unable to see the possibility of an estrangement, such as has occurred in Europe, between the people and the clergy in America, forget that modern democracy is twofold, political and economic, and that the latter form has become much the more important. By economic democracy is meant the movement toward a more general and more equitable distribution of economic power and goods and opportunities. At present this economic democracy shows, even in our country, a strong tendency to become secular if not anti-Christian. Here again we are dealing with the actual facts of today. Consequently, unless the clergy shall be able and willing to understand, appreciate, and sympathetically direct the aspirations of economic democracy, it will inevitably become more and more unchristian, and pervert all too rapidly a larger and larger proportion of our Catholic population.

A SELECTED BIBLIOGRAPHY

PRIMARY SOURCES:

"A Country Without Strikes," *Catholic World* 72 (November, 1900), 145-57.

A Living Wage: Its Ethical And Economic Aspects (New York: Macmillan, 1906).

"Is the Modern Spirit Anti-Religious?" *Catholic World* 85 (May, 1907), 182-93.

"The Fallacy of 'Bettering One's Position,'" *Catholic World* 86 (October 1907-March 1908), 145-156.

"The Cost of Christian Living," *Catholic World* 86 (October 1907-March 1908), 575-88.

Distributive Justice: The Right and Wrong of Our Present Distribution of Wealth (New York: Macmillan, 1916).

Social Reconstruction (New York: Macmillan, 1920).

Declining Liberty and Other Papers (New York: Macmillan, 1927).

Social Doctrine in Action: A Personal History (New York: Harper, 1941).

SECONDARY SOURCES:

Francis L. Broderick, *The Right Reverend New Dealer: John A. Ryan* (New York: Macmillan Co., 1963).

Charles E. Curran, "American and Catholic: American Catholic Social Ethics, 1880-1965," *Thought* 52 (March, 1977), 50-75.

_____, *American Catholic Social Ethics* (Notre Dame, Indiana: University of Notre Dame Press, 1982).

Patrick W. Gearty, *The Economic Thought of Monsignor John A. Ryan* (Washington, D. C.: Catholic University of America Press, 1953).

George G. Higgins, "The Underconsumption Theory in the Writings of Monsignor John A. Ryan," M.A. dissertation, Catholic University of America, 1942.

Theodora E. McGill, "A Bio-Bibliography of Monsignor John A. Ryan," M.A. dissertation, Catholic University of America, 1952.

Joseph M. McShane, "The Bishops' Program of Social Reconstruction of 1919: A Study in American Catholic Progressivism," unpublished, University of Chicago, Ph.D. dissertation, 1981.

Part VI

NEO-THOMISM AND CATHOLIC CULTURE, 1920-1960

9

Dorothy Day

Dorothy Day (1897-1980) believed that the human person realized the destiny of history only in a life of practical love that served the immediate needs of the neighbor without counting the costs and without demanding or expecting an effective result. The Spirit of Christ, present in the Christian, must be realized in history through the actions of persons who see themselves not as isolated individuals but as members one of another—united together in the creative and redemptive love of God which transcends all processes of history and yet is incarnated in the Christian community. This Christian personalism was not individualism; it was communitarian. Persons, not states or legislation or techniques or social programs or slogans or even monetary contributions, were responsible for other persons in need.

Dorothy Day was born in Brooklyn, New York on November 8, 1897 to John and Grace Satterlee Day. Her father was a sports writer who took his family from New York to San Francisco to Chicago in the early part of the twentieth century. When Dorothy was seventeen, she enrolled at the University of Illinois at Urbana and remained there for only two years, 1914-1916, joining the Socialist Party. In 1916, she went to New York City and became a reporter for the Socialist New York Call and later worked for The Masses. From 1916 to 1927, she was a Communist sympathizer, joined the International Workers of the World (i.e., the "Wobblies"), took a trip to Europe in 1920 to write her first novel (published in 1924 as The Eleventh Virgin), lived in a common law marriage with Forster Battingham, and gave birth to her first and only child, Tamar, in 1927. As the result of a desire to have her child baptized, she converted to Catholicism (1927). In 1932, she met Peter Maurin (1877-1949) and began to think more deeply about the meaning of her Catholicism and her mission in life. In the midst of the Depres-

253

sion she found her mission in life: service to those who were suffering from the economic and social wants. *Within this context she and Peter Maurin began to organize what has become known as the Catholic Worker Movement. On May 1, 1933, she began to publish The Catholic Worker to encourage more Christians to pay special attention to the needs of the outcast of society, to clarify Catholic social thought, and to provide examples of love in action. Until she died on November 29, 1980, she dedicated herself through her publications, speeches, public protests, prayer and personal sacrifices to the needs of the poor, world peace and human dignity.*

The following selections outline some of Dorothy Day's fundamental Christian aims, attitudes and programs: social justice, peace, communitarianism, voluntary poverty, clarification of thought through round-table discussions, houses of hospitality for the corporeal and spiritual works of mercy, personal responsibility for the poor rather than state responsibility and farming communes as agronomic universities. Throughout these selections Dorothy Day reflects on the personalist philosophy of Peter Maurin, who according to Day was the soul of the Catholic Worker movement.

TEXT

To Our Readers
The Catholic Worker, May, 1933, p. 4;
"CW Stand on the Use of Force,"
The Catholic Worker, September, 1938, p. 4;
"A Letter to Our Readers at the Beginning
or Our Fifteenth Year,"
The Catholic Worker, May, 1947, pp. 1-3;
"Peter Maurin," unpublished manuscript in
Dorothy Day-Catholic Worker Collection,
Marquette University Archives,
Series D-3, Box 2, 3

TO OUR READERS . . .

For those who are sitting on park benches in the warm spring sunlight.

For those who are huddling in shelters trying to escape the rain.

For those who are walking the streets in the all but futile search for work.

For those who think that there is no hope for the future, no recognition of their plight—this little paper is addressed.

It is printed to call their attention to the fact that the Catholic Church has a social program—to let them know that there are men of God who are working not only for their spiritual, but for their material welfare.

Filling a Need

It's time there was a Catholic paper printed for the unemployed.

The fundamental aim of most radical sheets is the conversion of its readers to radicalism and atheism.

Is it not possible to be radical and not atheist?

Is it not possible to protest, to expose, to complain, to point out abuses and demand reforms without desiring the overthrow of religion?

In an attempt to popularize and make known the encyclicals of the Popes in regard to social justice and the program put forth by the Church for the "reconstruction of the social order," this news sheet, *The Catholic Worker*, is started.

It is not as yet known whether it will be a monthly, a fort-nightly or a weekly. It all depends on the funds collected for the printing and distribution. Those who can subscribe, and those who can donate, are asked to do so.

This first number of *The Catholic Worker* was planned, written and edited in the kitchen of a tenement on Fifteenth Street, on subway platforms, on the "L," the ferry. There is no editorial office, no overhead in the way of telephone or electricity, no salaries paid.

The money for the printing of the first issue was raised by begging small contributions from friends. A colored priest in Newark sent us ten dollars and the prayers of his congregation. A colored sister in New Jersey, garbed also in holy poverty, sent us a dollar. Another kindly and generous friend sent twenty-five. The rest of it the editors squeezed out of their own earnings, and at that they were using money necessary to pay milk bills, gas bills, electric light bills.

By accepting delay the utilities did not know that they were furthering the cause of social justice. They were, for the time being, unwitting cooperators.

Next month someone may donate us an office. Who knows?

It is cheering to remember that Jesus Christ wandered this earth with no place to lay His head. *The foxes have holes and the birds of the air their nests, but the Son of Man has no place to lay His head.* And when we consider our fly-by-night existence, our uncertainty, we remember (with pride at sharing the honor), that the disciples supped by the seashore and wandered through corn fields picking the ears from the stalks wherewith to make their frugal meals.

CW STAND ON THE USE OF FORCE

Dear Father:

You are one of many priests and laymen who have written to us of *The Catholic Worker* these past two years on the stand we have taken in the Spanish conflict. Many times we have been misquoted, or sentences from articles or public speeches have been taken from their context and distorted, and our friends have written us with pain that our attitude should seem to be at variance with that of Catholic leaders.

I am writing this letter to explain as best I can the points which we are trying to bring out in *The Catholic Worker*. I am writing it with prayer because it is so hard to write of things of the spirit—it is so hard to explain. If we had made ourselves clear before, we should not have to keep restating our position. But perhaps conflict is good in that it brings about clarification of thought.

We all know that there is a frightful persecution of religion in Spain. Churches have been destroyed and desecrated, priests and nuns have been tortured and murdered in great numbers.

In the light of this fact it is inconceivably difficult to write as we do. It is folly—it seems madness—to say as we do—"we are opposed to the use of force as a means of settling personal, national, or international disputes." As a newspaper trying to affect public opinion, we take this stand. We feel that if the press and the public throughout the world do not speak in terms of the counsels of perfection, who else will?

We pray those martyrs of Spain to help us, to pray for us, to guide us in the stand we take. We speak in their name. Their blood cries out against a spirit of hatred and savagery which aims toward a peace founded upon victory, at the price of resentment and hatred enduring for years to come. Do you suppose they died, saying grimly: "All right—we accept martyrdom—we will not lift the sword to defend ourselves but the lay troops will avenge us!" This would be martyrdom wasted. Blood spilled in vain. Or rather did they say with St. Stephen, "Father, forgive them," and pray with love for their conversion. And did they not rather pray, when the light of Christ burst upon them, that love would overcome hatred, that men *dying* for faith, rather than *killing* for their faith, would save the world?

Truly this is the folly of the cross! But when we say "Saviour of the World, save Russia," we do not expect a glittering army to overcome the heresy.

As long as men trust to the use of force—only a superior, a more savage and brutal force will overcome the enemy. We use his own weapons, and we must make sure our own force is more savage, more bestial than his own. As long as we are trusting to force—we are praying for a victory by force.

We are neglecting the one means—prayer and the sacraments—by which whole armies can be overcome. "The King is not saved by a great army," David said. "Proceed as sheep and not wolves," St. John Chrysostom said.

St. Peter drew the sword and our Lord rebuked him. They asked our Lord to prove His Divinity and come down from the cross. But He suffered the "failure" of the cross. His apostles kept asking for a temporal Kingdom. Even with Christ Himself to guide and enlighten them they did not see the primacy of the spiritual. Only when the Holy Ghost descended on them did they see.

Today the whole world has turned to the use of force.

While we take this stand we are not condemning those who have seized arms and engaged in war.

Who of us as individuals if he were in Spain today, could tell what he would do? Or in China? From the human natural standpoint men are doing good to defend their faith, their country. But from the standpoint of the Supernatural—there is the "better way"—the way of the Saints—the way of love.

Who of those who are combating *The Catholic Worker* stand would despise the Christian way—the way of Christ? Not one.

Yet again and again it is said that Christianity is not possible—that it cannot be practiced.

Today the whole world is in the midst of a revolution. We are living through it now—all of us. History will record this time as a time of world revolution. And frankly, we are calling for Saints. The Holy Father in his call for Catholic Action, for the lay apostolate, is calling for Saints. We must prepare now for martyrdom—otherwise we will not be ready. Who of us if he were attacked now would not react quickly and humanly against such attack? Would we love our brother who strikes us? Of all at *The Catholic Worker* how many would not instinctively defend himself with any forceful means in his power? We must prepare. We must prepare now. There must be a disarmament of the heart.

Yes, wars will go on. We are living in a world where even "Nature itself travaileth and groaneth" due to the Fall. But we cannot sit back and say "human nature being what it is, you cannot get a man to overcome his adversary by love."

We are afraid of the word love and yet love is stronger than death, stronger than hatred.

If we do not, as the press, emphasize the law of love, we betray our trust, our vocation. We must stand opposed to the use of force.

St. Paul, burning with zeal, persecuted the church. But he was converted.

Again and again in the history of the church, the conquered overcome the conquerors.

We are not talking of passive resistance. Love and prayer are not passive, but a most active glowing force.

And we ask with grief who are they amongst us who pray with faith and with love, and so powerfully that they can move the mountains of hatred that stand in our path. The soul needs exercise as well as the body and if we do not exercise our soul in prayer now, we will be puny and ineffectual in the trials that await us.

We are not praying for victory for Franco in Spain, a victory won with the aid of Mussolini's son who gets a thrill out of bombing; with the aid of Mussolini who is opposing the Holy Father in his pronouncements on "racism"; with the aid of Hitler who persecutes the church in Germany. Nor are we praying for victory for the loyalists whose Anarchist, Communist and anti-God leaders are trying to destroy religion.

We are praying for the Spanish people—all of them our brothers in Christ—all of them Temples of the Holy Ghost, all of them members or potential members of the Mystical Body of Christ.

And we add daily to this prayer for peace: "Lord, teach us to pray." "Lord, I believe; help Thou my unbelief." "Lord, take away my heart of stone and give me a heart of flesh."

This editorial is not intended to be a complete statement of *The Catholic Worker's* stand on the Spanish war. Neither does it purport to be anything dogmatic, merely an expression of the sincere convictions of *The Catholic Worker* staff.

A LETTER TO OUR READERS AT THE
BEGINNING OF OUR FIFTEENTH YEAR

Dear Fellow Workers in Christ:

This merry month of May, this month of Mary, this most important month which marks the beginning of our fifteenth year, I have offered, with great temerity, to write the whole paper, aside from Peter's essays. We have a new farm and retreat house at Newburgh-on-the-Hudson, sixty miles from New York, and up there the men are ploughing and planting and building, Gerry Griffin and Jack Thornton, John Fillinger, Joe Cotter, Hans Tunnesen, Rocco and Frank Coyle. In a way I would like to have this issue of *The Catholic Worker* an anniversary issue, and give a resume of our life and work in neat and scholarly style. But being a woman, and a much-interrupted woman, I can only write a letter, a discursive letter, which none the less will be packed full of news and events and from which you will gain a picture, form an opinion, even perhaps make a decision. A decision to read a book, make a retreat, visit us on Mott street; a decision perhaps to consider yourself an apostle and search out some school of the apostolate to inform yourself more about God our King, and Heaven our country.

Each and every paragraph of this letter will be interrupted, I know, by visitors, by babies perhaps, by meals, by matters of great importance in that they have to do with human beings. And in the face of these interruptions, I must remember what I read of Cervantes recently—that he wrote his masterpiece, *"Don Quixote,"* while he lived in a four-room house with six women, and above a tavern full of roistering drinkers. Not much peace and quiet there.

Peter Maurin's program of action, in the face of the crisis of the day, a crisis that has continued these last fourteen years through a great depression and a great war, remains the same now as it did when first we met back in 1933.

    1.—To reach the man in the street with the social teachings of the Church.

    2.—To reach the masses through the practice of the corporal and spiritual works of mercy, at a personal sacrifice, which means voluntary poverty.

    3.—To build up a lay apostolate through round table discussions for the clarification of thought.

    4.—To found Houses of Hospitality for the practice of the works of mercy.

    5.—To found farming communes for the cure of unemployment. To solve the problem of the machine, for the restoration of property and the combatting of the servile state; for the building up of the family, the original community, the first unit of society.

To form our minds, Peter brought us things to read, Chesterton and Belloc and Gill and Cobbett and Father Vincent McNabb; the encyclicals of the recent Popes, from Pope Leo XIII down to the present day. "Making the encyclics click," he used to say with his bright and happy smile, at what he considered a happy phrase, something that

would stick in the mind of the hearer. Peter is a Frenchman (for those of
you who do not know him) and a peasant, and he has his own way of
saying things.

He introduced to us Leon Bloy, the pilgrim of the absolute, and
that great and terrible line of his, which converted the Maritains, "*There
is only one unhappiness, and that is*—NOT TO BE ONE OF THE SAINTS." He
showed us how Pope Pius XI called our attention in his encyclical on St.
Francis de Sales, to the fact that *we are all called to be saints*, layman and
religious, that this is our goal, union with God.

"If you have risen with Christ, seek the things which are above.
Mind the things that are above, not the things that are on earth. For
you have died and your life is hid with Christ in God." "Unless the seed
fall into the ground and die, itself remaineth alone. But if it die it
bringeth forth much fruit."

Peter quoted this encyclical on St. Francis de Sales, he quoted the
beatitudes, he quoted the Sermon on the Mount. And these ideas were
afterward elaborated in the retreats given at Maryfarm, Easton, which
are now being given at Maryfarm, Newburgh; retreats which emphasize
man's dignity as the son of God, the supernatural motive, as the little
way to God; the correlation of the spiritual and the material; making
one's work coincide with one's faith as a Christian. All summer we will
have these retreats at Newburgh, and after the retreats there will be discussions and work on the land, to raise the food for the bread-line at
Mott street.

This letter will be for our *prospective* readers, as well as for the
58,000 readers we now have throughout the world. So I will try to take
up Peter's program point by point and tell what we have been doing
these last fourteen years.

Reach All Nations, Reach All Men

To reach the man in the street. "The workers of the world have
been lost to the Church," Pope Pius XI is reported to have said to
Canon Cardijn, international head of the Young Christian Workers. It is
here that the apostolate of the WORD comes in, newspapers, leaflets,
magazines; THE CATHOLIC WORKER, a monthly, usually of eight pages,
but now cut down on account of the paper shortage, has been distributed from the very first in public squares, sold on street corners, distributed in front of meeting halls. At times the circulation which started at
2,500 went up to 150,000, at a time when labor was beginning to organize and there was a greater call for the paper for mass distribution.

At those times when such simple issues as the right of workers to
organize into unions of their own choosing were at stake, it was very

necessary to get out into industrial conflicts, in front of factories and on picket lines, to emphasize what the Popes have said in regard to the worker.

But there were also criticisms to make as to the acceptance by the unions of the industrial set-up as it was, private enterprise, competition, industrial capitalism.

Frankly, our position was that we had better work against the whole order—work for decentralization, in some cases even for abolition of the machine and the assembly line where it definitely went against the best interests of man and his needs and his nature. Since the unions were organized more for wages and hours, rather than for mutual aid and indoctrination, very often what we had to offer in the way of a program did not interest them. Our point of view was foreign if not hostile at times. Often it is a matter of criticism that we have not continued to work with unions as we did in 1933 through 1938. Frankly, it was because we were not interested in increasing armaments, big business, perpetuating the status quo, and working in many cases perhaps towards state ownership.

We must continue to protest injustice, bad working conditions, poor wages which are general now in face of the high cost of living; but our vision is of another system, another social order, a state of society where, as Marx and Engels put it, *"Each man works according to his ability and receives according to his need."* Or as St. Paul put it, *"Let your abundance supply their want."* Men are beginning to think of the annual wage, in the unions, but not the family wage. Usually it is "equal pay for equal work." But that holy Pope, Pius XI, said we should work, to deproletarize the worker, to get him out of the wage-earning class and into the propertied class, so that he would own his home, as well as his tools.

Join the Apostolate

We must continue to get out into the highways and byways to distribute the paper even if it is not the food the man in the street wants. Religion is morbid to most people, and indeed it is a matter of dying to self, in order to live for God and one's neighbor. Religion has too long been the opium of the people, the opiate of the people. I forget how the jingle in the first issue of INTEGRITY ran, but the sense of it was this:

John Smith puts on his hat and goes to Church on Sunday.
And John Smith goes to hell for what he does on Monday.

Not Saturday night, mind you, when he may be taking surcease from care in some tavern, but for the work he engages in, whether it is the advertising business, or a fat job in the Rubber Company or Copper or Nickel Mines, or a Steamship Company. We participate in the sin of others, we are all helping to make the kind of a world that makes for war.

Yes, let us get out into Union Square, along Forty Second street, in front of Madison Square Garden and distribute and sell *The Catholic Worker*. We have been doing that for many years, but we need to do much more of it. As the older ones get tired (and Stanley has become a tired radical in this job of selling the paper), let the younger students and workers take over the job of being fools for Christ. One seminarian sold the paper all one summer for us. One rainy night when we were going into a CIO meeting there he was, standing in the downpour shouting READ THE CATHOLIC WORKER—THE ONLY THING THAT ISN'T ALL WET!

Big Dan used to call out (in opposition to Communist salesmen, who shouted, Read the Daily Worker), "READ THE CATHOLIC WORKER DAILY."

Leaflets, pamphlets, papers, as well as more scholarly journals, are needed to reach the man in the street. Here is a letter which came last month:

> "We have been receiving a hundred CATHOLIC WORK-ERS a month and selling and distributing them in Columbus Circle. Do publish an appeal for more zeal on the part of Catholics in getting the Catholic message to the worker, to the poor, to the oppressed. There is a colored Catholic couple in Philadelphia and they would like a supply of fifty papers every month to distribute in their neighborhood."

Many an apostle has been found by selling Catholic literature on the street corner; he has been queried as to his positions and beliefs and has had to begin to study "to know the reason for the faith that is in him" in order to answer all the questions that are put to him. And many a time he just can't answer them and it's no use his trying.

Houses Needed for Hospitality

To reach the masses through the spiritual and the corporal works of mercy. Of course getting Catholic literature around is performing quite a few of those tasks. It is enlightening the ignorant and counseling the doubtful, comforting the afflicted, and you might even say that walking on a picket line is doing these things too, as well as rebuking the sinner. But when we talk of the works of mercy, we usually think of *feeding the hungry, clothing the naked, and sheltering the homeless.*

We have had to do them all, even to burying the dead. One does not necessarily have to establish, run, or live in a House of Hospitality, as Peter named the hospices we have been running around the country, in order to practice the works of mercy. The early Fathers of the Church said that every house should have a Christ's room. But it is generally only the poorest who are hospitable. A young college graduate hitchhiking across the county during the depression (he was trying to make up his mind about his vocation) said that the only place he found hospitality was among the Negroes and the Mexicans. Certainly priests' housekeepers did not extend any. He met so much misery and starvation even, that when he reached Los Angeles, he finally started a House of Hospitality there, and in that house he met with so many impossible cases that he turned more and more to the spiritual weapons, and now he is a priest, with the most powerful weapons of all in his hands.

Every house should have a Christ's room. The coat which hangs in your closet belongs to the poor. If your brother comes to you hungry and you say, Go be thou filled, what kind of hospitality is that? It is no use turning people away to an agency, to the city or the state or the Catholic Charities. It is you yourself who must perform the works of mercy. Often you can only give the price of a meal, or a bed on the Bowery. Often you can only hope that it will be spent for that. Often you can literally take off a garment if it only be a scarf and warm some shivering brother. But personally, at a personal sacrifice, these were the ways. Peter used to insist, to combat the growing tendency on the part of the State to take over. The great danger was the State taking over the job which our Lord Himself gave us to do, *"Inasmuch as you did it unto one of the least of these my brethren, you have done it unto me."*

Of course husbands must be considered, and wives must be considered, and children. One must look after one's own family it is true. But Fr. Coady said once, "We can all do ten times as much as we think we can do."

Right now we have two Houses of Hospitality in Detroit, the St. Martha House and the St. Francis House. In Cleveland there is the Martin de Porres House. In Pittsburgh, there is the St. Joseph House of Hospitality which was started by our group (the Bishop gave the use of a huge orphanage) and is now run by Father Rice and Joseph Lenz. In Harrisburg there is the Martin de Porres House. In Philadelphia, the House of Christ the Worker. In Rochester, St. Joseph's House of Hospitality for men and the Martha flat for women.

In the past there have been houses in Seattle, Sacramento, San Francisco, Los Angeles, St. Louis, Milwaukee, St. Paul, Minneapolis, Chicago, South Bend, Toledo, Troy, Buffalo, Boston, Washington, Baltimore, New Orleans, etc., but when the depression ended with the war boom, and there were again jobs for all, many of the houses closed. Of course there is always a need for such centers. There are always the lame and the halt and the blind. There are always the poor we will always have with us, as our Lord said. There are always those coming out of hospitals, mental asylums, jails, etc. There is the wayfarer that needs to be sheltered for a night and those who come and stay a lifetime and finally need to be buried. The war took many of our young men into the service, into conscientious objector camps, into the medical corps, into jails, and they were the ones who ran the houses and performed the works of mercy. There were only four houses for women, and of those two are still going; the Harrisburg house is a family center, to take care of the Negroes in the Seventh Street district in the shadow of the capitol.

Unpremeditated

At one time a thousand a day were fed in New York, probably more. Now there are perhaps four hundred or five hundred. The house is always filled (we have 36 rooms and two stores) but the line is smaller. We started fourteen years ago by inviting whoever came along to dinner. Many of our workers were recruited in that way. By the time three years had passed, we were given the use of 115 Mott street and the line began to stretch around the block. We never contemplated starting a BREAD LINE. All Peter had ever talked about were Houses of Hospitality and he had hoped that there could be craft shops, and discussion centers and libraries, and perhaps a chapel, and that these houses would be little cells of Christian living, radiating peace and brotherly love. But the evil of the day, the poverty in our rich country, the unemployment in the age of the machine was so great, and the disability, mental and physical, so appalling, that our houses grew and the lines grew with them.

But Peter never grows discouraged. "Discouragement is a temptation of the devil," he would say. "We must make the kind of society where people find it easier to be good," he would add very simply.

Clarification Through Discussion

Round table discussions go on everywhere, when two or three gather together. Perhaps there is too much of it, in an informal way, and not enough of it in a formal way. We have regular Friday night meetings, when speakers come and present a point of view, lead in a discussion, or give a spiritual conference. There are discussions when visitors gather together, and whole groups, classes from seminaries, colleges and schools, come together to ask questions and to enter into controversy. There are the retreats at Maryfarm, which in the past have been glimpses of heaven to a great many, an enlightenment, a conversion, a time of peace and study and rest.

Peter used to enter upon discussions on street corners, over restaurant tables, in public squares, as well as in the office, at all times of the day and night. He believed in catching people as they came, and often the discussions would go on all night. One is reminded of St. Paul, who talked so long that the young man fell off the window seat, out of the open window, and was picked up for dead; St. Paul had to revive him. And St. Catherine of Siena, it is said, talked until she put people to sleep and then woke them up to listen some more.

But Peter can talk and discuss no longer. He is over seventy, and his mind is tired, and his memory bad. He has been a great leader, and his writings still inspire. And now significantly enough, many young people all over the country are trying to put into effect his ideas, both in publishing, in running centers of training, in establishing themselves on the land, and here these discussions are being continued. If you cannot find enough people around Mott street to talk to about these ideas, and books that Peter has recommended, one can go to John Straub or Walter Marx in Washington, or the Center for Christ the King at Herman, Pennsylvania, or to Loveland, Ohio, where there are a number of families, as well as the great school of the apostolate for women, THE GRAIL. Or there is a center at Brookfield, Conn., where there are four families on the land. Everywhere, the discussions, started by Peter, are going on. The candle he has lit has been lighting many another candle and the light is becoming brighter.

Farm Centers Are Small Beginnings

There are these centers, and other farms too around the country which are centers of the lay apostolate, though not the communal farm that Peter envisaged at a time when unemployment was the tragedy of the day, and man had neither work nor bread. There is a Catholic Worker farm at Lyons, Michigan, where Louis and Justine Murphy live, and another Catholic Worker farm at Upton, Mass., where the O'Donnell, Paulson and Roach families live. Frank manages the St. Leo shop there and Carl Paulson and Mary make stained glass and do wood carving, etc. Both farms are called St. Benedict's Farm. There are 14 children at the Massachusetts farm. There is Our Lady of the Wayside Farm at Avon, Ohio, where Bill and Dorothy Gauchat live with their three children and are taking care of a little crippled baby (who cannot live) whose parents cannot care for it. This farm helps provide food for the House of Hospitality Bill manages in Cleveland.

Now there is Maryfarm, Newburgh, which is connected with 115 Mott street, and which we hope will soon be self sustaining, and not only self sustaining, but helping to feed the breadline at Mott street. We will be having retreats there during the summer, and it will be delightful to go by way of boat up the Hudson, a slow trip, but a fitting approach to a week of prayer and study. You can get there quickly by New York Central to Beacon in an hour and a half; then take the ferry to Newburgh and a bus to Coldenham for ten minutes or so. You ask to be let off on Route 17K at the Catholic Worker Farm which is opposite the Sunnybrook Fruit Farms. We have had our first retreat already, Easter week, dedicated to rejoicing.

This is a brief summary of the Catholic Worker and its aims and purposes in the lay apostolate. Often people ask us what is the keynote of Peter's message, and one could say at once, without hesitation, POVERTY. It is what sets him apart, it is what distinguishes him from the great mass of the teachers of the day. In a time when we are living in an acquisitive society, Peter Maurin is THE POOR MAN.

Last month there was a sensational story in all the New York papers, and probably reprinted all over the country, about two brothers, Langley and Homer Cohyer, who were misers and accumulators and who met with a horrible end. On receipt of a telephone call, police broke into a house on upper Fifth Avenue in the Harlem section, a four story house which in this housing shortage could have been converted into homes for four families. They found Homer, who had been blind and helpless, dead from starvation. His brother had disappeared. The house was so filled with junk that Langley had had to tunnel his way through to go in and out of the house to make their few purchases. In fear of intrusion, he had made booby traps with hundreds of pounds of old iron ready to fall on whoever threatened their privacy. One of these booby traps caught Langley who smothered to death within a few feet of his blind brother, who on account of the junk, could not reach either his brother or the window to call for help.

He slowly starved to death, while listening to the rats feeding on the corpse of Langley a few feet away.

This story seems to me a vision of hell, a very literal and appalling sample of the hell that awaits the acquisitive, the greedy, the accumulators, the seekers after markets, wealth, power, prestige, exclusiveness, empire, dominion, of everything opposed to the common good. Here were two old men who epitomized to the nth degree suspicion and hatred of their fellows, and a desire to gather together to themselves everything they could lay their hands on. "They were worth $100,000" the newspapers reported. What a strange use of words! They spent little. Among the things they collected were six grand pianos, dismantled cars, babies' cribs.

Peter, on the other hand, has accumulated nothing in this life. He has nothing but the suit on his back, the shoes on his feet. He has lived on Bowerys and Skid Roads all his life, not believing that his dignity needed to be maintained by residence at a decent address, or by stopping at a good hotel. To reach one's fellows by the practice of the works of mercy, AT A PERSONAL SACRIFICE,—this meant embracing voluntary poverty. Voluntary poverty as a means to an end, to publish a paper, to put out leaflets, to live on the land, to serve one's fellows. He has lived these ideas.

And so when people ask us how we get the funds to run Houses of Hospitality, to feed the hungry, clothe the naked, shelter the homeless, care for the sick and bury the dead, we can only reply that our own wages are a penny a day, and that by living in common we have enough to care for our brothers. The paper costs a cent a copy, or twenty-five cents a year. Many people send more. When our bills pile high, we send out an appeal, and usually this must be done twice a year, spring and fall; on St. Joseph's Day in March and St. Francis' Day in October. Always we get just enough to carry on. When there is some extraordinary project in view like the new farm at Newburgh, we make an especial appeal for that. Ask and you shall receive. That is, if the Lord wants you to have it. "I have no need of your goods," He has said, through the psalmist, and one of the ways we may know if it is God's will that we carry on this work, is by the response to our appeals. If He wants the work done, He will send the means to do it.

Light and Warmth Means Love

All this is set forth to show the validity, the vitality of Peter Maurin's ideas, of his vision. They said of the early Christians,—"SEE HOW THEY LOVE ONE ANOTHER," and we have seen in Peter's poverty how this love could be expressed, to live with the poor, to work with the poor, and to love the poor. And how great and wonderful a thing is this love which makes all work joyful and all burdens light. "Love is the fulfilling of the law." And HELL, Bernanos says, is not to love any more.

That love is not a matter of emotion, but a matter of the will, a matter of preference, one soon learns in work like this. To love your neighbor, to love your enemy, who only yesterday was your neighbor, your ally and now has become an enemy. Or so they say.

And what does this love mean in regard to Russia for instance?

What Is Our Stand on Russia?

We are fighting principalities and powers, not flesh and blood, and the Russians are our neighbors, our brothers in Christ, and not just a world power seeking empire. We are inclined to look upon the small nations as having much more to say, these days, and much clearer judgment than the mighty powers in the UNO. We are for disarmament and the outlawing of the atomic bomb, even if we die for it, even if we are deceived in the integrity of our brothers. We must lay down our lives as Christ did, "A New Commandment I give you, that you love your brother as I have loved you."

But what about the concentration camps, forced labor, domination of small countries? "The worst enemy of a man will be those of his own household." "Regard not the mote that is in thy brother's eye while disregarding the beam in thine own eye." What about our own problem of minorities; Negroes who are one tenth of our population, Chinese, Filipino, Japanese concentration camps, the recent deportation of Indonesians. Have we forgotten about these?

If your enemy hunger, give him to eat. There is always a solution in the practice of the works of mercy, at a personal sacrifice.

The Old Testament speaking of our Lord, foretelling Him, is full of the same thought. The epistle on Monday in Holy Week was from Isaias, "I have given my body to the strikers, and my cheeks to them that plucked them. I have not turned away my face from them that rebuked me and spit upon me. The Lord God is my helper."

To those who call us isolationist, we must remind them that the Good Samaritan did not leave the poor traveler by the road and run after the robbers. He ministered to the wounded, and fed and sheltered him, and did not seem in the least concerned for justice to be done to the thieves, or revenge being taken. Love, it is a beautiful word, but as Father Zossima said, LOVE IN PRACTICE IS A HARSH AND DREADFUL THING COMPARED TO LOVE IN DREAMS.

"PETER MAURIN"

When Peter talked about asceticism, it was matter-of-factly, as the word implies, "an exercise of one's religion. To him, religion and asceticism go together. It is inconceivable for instance that one can truly be "religious" and not embrace voluntary poverty.

And it is this emphasis on voluntary poverty that has led to much criticism and antagonism toward the movement, even while it has called forth the most attention and attracted the most admiration. Unfortunately, the admiration has come from those who contemplate from afar, and the criticism from those close to us has much of justice in it.

On account of the emphasis placed upon poverty in the past which led to heresies (an over-emphasis of one aspect of the truth, to the expense of others) probably not enough has been written about poverty in the present, especially here in the United States, when modern plumbing seems to epitomize culture and civilization.

When Jesus gathered his disciples and the multitude around Him to preach the Sermon on the Mount, He was not just addressing the disciples when He said, "Ye are the salt of the earth." He was addressing the poor. The rest of His discourse was meant for them, the Beatitudes were for them, so He meant also to call them the salt of the earth. The poor are the salt of the earth; the truly poor,—the poor in spirit.

What a mysterious thing poverty is. To the religious-minded, it has had an enormous attraction down through the ages. To simplify one's life, to cut out the superfluous, to go against the sensual inclinations of one's own nature,—Christian and non-Christian have emphasized these teachings.

There is William James' panegyric on poverty.

"When we gravely ask ourselves whether this wholesale organization of irrationality and crime (war) be our only bulwark against effeminacy, we stand aghast at the thought, and think more kindly of ascetic religion. One hears of the mechanical equivalent of heat. What we need now to discover in the social realm is the moral equivalent of war: something heroic that will speak to men as universally as war does, and yet will be as compatible with their spiritual selves as war has proved itself to be incompatible. I have often thought that in the old monkish poverty-worship, in spite of the pedantry which infested it, there might be something like that moral equivalent of war which we are seeking. May not voluntarily accepted poverty be "the strenuous life," without the need of crushing weaker peoples? Poverty indeed IS the strenuous life,—without brass bands or uniforms or hysteric popular applause or lies or circumlocutions; and when one sees the way in which wealth-giving enters as an ideal into the very bone and marrow of our generation, one wonders whether a revival of the belief that poverty is a worthy religious vocation may not be the transformation of military courage and the spiritual reform which our time stands most in need of. Among us English-speaking peoples especially do the praises of poverty need once more to be boldly sung. We have grown literally afraid to be poor. We despise anyone who elects to be poor in order to simplify and save his inner life. If he does not join the general scramble and cant with the money-making street, we deem him spiritless and lacking in ambition. We have lost the power even of imagining what the ancient idealization of poverty could have meant: the liberation from material attachments, the unbribed soul, the manlier indifference, the paying our way by what we are to do and not by what we have, the right to fling away our life at any moment irresponsibly,—the more athletic trim, in short, the moral fighting shape. When we of the so-called better classes are scared as men were never scared in history at material ugliness and hardship; when we put off marriage until our house can be artistic, and quake at the thought of having a child without a bank-account and doomed to manual labor, it is time for thinking men to protest against so unmanly and irreligious a state of opinion. It is true that so far as wealth gives time for ideal ends and exercise to ideal energies; wealth is better than poverty and ought to be chosen. But wealth does this in only a portion of the actual cases. Elsewhere the desire to gain wealth and the fear to lose it are our chief breeders of cowardice and propagators of corruption. There are thousands of conjunctures in which a wealth-bound man must be a slave, whilst a man for whom poverty has no terrors becomes a free man. Think of the strength which personal indifference to poverty would give us if we were devoted to unpopular causes. We need no longer hold our tongues or fear to vote the revolutionary or reformatory ticket. Our stocks might fall, our hopes of promotion vanish, our salaries stop, our club doors close in our faces; yet while we lived we would imperturbably bear witness to the spirit, and our example would help us to set free our generation. The cause would need its funds, but we its servants would be potent in proportion as we personally were contented with our poverty. I recommend this matter to your serious pondering, for it is certain that the prevalent fear of poverty among the educated classes is the worst moral disease from which our civilization suffers."

One of our Italian neighbors has an extravagant fear of poverty. When we took over one of the apartments in the front building there were so many locks and bars and bolts that one would have thought there was a vendetta in the neighborhood.

I looked at those bolts and bars. The family was not afraid of public opinion—it was the strongest family in the neighborhood. They were not afraid of the law—the matriarch of the family sold liquor in her kitchen, without a license, as many of the families did, and other members had gotten into trouble with the law. They were not afraid of God Himself, since none of them went to Church. They were afraid of neither God nor man, but they were afraid of losing their money. That was the greatest terror life had to offer.

There is Saint Francis—the heart leaps at the thought of him— loved by Catholic and non-Catholic. Once a priest pointed to a statue of Saint Francis and said sadly, "There is the last Franciscan."

Bernanos, in his *Diary of a Country Priest.* understood poverty, and Leon Bloy, who wrote *The Woman Who Was Poor.*

Poverty is hard to understand. It is an inexhaustible mine of wisdom. "Those who are in honor are without understanding." the Psalmist said.

Christ did not try to rescue people from their poverty. He came to preach the Gospel. When He fed the multitude and there are two stories of such miracles in the Gospel, the people must have wanted Him to go on feeding them. But He fed them once, taking compassion on them so that they did not go away hungry. It must have been a suffering all through His life, not to feed people in their poverty. It was one of the temptations of the devil who said to Him, "Turn these stones into bread." It would have been so easy for Him to feed them, to relieve their hunger. He must have seen many hungry, many suffering, many begging. Remembering this, and living in poverty ourselves is the only way we can endure life which is so filled with suffering these days.

Yet by poverty we do not mean destitution. Daniel-Rops in *The Poor and Ourselves* makes a distinction between poverty and destitution. To us, voluntary poverty has been a mine of wealth and wisdom; a means to an end. And amongst us all, Peter has most exemplified the man who was poor.

A SELECTED BIBLIOGRAPHY

PRIMARY SOURCES:

The Eleventh Virgin (New York: Boni, 1924).

From Union Square to Rome (Silver Spring, Md.: The Preservation of the Faith Press, 1938).

House of Hospitality (New York: Sheed and Ward, 1939).

The Long Loneliness (New York: Harper and Row, 1959).

Therese (Notre Dame, Indiana: Fides Publishers, 1960).

Loaves and Fishes (New York: Harper, 1963).

On Pilgrimage: The Sixties (New York: Curtis, 1972).

Articles in *The Catholic Worker*, 1933-1980.

SECONDARY SOURCES:

Marc H. Ellis, *Peter Maurin: Prophet in the Twentieth Century* (New York: Paulist Press, 1981).

John Hellman, *Emmanuel Mounier and the New Catholic Left, 1930-1950* (Buffalo: University of Toronto Press, 1981).

Wayne Lobue, "Public Theology and the Catholic Worker," *Cross Currents* 26 (Autumn, 1976), 270-85.

William Miller, *Dorothy Day: A Biography* (San Francisco: Harper and Row, 1982).

_____, *A Harsh and Dreadful Love: Dorothy Day and the Catholic Worker Movement* (New York: Doubleday, 1973).

David O'Brien, "Dorothy Day and History," *Commonweal*, December 19, 1980.

Mel Piehl, *Breaking Bread: The Catholic Worker and the Origin of Catholic Radicalism in America* (Philadelphia: Temple University Press, 1982).

Nancy Roberts, *Dorothy Day and the Catholic Worker* (New York: State University of New York Press, 1984).

10

Dom Virgil Michel, O.S.B.

DOM VIRGIL MICHEL, O.S.B.: LITURGICAL REFORMER

Dom Virgil (nee George) Michel, O.S.B. (1890-1938), was the foremost spokesman for the liturgical revival in American Catholicism during the early twentieth century. Combining interests in sociology, economics, politics, education, philosophy, and art with his study of liturgy, Michel developed a liturgical movement in the United States that differed significantly from its European Catholic precursor. He contributed to a renewed understanding of the liturgy by emphasizing the liturgy's potential for social reform. The liturgy expressed a Christian community of justice as well as faith. For Michel, this meant that a renewal of the social order must be tied to a revival of the liturgy, and that a revived concern for the liturgy demanded a corresponding concern for social reconstruction. The European liturgical movement reflected little of this emphasis upon social justice and reform. It did not have the pragmatic and activist orientation that Michel gave to the American Catholic movement. Michel's movement, of course, was not a popular movement in American Catholicism, but it did anticipate the liturgical renewal fostered by the Second Vatican Council.

George Michel was born in St. Paul, Minnesota to Fred and Mary Griebler Michel, immigrants from Germany. George received his elementary education in St. Paul, entered St. John's Preparatory School in Collegeville, Minnesota in 1903, and was graduated in 1909 from St. John's University with a Bachelor's degree in Latin. Immediately after college, he entered the Benedictine Order at St. John's Abbey and was ordained in 1916. From 1916 to 1918, he studied at the Catholic University of America and received a doctorate in English, writing a dissertation on Orestes Brownson's literary principles. From 1918 to 1924 he taught various disciplines at St. John's. He, then, studied philosophy at Sant 'Anselmo in Rome and at the University of Louvain during 1924 and 1925. In 1926, back at St. John's, he began to publish *Orate Fratres*, the organ of the liturgical movement he instituted. In 1930, exhausted with teaching and editing responsibilities, he retired from St. John's to serve in the Indian missions in Northern Minnesota for three years. In 1933, he returned to St. John's as Dean of the University. After a brief illness in November of 1938, he died at St. John's.

The following selection was originally an address given to the Minnesota branch of the Central-Verein Society during its thirty-seventh annual convention at Mankato, Minnesota on September 22, 1934. Stressing one of the primary themes of the Central-Verein, social reconstruction through local solidarity rather than through state intervention, Michel presented the liturgy as the basis of a common solidarity and as the teacher of organic fellowship and the dignity of the individual. The liturgy teaches most effectively, however, by doing. Teaching is always inseparable from practice. The liturgy, therefore, should not only express and teach human solidarity, but it should also enable the Christian community to be an agent of social regeneration.

TEXT

"THE LITURGY THE BASIS OF SOCIAL REGENERATION"

Source: Orate Fratres, IX (1934/35), 536-545

At the first mention of the subject of this address one might be inclined to ask: What has the liturgy to do with social reconstruction or the social question? Can the liturgy help to give jobs or raise wages? Can there be any connection between the liturgy and the social problem?

It is now seven years ago that the Central Bureau of the Central-Verein published a pamphlet that was more than usually distinguished for its keen Christian sense as well as its historical vision. It was entitled *The True Basis of Christian Solidarity* and it carried the explanatory subtitle: "The Liturgy an Aid to the Solution of the Social Question."

The moment we deal with the problem of social regeneration, we shall do well to have recourse to the classic Catholic text on the question, the encyclical *Quadragesimo Anno* of the present Holy Father "on Reconstructing the Social Order."

The very idea of social regeneration or reconstruction implies that there is something very much awry with our present social order. Pius

XI refers to this fact in the following brief sentence: "Nowadays, as more than once in the history of the Church, we are confronted with a world which in large measure has almost fallen back into paganism." In analysing conditions the Pontiff speaks of a double danger. This is how he expresses it when he discusses the particular question of private property: "There is, therefore, a double danger to be avoided. On the one hand, if the social and public aspect of ownership be denied or minimized, the logical consequence is Individualism, as it is called; on the other hand, the rejection or diminution of its private and individual character necessarily leads to some form of Collectivism. To disregard these dangers would be to rush headlong into the quicksands of Modernism."

These, then, are the two dangers the Holy Father warns us to avoid if society is to be regenerated; they are the products of an un-Christian view of life and are therefore pagan at heart; and they are both current symptoms of a diseased social order.

INDIVIDUALISM

I shall deal first with individualism. Christianity has always upheld the supreme value of each individual soul, and so has always been the champion of a moderate form of individualism. It could do no less since the whole Christian view of life, both natural and supernatural, is dependent on the existence of individual human responsibility for one's action and conduct. Christianity has always stood for a proper appreciation of human personality and has always opposed the treatment of men as if they were animals or mechanical robots.

When the great break occurred four centuries ago in the Christian tradition that had been developing for centuries, it showed itself precisely in the question of individualism. For many persons the individual conscience was then made the supreme judge in all matters of religion; each man became his own highest authority in the interpretation of the scriptural word of God. At the height of the eighteenth-century enlightenment the principle of extreme individualism had entered into the entire field of social life. All authority superior to man was denied, and human traditions were laughed out of court. There was then no longer any master superior to man. Man was his own supreme authority, his own sole lawgiver, not only in religion but in all the fields of human conduct, especially also in economic life. Man no longer had any real duties towards his fellowmen. He had a duty only towards his own self, and that duty was the pleasant one of looking after his own best interests in his own chosen way and not bothering about anyone else. This principle of extreme individualism was then given moral justification by the view that if every individual looks to his own best personal interest and makes that his supreme law in life, then the good of society will also be best attained.

What actually happened thereupon was that this principle of exaggerated individualism made of society a battle-ground of each against all. This was a condition not of dignified human personalities and life, but a human version of the law of the jungle. It was a raw "struggle for existence and survival of the fittest" disguised under the phrase of "free competition."

Here is what *Quadragesimo Anno* has to say on this point: "Just as the unity of human society cannot be built upon class warfare, so the proper ordering of economic affairs cannot be left to free competition alone. From this source have proceeded in the past all the errors of the 'Individualistic' school. This school, ignorant or forgetful of the social and moral aspects of economic matters, teaches that the State should refrain in theory and practice from interfering therein, because these possess in free competition and open markets a principle of self-direction better able to control them than any created intellect. Free competition, however, though within certain limits just and productive of good results, cannot be the ruling principle of the economic world. This has been abundantly proved by the consequences that have followed from the free rein given to these dangerous individualistic ideals."

Such is one of the dangers alluded to by the Holy Father. And it is pagan in nature because it contradicts true Christian principles of social life. It has developed, moreover, during the past four centuries step by step with the gradual abandonment of traditional Christianity. As the mighty of the world went on from an abandonment of the Church of Christ to a denial of the divinity of Christ and then to a denial of God, so did the jungle law and pagan principle of the right of the strong and the fortunate spread ever wider into every field of human life.

The other danger pointed out by the Holy Father is called by him Collectivism, the opposite extreme to Individualism. In the sense in which the Papal encyclical refers to Collectivism, it is just as pagan, just as un-Christian as Individualism; and it is just as one-sided as the latter. Just as the undue stressing of the individual led to the neglect of the social nature of human life, so the undue stressing of the social nature of man leads to a one-sided neglect of his individual rights as a human person.

"It is true, indeed," says our encyclical, "that a just freedom of action should be left to individual citizens and families." Hence this Collectivism is wrong in fact and principle. To quote again: "Just as it is wrong to withdraw from the individual and commit to the community at large what private enterprise and industry can accomplish, so too it is an injustice, a grave evil and a disturbance of the right order for a larger and higher organization to arrogate to itself functions which can be performed efficiently by smaller and lower bodies. . . . Of its very nature the true aim of all social activity should be to help individual members of the social body, but never to destroy or absorb them."

That is the true danger of Collectivism: that it destroys or absorbs the individual. For it the individual does not count for anything. Authority and obedience is everything, and the human person nothing. That this danger is real today a glance at the face of Europe sufficiently proves. We may express it in one word: the totalitarian State. And we shall do well to remind ourselves that similar State absolutism, and supreme and arbitrary political power over life and death was a characteristic of pre-Christian pagan kingdoms and empires. No wonder that where the principles of the totalitarian State have been followed to the full, in Russia and Germany, for instance, we have a conscious espousal and enforcement of atheism on the one hand and a barbaric revival of pagan religion on the other. Such Collectivism is as much the antithesis of Christianity as is Individualism.

THE CHRISTIAN PRINCIPLE

Now what is the Christian principle over against these two pagan extremes? It is such a mutual balancing and limitation of the two as brings them into harmony. Pius XI refers to this principle at various times. Speaking of the question of Capital and Labor he states it as follows: "In the first place, due consideration must be had for the double character, individual and social, of Capital and Labor, in order that the dangers of Individualism and Collectivism be avoided."

It is this double character, the harmonious fusion of the two elements of human nature, the individual and the social, that we must not only keep in mind, but that must again become dominant in all human life. How can that be done?

Pius XI answers by referring to a "new diffusion throughout the world of the Gospel spirit, which is a spirit of Christian moderation and of universal charity." By reason of it, he says, "we confidently look forward to that complete and much desired renewal of human society, and to 'the Peace of Christ in the Kingdom of Christ.'"

Now this renewal of human society, which must needs bring about a harmonious relation between men, one of cooperation and mutual aid and not one of mutual strife and cut-throat competition, must have its origin and inspiration in religion. The Holy Father quotes his great predecessor Leo XIII to that effect: "For the 'foundation of social laws being thus laid in religion, it is not hard to establish the relations of members one to another, in order that they may live together in concord and achieve prosperity.'"

He is indeed very emphatic on this point: "If We examine matters diligently and thoroughly We shall perceive clearly that this longed-for social reconstruction must be preceded by a profound renewal of the Christian spirit, from which multitudes engaged in industry in every country have unhappily departed. Otherwise, all our endeavors will be futile, and our social edifice will be built, not upon a rock, but upon shifting sand."

Now the question logically arises: Where are we to find this Christian spirit that is essential to the successful regeneration of the social order? The answer was given long ago by the saintly Pius X in a statement that many of you have undoubtedly heard repeated time and again. He first of all expressed it as his keenest desire "that the true Christian spirit flourish again and become more firmly grounded in all the faithful." Then he pointed out the great need "of deriving this spirit from its primary and indispensable source, which is active participation in the sacred mysteries and the public and solemn prayers of the Church."

With this we have come to the liturgy. For the liturgy is nothing else than the solemn and public worship of the Church, her official prayers and blessings, the sacraments, and above all the holy Sacrifice of Christ, the Mass. Pius X not only called this liturgy the indispensable source of the true Christian spirit, but added that the faithful must derive this spirit from the Church's worship by active participation: therefore, not by passive bodily presence, but by being present in such a manner that mind and heart are actively joined to the official worship and take intelligent part in the holy action.

There is no time here to dwell on the meaning of active participation, nor to analyse further the nature of the elements that make up the Church's liturgy. I shall proceed at once to the question: What is the basic idea of this liturgy?

It is that of the Mystical Body of Christ—a concept that was not only well known to the early Christians but also a primary inspiration for all their conduct and life. It was constantly preached by the Church Fathers and taught by the Church down to our own day, but it has often, among the faithful of all ranks, been left in the background, even quite forgotten, especially since the growing dominance of an un-Christian individualism.

The doctrine of the Mystical Body was explained by Christ under the example of the vine and the branches and by St. Paul under the picture of the human body composed of head and members. When through the liturgical initiation of Baptism we enter the Church, by that same fact we become intimately united with Christ as members of the Mystical Body of which He is the Head. Christ is then most truly and supernaturally our Brother, we are all children of God in a very special and sublime manner; we are all brethren together who are intimately united in the one Christ. In this holy fellowship we find a harmonious combination of the two complementary factors of humankind, that is, organic fellowship coupled with full respect for human personality and individual responsibility.

This is not merely an abstract doctrine or truth of our Christian lives, but one that should be the basis of our every thought and action as Christians. The active character of it is seen for instance in what our catechism has taught us about the communion of the saints and the common treasury of supernatural merits in the Church. By becoming members of the Mystical Body of Christ through Baptism, we no longer belong to ourselves alone but above all to Christ and His cause. All our good actions and merits likewise, which we perform only through Christ, belong strictly to Christ for attaining the purposes of Christ. Thus all the merits of Christ, which exceed all human needs, and those of His members, form a common treasury of grace and merits, which are in turn applied to all the members according to their needs and their desert. This is the highest type of Christian solidarity—a supernatural living solidarity or fellowship—not only in theory but also in practice.

Similarly the liturgy of the Church not only makes and keeps us members of this fellowship, but it always puts the idea of fellowship in Christ into full practice. Just in so far as we participate in the liturgy after the mind of Christ do we also live and breathe this supernatural social unity of all members in Christ. This is why the liturgy is so truly the primary and indispensable source of the true Christian spirit: it not only teaches us what this spirit is but also has us live this spirit in all its enactments. In the liturgy the teaching is inseparable from the putting into practice.

I shall have to content myself with one of two examples of this truth. The sacrament of the Eucharist, holy Communion, is called by St. Thomas the sacrament of the unity of the Mystical Body of Christ. When we receive Communion we may be inclined to think of it as Christ coming into our hearts and becoming our own exclusive possession, and we think with gratitude of the infinite Christ confining Himself within the limits of our small heart. When twenty persons receive

Communion at Mass and go back to their separate pews, this would almost imply that there were now twenty Christs extant among the pews. We know, of course, that this is not the Catholic doctrine. When twenty or more individuals receive Communion they have all been intimately united to one and the same sacramental Christ. Christ is not divided or really multiplied among them after Communion; rather are they all contained in one and the same Christ, and thus united most closely into a single supernatural fellowship with Him. The early Christians understood this very well. And therefore they had no difficulty in transferring this intimate fellowship of love that was wrought among them in holy Communion into every action of their daily lives. They also understood that Communion was God's answering gift to the offering they had made in an earlier part of the Mass. At the Offertory they all entered with full understanding and heart into the Offertory procession that was a universal custom of the Church for many centuries. What was the real meaning of this Offertory procession?

First of all, everyone who assisted at Mass brought his own individual gift to God, something of his own, something he had raised or worked to acquire, something that he could have used for his own support and that therefore stood for himself. In bringing to the altar this gift, which was generally a portion of bread or wine, olive oil, or some such product, he was fully conscious of thereby dedicating his whole self to God, of giving body and soul, mind and heart to his Maker, and of doing so not only by internal intention but also by external action. Moreover no one brought his gift in isolation from his brethren. All joined together in the Offertory procession and together brought their gifts as one single common offering to God, each one offering not only himself and for himself but each one offering all and for all. It was thus a beautiful example as well as realization of true Christian solidarity and love.

Of the gifts offered, some bread and wine were laid on the altar to be the essential elements of the Sacrifice of Mass, and all the rest of the one common offering was laid aside on tables to be used for the poor and the needy. Thus the common offering made by them to God became at the same time a common act of love and charity to the poor and the needy, so that in one and the same collective but unitary action they worshiped God directly and served Him indirectly in their fellowmen. Such was the sublime lesson of Christian solidarity that was brought home to the early Christians increasingly by their active participation in the liturgy. It was brought home to them not only as a truth learned, but as a principle put into regular practice, which by repetition formed a permanent attitude and habit of mind. No wonder that they lived so true to this genuine Christian spirit in all the actions of their daily lives!

The liturgy is replete with instances of the actual working out of this Christian fellowship and solidarity, this mutual Christian love which cannot bear to see a member suffer without an attempt to aid him. We are all aware of the fact that no Mass is offered without an official commemoration of the poor souls in purgatory. This is but another illustration of the general principle of Christian solidarity between the different divisions of the fellowship.

Sometimes we view the sacrament of Confession as a striking instance of God's dealing solely with the individual. But here too we have another example of the same solidary Christian spirit. Here too the merits of the common treasury of all is drawn upon for the needs of the individual member. This is beautifully expressed in the official prayer recited by the priest after the sacramental absolution. In a most offhand way the good works of the individual in question and of all the saints and of Christ are mentioned together: "May the passion of our Lord Jesus Christ, the merits of the blessed Virgin Mary and of all the saints, whatever good thou mayest do and whatever evil thou mayest have to endure, profit thee unto the remission of sins, increase of grace, and glory in the life without end. Amen."

This, then, is the true Christian spirit and first and last the supreme lesson of the liturgy as the official worship and life of the Mystical Body of Christ. And this spirit must needs be the source of all further extension and application of the principles of solidarity and fellowship in our common life and civilization.

So it is pointed out by the Holy Father himself. For him this mutual supernatural relationship of men united in Christ is the model towards which all social regeneration must strive. Speaking of the proper economic relations between men he says, for instance: "Where this harmonious proportion is kept, man's various economic activities combine and unite into one single organism and become as members of a common body, lending each other mutual help and service." Again: "Then only will it be possible to unite all in a harmonious striving for the common good, when all sections of society have the intimate conviction that they are members of a single family and children of the same heavenly Father, and further, that they are one body in Christ and everyone members one of another."

The whole trend of ideas I have tried to bring before you is admirably expressed in a quotation from one of the most active and inspiring as well as profound apostles of Catholic Action in our day, Christopher Dawson. "The Mystical Body," he says, "is the link between the liturgy and sociology: and in proportion as men are brought to realize, through the liturgy, their position as members of that Body, will their actions in the social sphere be affected thereby. . . . A visible manifestation of incorporation into Christ, a visible united action on the part of the members, cannot fail to revive and foster in them a determination to carry their Christ-life into the social and economic sphere."

In conclusion, I may summarize in what happens to take on the form of a logical syllogism:

Pius X tells us that the liturgy is the indispensable source of the true Christian spirit; Pius XI says that the true Christian spirit is indispensable for social regeneration.

Hence the conclusion: The liturgy is the indispensable basis of Christian social regeneration.

A SELECTED BIBLIOGRAPHY

PRIMARY SOURCES:

The Critical Principles of Orestes A. Brownson (Washington, D.C.: 1918).

The Liturgical Apostolate (Collegeville, Minn.: The Liturgical Press, 1926).

My Sacrifice and Yours (Collegeville: The Liturgical Press, 1926).

[with Martin B. Hellriegel] *The Liturgical Movement* (Collegeville: The Liturgical Press, 1930).

Philosophy of Human Conduct (Minneapolis: Burgess Publishing Co., 1936).

The Liturgy of the Church (New York: Macmillan, 1937).

Christian Social Reconstruction (Milwaukee: Bruce, 1937).

Our Life in Christ (Collegeville: The Liturgical Press, 1939).

The Christian in the World (Collegeville: The Liturgical Press, 1939).

SECONDARY SOURCES:

Colman Barry, O.S.B., *Worship and Work: St. John's Abbey, and University, 1856-1956* (Collegeville: St. John's Abbey, 1956).

Jeremy Hall, O.S.B., *The Full Stature of Christ: The Ecclesiology of Dom Virgil Michel* (Collegeville: The Liturgical Press, 1976).

Paul B. Marx, O.S.B., *Virgil Michel and the Liturgical Movement* (Collegeville: The Liturgical Press, 1957).

David J. O'Brien, *American Catholics and Social Reform: The New Deal Years* (New York: Oxford University Press, 1968).

11

John Courtney Murray

John Courtney Murray, S.J. (1904-1967) was the principal American Catholic theoretician on religious liberty. Murray believed that the post World-War II world demanded two major tasks from the American Catholic theologian before Catholics could cooperate with fellow Christians and Jews in attacking the social crises of the era. On the one hand, the theologian had to overcome Protestant and Jewish suspicions of Catholic political goals before cooperation was possible. This was the perennial problem in American Catholicism. On the other hand, he had to refute a secularist interpretation of separation of church and state that relegated religion to the sacristy or to the "private" sphere of individual conscience. The theologian had to develop an adequate response to these problems in order to secure the freedom of the church as an organized community in American society. Thus, Murray's work on religious liberty was preliminary to the more fundamental task of discussing the positive role of Christians and churches in society.

John Courtney Murray was born in New York City to Michael John and Margaret Courtney Murray. At the age of sixteen, after receiving primary and secondary education in New York City, he joined the Society of Jesus. In 1926, he was a graduate from Weston College in Massachusetts and in 1927 received a Master's degree from Boston College. From 1927 to 1930 he taught Latin and English literature in the Philippines. In 1930 he returned to the United States to study theology for the next four years at Woodstock College in Maryland. After ordination to the priesthood on June 25, 1933, he was sent to the Gregorian University in Rome to obtain a doctorate in theology. In 1937, after receiving the doctorate, he returned to Woodstock College where he taught theology until his death in 1967. In 1963, he was appointed a

*peritus at the Second Vatican Council where he became a primary con-
tributor to the Council's Declaration on Religious Liberty.*

*In the following selection Murray argues that the American doc-
trine of religious liberty is a political and not a religious proposition.
American Catholic assent to the first amendment, therefore, is
grounded on moral principle and public philosophy rather than religious
belief or theology. He also maintains that because the state is not juridically omnipotent in America, there is room for an independent exercise
of an authority not derived from the state—i.e., for ecclesiastical authority. Thus, he concludes that the freedom of religion guaranteed by
the Constitution provides for the possibility of religious integrity as well
as civil and political unity. The wisdom and validity of this constitutional provision is grounded in and has been tested by the American
experience.*

TEXT

"CIVIL UNITY AND RELIGIOUS INTEGRITY: THE ARTICLES OF PEACE"

Source: John Courtney Murray, S.J.,
*We Hold These Truths: Catholic Reflections
on the American Proposition*
(New York: Sheed and Ward, 1960), 55-85.

The unity asserted in the American device, "E pluribus unum" (as
I have adapted its meaning) is a unity of a limited order. It does not go
beyond the exigencies of civil conversation, taken in the sense already
defined.[1] This civil unity therefore must not hinder the various religious
communities in American society in the maintenance of their own distinct identities. Similarly, the public consensus, on which civil unity is
ultimately based, must permit to the differing communities the full
integrity of their own religious convictions. The one civil society contains within its own unity the communities that are divided among
themselves; but it does not seek to reduce to its own unity the differences
that divide them. In a word, the pluralism remains as real as the unity.
Neither may undertake to destroy the other. Each subsists in its own
order. And the two orders, the religious and the civil, remain distinct,
however much they are, and need to be, related. All this, I take it, is
integral to the meaning attached in America to the doctrine of religious

freedom and to its instrumental companion-doctrine called (not felici-
tously) separation of church and state. I use the word "doctrine" as lawyers or political philosophers, not theologians, use it.

We come therefore to the second question. It concerns the American solution to the problem put by the plurality of conflicting religions
within the one body politic. In its legal form (there are other forms, as I
shall later say) the solution is deposited in the First Amendment to the
Federal Constitution: "Congress shall make no law respecting an establishment of religion or prohibiting the free exercise thereof. . . ." What
then is the Catholic view of this constitutional proviso?

In 1790 Edmund Burke published his *Reflections on the Revolution in
France*. When he comes to his defense of English institutions ("an established Church, an established monarchy, an established aristocracy, and
an established democracy"), he says: "First I beg leave to speak of our
Church Establishment, which is the first of our prejudices—not a prejudice destitute of reason, but involving in it profound and extensive wisdom. I speak of it first. It is first, and last, and midst in our minds." In
that same year the people of the states newly formed into the American
Federal Republic were debating the ten amendments to the Constitution, submitted to them for ratification. The ratification was complete in
1791, and in that year the legal rule against any establishment of religion was on its way to becoming, where it had not already become, the
first of our prejudices. There is a contrast here, a clash of prejudices,
which still endures. The clash ought to be mentioned at the outset of
our present question, primarily because it should teach one the dangers
of doctrinaire judgments. Such judgments are always in peril of falsity;
they are particularly so in the delicate matter of the legal regulation of
religion in society. We have a special prejudice in this matter, which is
specifically American, because its origins are in our particular context
and its validity has been demonstrated by the unique course of American history.

The subject might almost be left right here, if it could be generally
admitted that the First Amendment expresses simply an American prejudice, in Burke's sense of the word. A prejudice is not necessarily an
error; to be prejudiced is not necessarily to be unreasonable. Certain
pre-judgments are wholesome. Normally, they are concrete judgments
of value, not abstract judgments of truth. They are not destitute of reason, but their chief corroboration is from experience. They are part of
the legacy of wisdom from the past; they express an ancestral consensus.
Hence they supply in the present, as Russell Kirk puts it, "the half-
intuitive knowledge which enables men to meet the problems of life
without logic-chopping." The American Catholic is entirely prepared to

accept our constitutional concept of freedom of religion and the policy of no establishment as the first of our prejudices. He is also prepared to admit that other prejudices may obtain elsewhere—in England, in Sweden, in Spain. Their validity in their own context and against the background of the history that generated them does not disturb him in his conviction that his own prejudice, within his own context and against the background of his own history, has its own validity.

American Catholics would even go as far as to say of the provisions of the First Amendment what Burke, in his *Reflections*, said of the English Church Establishment, that they consider it as "essential to their state; not as a thing heterogeneous and separable, something added from accommodation, what they may either keep up or lay aside, according to their temporary ideas of convenience. They consider it as the foundation of their whole Constitution, with which, and with every part of which, it holds an indissoluble union." The prejudice formulated in the First Amendment is but the most striking aspect of the more fundamental prejudice that was the living root of our constitutional system—the prejudice in favor of the method of freedom in society and therefore the prejudice in favor of a government of limited powers, whose limitations are determined by the consent of the people. The American people exempted from their grant of power to government any power to establish religion or to prohibit the free exercise thereof. The Catholic community, in common with the rest of the American people, has historically consented to this political and legal solution to the problem created by the plurality of religious beliefs in American society. They agree that the First Amendment is by no means destitute of reason; that it involves profound and extensive wisdom; that its wisdom has been amply substantiated by history. Consequently, they share the general prejudice which it states; often enough both in action and in utterances they have made this fact plain. And that should be the end of the matter.

THEOLOGIES OF THE FIRST AMENDMENT

But, as it happens, one is not permitted thus simply to end the matter. I leave aside the practical issues that have arisen concerning the application of the First Amendment. The question here is one of theory, the theory of the First Amendment in itself and in its relation to Catholic theories of freedom of religion and the church-state relation. It is customary to put to Catholics what is supposed to be an embarrassing question: Do you really believe in the first two provisions of the First

Amendment? The question calls to mind one of the more famous among the multitudinous queries put by Boswell to Dr. Johnson, "whether it is necessary to believe all the Thirty-Nine Articles." And the Doctor's answer has an applicable point: "Why, sir, that is a question which has been much agitated. Some have held it necessary that all be believed. Others have considered them to be only articles of peace, that is to say, you are not to preach against them."

An analogous difference of interpretation seems to exist with regard to the first two articles of the First Amendment.

On the one hand, there are those who read into them certain ultimate beliefs, certain specifically sectarian tenets with regard to the nature of religion, religious truth, the church, faith, conscience, divine revelation, human freedom, etc. In this view these articles are invested with a genuine sanctity that derives from their supposed religious content. They are dogmas, norms of orthodoxy, to which one must conform on pain of some manner of excommunication. They are true articles of faith. Hence it is necessary to believe them, to give them a religiously motivated assent.

On the other hand, there are those who see in these articles only a law, not a dogma. These constitutional clauses have no religious content. They answer none of the eternal human questions with regard to the nature of truth and freedom or the manner in which the spiritual order of man's life is to be organized or not organized. Therefore they are not invested with the sanctity that attaches to dogma, but only with the rationality that attaches to law. Rationality is the highest value of law. In further consequence, it is not necessary to give them a religious assent but only a rational civil obedience. In a word, they are not articles of faith but articles of peace, that is to say, you may not act against them, because they are law and good law.

Those who dogmatize about these articles do not usually do so with all the clarity that dogmas require. Nor are they in agreement with one another. The main difference is between those who see in these articles certain Protestant religious tenets and those who see in them certain ultimate suppositions of secular liberalism. The differences between those two groups tend to disappear in a third group, the secularizing Protestants, so called, who effect an identification of their Protestantism with American secular culture, consider the church to be true in proportion as its organization is commanded by the norms of secular democratic society, and bring about a coincidence of religious and secular-liberal concepts of freedom. . . .

This is not the place to argue the question, whether and how far any of these views can be sustained as an historical thesis. What matters here is a different question, whether any of them can serve as a rule of interpretation of the First Amendment. What is in question is the meaning and the content of the first of our American prejudices, not its genesis. Do these clauses assert or imply that the nature of the church is such that it inherently demands the most absolute separation from the state? Do they assert or imply that the institutional church is simply a voluntary association of like-minded men; that its origins are only in the will of men to associate freely for purposes of religion and worship; that all churches, since their several origins are in equally valid religious inspirations, stand on a footing of equality in the face of the divine and evangelical law; that all ought by the same token to stand on an equal footing in the face of civil law? In a word, does separation of church and state in the American sense assert or imply a particular sectarian concept of the church?

Further, does the free-exercise clause assert or imply that the individual conscience is the ultimate norm of religious belief in such wise that an external religious authority is inimical to Christian freedom? Does it hold that religion is a purely private matter in such wise that an ecclesiastical religion is inherently a corruption of the Christian Gospel? Does it maintain that true religion is religion-in-general, and that the various sects in their dividedness are as repugnant religiously as they are politically dangerous? Does it pronounce religious truth to be simply a matter of personal experience, and religious faith to be simply a matter of subjective impulse, not related to any objective order of truth or to any structured economy of salvation whose consistence is not dependent on the human will?

The questions could be multiplied, but they all reduce themselves to two. Is the no-establishment clause a piece of ecclesiology, and is the free-exercise clause a piece of religious philosophy? The general Protestant tendency, visible at its extreme in the free-church tradition, especially among the Baptists, is to answer affirmatively to these questions. Freedom of religion and separation of church and state are to be, in the customary phrase, "rooted in religion itself." Their substance is to be conceived in terms of sectarian Protestant doctrine. They are therefore articles of faith; not to give them a religious assent is to fall into heterodoxy.

The secularist dissents from the Protestant theological and philosophical exegesis of the first of our prejudices. But it is to him likewise an article of faith (he might prefer to discard the word, "faith," and speak rather of ultimate presuppositions). Within this group also there are differences of opinion. Perhaps the most sharpened view is taken by those who in their pursuit of truth reject not only the traditional methods of Christian illumination, both Protestant and Catholic, but also the reflective methods of metaphysical inquiry.

These men commit themselves singly to the method of scientific empiricism. There is therefore no eternal order of truth and justice; there are no universal verities that require man's assent, no universal moral law that commands his obedience. Such an order of universals is not empirically demonstrable. Truth therefore is to be understood in a positivistic sense; its criteria are either those of science or those of practical life, i.e., the success of an opinion in getting itself accepted in the market place. With this view of truth there goes a corresponding view of freedom. The essence of freedom is "non-committalism." I take the word from Gordon Keith Chalmers. He calls it a "sin," but in the school of thought in question it is the highest virtue. To be uncommitted is to be in the state of grace; for a prohibition of commitment is inherent in the very notion of freedom. The mind or will that is committed, absolutely and finally, is by definition not free. It has fallen from grace by violating its own free nature. In the intellectual enterprise the search for truth, not truth itself or its possession, is the highest value. In the order of morals the norm for man is never reached by knowledge. It is only approximated by inspired guesses or by tentative practical rules that are the precipitate of experience, substantiated only by their utility.

This school of thought, which is of relatively recent growth in America, thrusts into the First Amendment its own ultimate views of truth, freedom, and religion. Religion itself is not a value, except insofar as its ambiguous reassurances may have the emotional effect of conveying reassurance. Roman Catholicism is a disvalue. Nevertheless, religious freedom, as a form of freedom, is a value. It has at least the negative value of an added emancipation, another sheer release. It may also have the positive value of another blow struck at the principle of authority in any of its forms; for in this school authority is regarded as absolutely antinomous to freedom.

Furthermore, this school usually reads into the First Amendment a more or less articulated political theory. Civil society is the highest societal form of human life; even the values that are called spiritual and moral are values by reason of their reference to society. Civil law is the highest form of law and it is not subject to judgment by prior ethical canons. Civil rights are the highest form of rights; for the dignity of the person, which grounds these rights, is only his civil dignity. The state is purely the instrument of the popular will, than which there is no higher sovereignty. Government is to the citizen what the cab-driver is to the passenger (to use Yves Simon's descriptive metaphor). And since the rule of the majority is the method whereby the popular will expresses itself, it is the highest governing principle of statecraft, from which there is no appeal. Finally, the ultimate value within society and state does not consist in any substantive ends that these societal forms may pursue; rather it consists in the process of their pursuit. That is to say, the ultimate value resides in the forms of the democratic process itself, because these forms embody the most ultimate of all values, freedom. There are those who pursue this theory to paradoxical lengths—perhaps more exactly, to the lengths of logical absurdity—by maintaining that if the forms of democracy perish through the use of them by men intent on their destruction, well then, so be it.

Given this political theory, the churches are inevitably englobed within the state, as private associations organized for particular purposes. They possess their title to existence from positive law. Their right to freedom is a civil right, and it is respected as long as it is not understood to include any claim to independently sovereign authority. Such a claim must be disallowed on grounds of the final and indivisible sovereignty of the democratic process over all the associational aspects of human life. The notion that any church should acquire status in public life as a society in its own right is per se absurd; for there is only one society, civil society, which may so exist. In this view, separation of church and state, as ultimately implying a subordination of church to state, follows from the very nature of the state and its law; just as religious freedom follows from the very nature of freedom and of truth.

The foregoing is a sort of anatomical description of two interpretations of the religion clauses of the First Amendment. The description is made anatomical in order to point the issue. If these clauses are made articles of faith in either of the described senses, there are immediately in this country some 35,000,000 dissenters, the Catholic community. Not being either a Protestant or a secularist, the Catholic rejects the religious position of Protestants with regard to the nature of the church, the meaning of faith, the absolute primacy of conscience, etc.; just as he rejects secularist views with regard to the nature of truth, freedom, and civil society as man's last end. He rejects these positions as demonstrably erroneous in themselves. What is more to the point here, he rejects the notion that any of these sectarian theses enter into the content or implications of the First Amendment in such wise as to demand the assent of all American citizens. If this were the case the very article that bars any establishment of religion would somehow establish one. (Given the controversy between Protestant and secularist, there would be the added difficulty that one could not know just what religion had been established.)

If it be true that the First Amendment is to be given a theological interpretation and that therefore it must be "believed," made an object of religious faith, it would follow that a religious test has been thrust into the Constitution. The Federal Republic has suddenly become a voluntary fellowship of believers either in some sort of free-church Protestantism or in the tenets of a naturalistic humanism. The notion is preposterous. The United States is a good place to live in; many have found it even a sort of secular sanctuary. But it is not a church, whether high, low, or broad. It is simply a civil community, whose unity is purely political, consisting in "agreement on the good of man at the level of performance without the necessity of agreement on ultimates" (to adopt a phrase from the 1945 Harvard Report on General Education in a Free Society). As regards important points of ultimate religious belief, the United States is pluralist. Any attempt at reducing this pluralism by law, through a process of reading certain sectarian tenets into the fundamental law of the land, is prima facie illegitimate and absurd. . . .

ARTICLES OF PEACE

From the standpoint both of history and of contemporary social reality the only tenable position is that the first two articles of the First Amendment are not articles of faith but articles of peace. Like the rest of the Constitution these provisions are the work of lawyers, not of theologians or even of political theorists. They are not true dogma but only good law. That is praise enough. This, I take it, is the Catholic view. But in thus qualifying it I am not marking it out as just another "sectarian" view. It is in fact the only view that a citizen with both historical sense and common sense can take.

That curiously clairvoyant statesman, John C. Calhoun, once observed that "this admirable federal constitution of ours is superior to the wisdom of any or all the men by whose agency it was made. The force of circumstances and not foresight or wisdom induced them to adopt many of its wisest provisions." The observation is particularly pertinent to the religion clauses of the First Amendment. If history makes one thing clear it is that these clauses were the twin children of social necessity, the necessity of creating a social environment, protected by law, in which men of differing religious faiths might live together in peace. In his stimulating book, *The Genius of American Politics*,[2] Prof.

Daniel Boorstin says: "The impression which the American has as he looks about him is one of the inevitability of the particular institutions under which he lives." This mark of inevitability is an index of goodness. And it is perhaps nowhere more strikingly manifest than in the institutions which govern the relation of government to religion. These institutions seem to have been performed in the peculiar conditions of American society. It did indeed take some little time before the special American solution to the problem of religious pluralism worked itself out; but it is almost inconceivable that it should not have worked itself out as it did. One suspects that this would have been true even if there had been no Williamses and Penns, no Calverts and Madisons and Jeffersons. The theories of these men, whatever their merits, would probably have made only literature not history, had it not been for the special social context into which they were projected. Similarly, the theories of these men, whatever their defects, actually made history because they exerted their pressure, such as it was, in the direction in which historical factors were already moving the new American society.

To say this is not of course to embrace a theory of historical or social determinism. It is only to say that the artisans of the American Republic and its Constitution were not radical theorists intent on constructing a society in accord with the a priori demands of a doctrinaire blueprint, under disregard for what was actually "given" in history. Fortunately they were, as I said, for the most part lawyers. And they have a strong sense of that primary criterion of good law which is its necessity or utility for the perservation of the public peace, under a given set of conditions. All law looks to the common good, which is normative for all law. And social peace, assured by equal justice in dealing with possibly conflicting groups, is the highest integrating element of the common good. This legal criterion is the first and most solid ground on which the validity of the First Amendment rests. . . .

On these grounds it is easy to see why the Catholic conscience has always consented to the religion clauses of the Constitution. They conform to the highest criterion for all legal rulings in this delicate matter. The criterion is moral; therefore the law that meets it is good, because it is for the common good. Therefore the consent given to the law is given on grounds of moral principle. To speak of expediency here is altogether to misunderstand the moral nature of the community and its collective moral obligation toward its own common good. The origins of our fundamental law are in moral principle; the obligations it imposes are moral obligations, binding in conscience. One may not, without moral fault, act against these articles of peace.

THE DISTINCTION OF CHURCH AND STATE

If the demands of social necessity account for the emergence in America of religious freedom as a fact, they hardly account for certain peculiarities of the first of our prejudices and for the depth of feeling that it evokes. Another powerful historical force must be considered, namely, the dominant impulse toward self-government, government by the people in the most earnest sense of the word. Above all else the early Americans wanted political freedom. And the force of this impulse necessarily acted as a corrosive upon the illegitimate "unions" of church and state which the post-Reformation era had brought forth. The establishments of the time were, by and large, either theocratic, wherein the state was absorbed in the church, or Erastian, wherein the church was absorbed in the state. In both cases the result was some limitation upon freedom, either in the form of civil disabilities imposed in the name of the established religion, or in the form of religious disabilities imposed in the name of the civil law of the covenanted community. The drive toward popular freedom would with a certain inevitability sweep away such establishments. Men might share the fear of Roger Williams, that the state would corrupt the church, or the fear of Thomas Jefferson, that the church would corrupt the state. In either case their thought converged to the one important conclusion, that an end had to be put to the current confusions of the religious and political orders. The ancient distinction between church and state had to be newly reaffirmed in a manner adapted to the American scene. Calvinist theocracy, Anglican Erastianism, Gallican absolutism—all were vitiated by the same taint: they violated in one way or another this traditional distinction.

The dualism of mankind's two hierarchically ordered forms of social life had been Christianity's cardinal contribution to the Western political tradition, as everyone knows who has looked into the monumental work of the two Carlyles, *Medieval Political Thought in the West*. Perhaps equally with the very idea of law itself it had been the most fecund force for freedom in society. The distinction had always been difficult to maintain in practice, even when it was affirmed in theory. But when it was formally denied the result was an infringement of man's freedom of religious faith or of his freedom as a citizen—an infringement of either or both. Hence the generalized American impulse toward freedom inevitably led to a new and specially emphatic affirmation of the traditional distinction. . . .

The point is that the distinction of church and state, one of the central assertions of this Western tradition [of politics] found its way into the Constitution. There it received a special embodiment, adapted to the peculiar genius of American government and to the concrete conditions of American society.

How this happened need not concern us here. Certainly it was in part because the artisans of the Constitution had a clear grasp of the distinction between state and society, which had been the historical product of the distinction between church and state, inasmuch as the latter distinction asserted the existence of a whole wide area of human concerns which were remote from the competence of government. Calhoun's "force of circumstances" also had a great deal of influence; here again it was a matter of the Fathers building better than they knew. Their major concern was sharply to circumscribe the powers of government. The area of state—that is, legal—concern was limited to the pursuit of certain enumerated secular purposes (to say that the purposes are secular is not to deny that many of them are also moral; so for instance the establishment of justice and peace, the promotion of the general welfare, etc.). Thus made autonomous in its own sphere, government was denied all competence in the field of religion. In this field freedom was to be the rule and method; government was powerless to legislate respecting an establishment of religion and likewise powerless to prohibit the free exercise of religion. Its single office was to take legal or judicial steps necessary on given occasions to make effective the general guarantee of freedom.

The concrete applications of this, in itself quite simple, solution have presented great　historical and legal difficulties. This has been inevitable, given the intimacy with which religion is woven into the whole social fabric, and given, too, the evolution of government from John Adams' "plain, simple, intelligible thing, quite comprehensible by common sense," to the enormously complicated and sprawling thing which now organizes a great part of our lives, handles almost all education, and much social welfare. In particular, we have not yet found an answer to the question whether government can make effective the primary intention of the First Amendment, the guarantee of freedom of religion, simply by attempting to make more and more "impregnable" what is called, in Rogers Williams' fateful metaphor, the "wall of separation" between church and state. However, what concerns us here is the root of the matter, the fact that the American Constitution embodies in a special way the traditional principle of the distinction between church and state.

For Catholics this fact is of great and providential importance for one major reason. It serves sharply to set off our constitutional system from the system against which the Church waged its long-drawn-out fight in the nineteenth century, namely, Jacobinism, or (in Carlton Hayes's term) sectarian Liberalism, or (in the more definitive term used today) totalitarian democracy.

It is now coming to be recognized that the Church opposed the "separation of church and state" of the sectarian Liberals because in theory and in fact it did not mean separation at all but perhaps the most drastic unification of church and state which history had known. The Jacobin "free state" was as regalist as the *ancien régime*, and even more so. Writing as a historian, de Tocqueville long ago made this plain. And the detailed descriptions which Leo XIII, writing as a theologian and political moralist, gave of the Church's "enemy" make the fact even more plain. Within this "free state" the so-called "free church" was subject to a political control more complete than the Tudor or Stuart or Bourbon monarchies dreamed of. The evidence stretches all the way from the Civil Constitution of the Clergy in 1790 to the Law of Separation in 1905. . . .

The American thesis is that government is not juridically omnipotent. Its powers are limited, and one of the principles of limitation is the distinction between state and church, in their purposes, methods, and manner of organization. The Jacobin thesis was basically philosophical; it derived from a sectarian concept of the autonomy of reason. It was also theological, as implying a sectarian concept of religion and of the church. In contrast, the American thesis is simply political. It asserts the theory of a free people under a limited government, a theory that is recognizably part of the Christian political tradition, and altogether defensible in the manner of its realization under American circumstances.

It may indeed be said that the American constitutional system exaggerates the distinction between church and state by its self-denying ordinances. However, it must also be said that government rarely appears to better advantage than when passing self-denying ordinances. In any event, it is one thing to exaggerate a traditional distinction along the lines of its inherent tendency; it is quite another thing to abolish the distinction. In the latter case the result is a vicious monistic society; in the former, a faultily dualistic one. The vice in the Jacobin system could only be condemned by the Church, not in any way condoned. The fault in the American system can be recognized as such, without condemnation. There are times and circumstances, Chesterton jocosely said, when it is necessary to exaggerate in order to tell the truth. There are also times and circumstances, one may more seriously say, when some exaggeration of the restrictions placed on government is necessary in order to insure freedom. These circumstances of social necessity were and are present in America.

THE FREEDOM OF THE CHURCH

Here then is the second leading reason why the American solution to the problem of religious pluralism commends itself to the Catholic conscience. Pius XII states, as the two cardinal purposes of a Concordat, first, "to assure to the Church a stable condition of right and of fact within society," and second, "to guarantee to her a full independence in the fulfillment of her divine mission." It may be maintained that both of these objectives are sufficiently achieved by the religious provisions of the First Amendment. It is obvious that the Church in America enjoys a stable condition in fact. That her status at law is not less stable ought to be hardly less obvious, if only one has clearly in mind the peculiarity of the American affirmation of the distinction between church and state. This affirmation is made through the imposition of limits on government, which is confined to its own proper ends, those of temporal society. In contrast to the Jacobin system in all its forms, the American Constitution does not presume to define the Church or in any way to supervise her exercise of authority in pursuit of her own distinct ends. The Church is entirely free to define herself and to exercise to the full her spiritual jurisdiction. It is legally recognized that there is an area which lies outside the competence of government. This area coincides with the area of the divine mission of the Church, and within this area the Church is fully independent, immune from interference by political authority.

The juridical result of the American limitation of governmental powers is the guarantee of the Church of a stable condition of freedom as a matter of law and right. It should be added that this guarantee is made not only to the individual Catholic but to the Church as an organized society with its own law and jurisdiction. The reason is that the American state is not erected on the principle of the unity and indivisibility of sovereignty which was the post-Renaissance European development. Nowhere in the American structure is there accumulated the plenitude of legal sovereignty possessed in England by the Queen in Parliament. In fact, the term "legal sovereignty" makes no sense in America, where sovereignty (if the alien term must be used) is purely political. The United States has a government, or better, a structure of governments operating on different levels. The American state has no sovereignty in the classic Continental sense. Within society, as distinct from the state, there is room for the independent exercise of an authority which is not that of the state. This principle has more than once been affirmed by American courts, most recently by the Supreme Court in the *Kedroff* case. The validity of this principle strengthens the stabililty of the Church's condition at law. . . .

THE AMERICAN EXPERIENCE

One final ground for affirming the validity of the religion clauses of the First Amendment as good law must be briefly touched on. Holmes's famous dictum, "The life of the law is not logic but experience," has more truth in it than many other Holmesian dicta. When a law ceases to be supported by a continued experience of its goodness, it becomes a dead letter, an empty legal form. Although pure pragmatism cannot be made the philosophy of law, nonetheless the value of any given law is importantly pragmatic. The First Amendment surely passes this test of good law. In support of it one can adduce an American experience. One might well call it *the* American experience in the sense that it has been central in American history and also unique in the history of the world.

This experience has three facets, all interrelated.

First, America has proved by experience that political unity and stability are possible without uniformity of religious belief and practice, without the necessity of any governmental restrictions on any religion. Before the days of the Federal Republic some men had tried to believe that this could be so; thus for instance the *politiques* in France, in their attack upon the classic Gallican and absolutist thesis, "One law, one faith, one king." But this thesis, and its equivalents, had not been disproved. This event was accomplished in the United States by an argument from experience. For a century and a half the United States has displayed to the world the fact that political unity and stability are not necessarily dependent on the common sharing of one religious faith.

The reach of this demonstration is, of course, limited. Granted that the unity of the commonwealth can be achieved in the absence of a consensus with regard to the theological truths that govern the total life and destiny of man, it does not follow that this necessary civic unity can endure in the absence of a consensus more narrow in its scope, operative on the level of political life, with regard to the rational truths and moral precepts that govern the structure of the constitutional state, specify the substance of the common weal, and determine the ends of public policy. Nor has experience yet shown how, if at all, this moral consensus can survive amid all the ruptures of religious division, whose tendency is inherently disintegrative of all consensus and community. But this is a further question, for the future to answer. I shall have occasion in later chapters to discuss this whole question of the American consensus and its present condition among us.

The second American experience was that stable political unity, which means perduring agreement on the common good of man at the level of performance, can be strengthened by the exclusion of religious differences from the area of concern allotted to government. In America we have been rescued from the disaster of ideological parties. They are a disaster because, where such parties exist, power becomes a special kind of prize. The struggle for power is a partisan struggle for the means whereby the opposing ideology may be destroyed. It has been remarked that only in a disintegrating society does politics become a controversy over ends; it should be simply a controversy over means to ends already agreed on with sufficient unanimity. The Latin countries of Europe have displayed this spectacle of ideological politics, a struggle between a host of "isms," all of which pretend to a final view of man and society, with the twin results of governmental paralysis and seemingly irremediable social division. In contrast, the American experience of political unity has been striking. (Even the Civil War does not refute this view; it was not an ideological conflict but simply, in the more descriptive Southern phrase, a war between the states, a conflict of interests.) To this experience of political unity the First Amendment has made a unique contribution; and in doing so it has qualified as good law.

The third and most striking aspect of the American experience consists in the fact that religion itself, and not least the Catholic Church, has benefited by our free institutions, by the maintenance, even in exaggerated form, of the distinction between church and state. Within the same span of history the experience of the Church elsewhere, especially in the Latin lands, has been alternately an experience of privilege or persecution. The reason lay in a particular concept of government. It was alternatively the determination of government to ally itself either with the purposes of the Church or with the purposes of some sect or other (sectarian Liberalism, for instance) which made a similar, however erroneous claim to possess the full and final truth. The dominant conviction, whose origins are really in pagan antiquity, was that government should represent transcendent truth and by its legal power make this truth prevail. However, in the absence of social agreement as to what the truth really was, the result was to involve the Catholic truth in the vicissitudes of power. It would be difficult to say which experience, privilege or persecution, proved in the end to be the more damaging or gainful to the Church.

In contrast, American government has not undertaken to represent transcendental truth in any of the versions of it current in American society. It does indeed represent the commonly shared moral values of the community. It also represents the supreme religious truth expressed in the motto on American coins: "In God we trust." The motto expresses the two truths without which, as the Letter to the Hebrews says, "nobody reaches God's presence," namely, "to believe that God exists and that he rewards those who try to find him" (Hebrews 11:6). For the rest, government represents the truth of society as it actually is; and the truth is that American society is religiously pluralist. The truth is lamentable; it is nonetheless true. Many of the beliefs entertained within society ought not to be believed, because they are false; nonetheless men believe them. It is not the function of government to resolve the dispute between conflicting truths, all of which claim the final validity of transcendence. As representative of a pluralist society, wherein religious faith is—as it must be—free, government undertakes to represent the principle of freedom.

In taking this course American government would seem to be on the course set by Pius XII for the religiously pluralist international community, of which America offers, as it were, a pattern in miniature. In the discourse already cited he distinguishes two questions: "The first concerns the objective truth and the obligation of conscience toward that which is objectively true and good." This question, he goes on, "can hardly be made the object of discussion and ruling among the individual states and their communities, especially in the case of a plurality of religious confessions within the same community." In other words, government is not a judge of religious truth; parliaments are not to play the theologian. In accord with this principle American government does not presume to discuss, much less rule upon the objective truth or falsity of the various religious confessions within society. It puts to itself only Pius XII's second question, which concerns "the practical attitude" of government in the face of religious pluralism. It answers this question by asserting that in the given circumstances it has neither the mandate nor the duty nor the right to legislate either in favor of or against any of the religious confessions existent in American society, which in its totality government must represent. It will therefore only represent their freedom, in the face of civil law, to exist, since they do in fact exist. This is precisely the practical attitude which Pius XII recognizes as right, as the proper moral and political course.

In consequence of this American concept of the representative function of government the experience of the Church in America, like the general American experience itself, has proved to be satisfactory when one scans it from the viewpoint of the value upon which the Church sets primary importance, namely, her freedom in the fulfillment of her spiritual mission to communicate divine truth and grace to the souls of men, and her equally spiritual mission of social justice and peace. The Church has not enjoyed a privileged status in public life; at the same time she has not had to pay the price of this privilege. A whole book could be written on the price of such legal privilege. Another book could be written on the value of freedom without privilege. In fact, both books have been written, on the metaphorical pages of history. And looking over his own continually unrolling historical manuscript the American Catholic is inclined to conclude that his is a valid book.

It does not develop a doctrinal thesis, but it does prove a practical point. The point is that the goodness of the First Amendment as constitutional law is manifested not only by political but also by religious experience. By and large (for no historical record is without blots) it has been good for religion, for Catholicism, to have had simply the right of freedom. This right is at the same time the highest of privileges, and it too has its price. But the price has not been envy and enmity, the coinage in which the Church paid for privilege. It has only been the price of sacrifice, labor, added responsibilities; and these things are redemptive.

CONCLUSION

In the final analysis any validation of the First Amendment as good law—no matter by whom undertaken, be he Protestant, Catholic, Jew, or secularist—must make appeal to the three arguments developed above—the demands of social necessity, the rightfulness within our own circumstances of the American manner of asserting the distinction between church and state, and the lessons of experience. Perhaps the last argument is the most powerful. It is also, I may add, the argument which best harmonizes with the general tone which arguments for our institutions are accustomed to adopt. . . .

The Catholic Church in America is committed to this prejudice of religious liberty by the totality of her experience in American history. As far as I know, the only ones who doubt the firmness, the depth, the principled nature of this commitment are not Catholics. They speak without knowledge and without authority; and the credence they command has its origins in emotion. If perhaps what troubles them is the fact that the commitment is limited, in the sense that it is not to the truth and sanctity of a dogma but only to the rationality and goodness of a law, they might recall the story of Pompey. After the capture of Jerusalem in 63 B.C. he went to the Temple and forced his way into the Holy of Holies. To his intense astonishment he found it empty. He should not have been astonished; for the emptiness was the symbol of the absence of idolatry. It symbolized the essential truth of Judaism, that One is the Lord. Professor Boorstin, who recounts the tale, adds: "Perhaps the same surprise awaits the student of American culture [or, I add, the American Constitution] if he finally manages to penetrate the arcanum of our belief. And for a similar reason. Far from being disappointed, we should be inspired that in an era of idolatry, when so many nations have filled their sanctuaries with ideological idols, we have had the courage to refuse to do so."

The American Catholic is on good ground when he refuses to make an ideological idol out of religious freedom and separation of church and state, when he refuses to "believe" in them as articles of faith. He takes the highest ground available in this matter of the relations between religion and government when he asserts that his commitment to the religion clauses of the Constitution is a moral commitment to them as articles of peace in a pluralist society.

NOTES

1. [Ed. By "E pluribus unum," Murray means that in the United States we have "one society subsisting amid multiple pluralisms," one of which is religious pluralism. The unity of which he speaks here is founded in a certain American consensus that acknowledges: 1. the nation to be under God; 2. the tradition of natural law; 3. the principle of consent; 4. the necessity of virtue for freedom; 5. the inalienability of human rights and responsibilities.]

2. Chicago: University of Chicago Press, 1953.

A SELECTED BIBLIOGRAPHY

PRIMARY SOURCES:

[with Edward S. Corwin], *Religion and the State; the Supreme Court as National School Board* (Durham, N.C.: Duke University Press, 1949).

[with Walter Millis], *Foreign Policy and the Free Society* (New York: Oceana Publications, 1958).

We Hold These Truths (New York: Sheed and Ward, 1960).

The Problem of God: Yesterday and Today (New Haven: Yale University Press, 1964).

The Problem of Religious Freedom (Westminster, Md.: Newman Press, 1965).

(ed.), *Freedom and Man* (N.Y.: P.J. Kennedy, 1965).

(ed.), *Religious Liberty: An End and a Beginning* (N.Y.: Macmillan, 1966).

Articles in *Theological Studies* and *America*, 1942-1967.

SECONDARY SOURCES:

Faith E. Burgess, *The Relationship between Church and State According to John Courtney Murray, S.J.* (Ph.D. dissertation, University of Basle, 1971; Dusseldorf: Rudolf Stehle, 1971).

Walter J. Burghart, S.J. (ed.), *Religious Freedom 1965-1975: A Symposium on an Historic Document* (Ramsey N.J.: Paulist Press, 1977).

John Coleman, S.J., "Vision and Praxis in American Theology: Orestes Brownson, John A. Ryan, and John Courtney Murray," *Theological Studies* 37 (March, 1976), 3-40.

John M. Cuddihy, *No Offense: Civil Religion and Protestant Taste* (New York: Seabury Press, 1978).

David Hollenbach, S.J. *et alii*, "J. C. Murray's Unfinished Agenda," *Theological Studies* XL (Dec., 1979), 700-716.

David Hollenbach, S.J., "Public Theology in America: Some Questions for Catholicism after John Courtney Murray," *Theological Studies* 37 (June, 1976), 290-303.

Thomas L. Love, *John Courtney Murray's Contemporary Church-State Theory* (Garden City, N.Y.: Doubleday, 1965).

Donald E. Pelotte, S.S.S., *John Courtney Murray: Theologian in Conflict* (New York: Paulist Press, 1975).